OXFORD WORLD'S CLASSICS

SWANN IN LOVE

MARCEL PROUST (1871–1922) is best known as the author of the seven-volume masterpiece *A la recherche du temps perdu* (*In Search of Lost Time*, 1913–27). He was born in Auteuil, on the west of Paris, to well-to-do parents; at the age of 10 he suffered a near-fatal asthma attack and his life from that point onward was marked by ill health. He began writing reviews, short stories, and society journalism whilst studying at the Lycée Condorcet and published a collection of these pieces, *Les Plaisirs et les jours* (*Pleasures and Days*) in 1896. Family connections and schoolfriends gave him access to the highest Parisian social circles, on which he would later draw for his portrayal of the society life in *In Search of Lost Time*. His first attempt at an extended narrative (posthumously published as *Jean Santeuil*, 1952) was abandoned; subsequent stages in his apprenticeship as a writer include translating works by the English art historian and social critic John Ruskin and producing dazzling pastiches of major French writers. Finally, during 1908–9, whilst working on a critical essay taking to task the great nineteenth-century critic Sainte-Beuve, Proust began to draft fragments of a first-person narrative that coalesced into what would become *In Search of Lost Time*. The first volume, containing *Swann in Love*, appeared in 1913. Unfit for military service, Proust spent the wartime years expanding his novel, the subsequent volumes of which appeared between 1919 and 1927. Proust's devotion to his work, sleeping by day then writing and making additions and revisions through the night, was ruinous for his already fragile health and he died in 1922, while still engaged in the corrections to his final volumes.

BRIAN NELSON is Professor Emeritus (French Studies and Translation Studies) at Monash University, Melbourne, and a Fellow of the Australian Academy of the Humanities. His publications include *The Cambridge Introduction to French Literature*, *The Cambridge Companion to Zola*, *Zola and the Bourgeoisie*, and translations of Zola's *Earth* (with Julie Rose), *The Fortune of the Rougons*, *The Belly of Paris*, *The Kill*, *Pot Luck*, and *The Ladies' Paradise*. He was awarded the New South Wales Premier's Prize for Translation in 2015.

ADAM WATT is Professor of French and Comparative Literature at the University of Exeter. He has published widely on the life and works of Marcel Proust. His books include a monograph *Reading in Proust's* A la recherche: *le délire de la lecture* (Oxford University Press, 2009); an illustrated biography, *Marcel Proust* (Reaktion Books, 2013; Chinese edition, Lijian Publishing, 2015); and, as editor, *Marcel Proust in Context* (Cambridge University Press, 2013).

OXFORD WORLD'S CLASSICS

*For over 100 years Oxford World's Classics have brought
readers closer to the world's great literature. Now with over 700
titles—from the 4,000-year-old myths of Mesopotamia to the
twentieth century's greatest novels—the series makes available
lesser-known as well as celebrated writing.*

*The pocket-sized hardbacks of the early years contained
introductions by Virginia Woolf, T. S. Eliot, Graham Greene,
and other literary figures which enriched the experience of reading.
Today the series is recognized for its fine scholarship and
reliability in texts that span world literature, drama and poetry,
religion, philosophy and politics. Each edition includes perceptive
commentary and essential background information to meet the
changing needs of readers.*

OXFORD WORLD'S CLASSICS

MARCEL PROUST

Swann in Love

Translated by
BRIAN NELSON

With an Introduction and Notes by
ADAM WATT

OXFORD
UNIVERSITY PRESS

OXFORD
UNIVERSITY PRESS

Great Clarendon Street, Oxford, OX2 6DP,
United Kingdom

Oxford University Press is a department of the University of Oxford.
It furthers the University's objective of excellence in research, scholarship,
and education by publishing worldwide. Oxford is a registered trade mark of
Oxford University Press in the UK and in certain other countries

Translation © Brian Nelson 2017
Editorial material © Adam Watt 2017

The moral rights of the authors have been asserted

First published as an Oxford World's Classics paperback 2017

Impression: 2

Published in the United States of America by Oxford University Press
198 Madison Avenue, New York, NY 10016, United States of America

British Library Cataloguing in Publication Data

Data available

Library of Congress Control Number: 2017935259

ISBN 978–0–19–874489–4

Printed in Great Britain by
Clays Ltd, Elcograf S.p.A.

CONTENTS

INTRODUCTION

SWANN IN LOVE is a brilliant, devastating novella that tells of infatuation, love, jealousy, and suffering. It is a love story that illuminates the fragilities and foibles of human subjects when in the grip of desire, set against the backdrop of Paris during the last decades of the nineteenth century, the time of the *Belle Epoque*.[1] This is the tale of Charles Swann, a highly cultured man-about-town, and the psychological turmoil into which he is plunged when he falls for a young woman by the name of Odette de Crécy. *Swann in Love* is an integral part of the complex narrative structure of the seven-volume novel *In Search of Lost Time* (*A la recherche du temps perdu*, 1913–27) by Marcel Proust (1871–1922). It takes up approximately one third of the first volume, *Swann's Way*, sandwiched between the opening section ('Combray'), which tells of the narrator-protagonist's childhood in the village of that name, during which Swann is introduced as a family friend, and the much shorter closing section 'Place-names: the name', which reflects on a much later stage in the narrator's life. The chronology here is complex: *Swann in Love* tells of a period in Swann's life that pre-dates the narrator's birth. It is an extended flashback, therefore, providing the backstory to the elegant and somewhat enigmatic figure we meet in 'Combray'. Chronologically, the events of *Swann in Love* are the earliest in Proust's narrative, and Swann's relationship with Odette provides a blueprint of sorts for many other amorous relationships we encounter later in *In Search of Lost Time*. It is thus a crucial building block in the edifice of Proust's novel yet at the same time it is a stand-alone novella that can be very fruitfully read as such. In this it is something of an oddity. Proust, the story goes, is all about heft and stamina: it is about hand- and eye-wearying tomes that pile up to a total of over three thousand pages of text. Yet here is *Swann in Love*, a sprightly, slender volume that one might read in two or three

---

[1] Readers seeking further historical and cultural-historical background to the period of Proust's novel are well served by Robert Gildea's *Children of the Revolution: The French 1799–1914* (London: Allen Lane, 2008) and, particularly for its focus on time and space as seen through the prism of the arts in the period, Stephen Kern, *The Culture of Time and Space: 1880–1918* (Cambridge, MA, and London: Harvard University Press, 2003 [1983]).

sittings, neither a sprawling epic nor a fearsome modernist puzzle, but more straightforwardly a love story: *Un amour de Swann*, to give it its French title. Readers who choose to read the whole of *In Search of Lost Time* spend a great many hours in the company of the book's narrator. It is perhaps the greatest first-person narrative of all time. From this perspective, too, *Swann in Love* is at odds with the rest of the *Search*, since the first-person narrator makes only a handful of fleeting appearances: the text is otherwise exclusively, intimately (and at times agonizingly) focused on Charles Swann and the love affair that shapes his life.

For many years various editions of *Un amour de Swann* have been available to readers of French, providing an affordable, approachable taster for those whose interest in Proust has been piqued but who are perhaps not quite ready for the long-haul commitment to *In Search of Lost Time* as a whole. The present volume now offers that same opportunity to English-language readers, in a new translation by Brian Nelson. Until now, those intent on broaching Proust's novel have been obliged to start with the 400-plus pages of *Swann's Way*, or pick one of the other six weighty volumes at random.[2] *Swann in Love* provides an excellent alternative access route to Proust's writing. Many readers (and this was also true in Proust's day) find the often inward-looking, associative, slow-moving nature of the writing in 'Combray' hard to get used to. Proust's famously long and complex sentences—which typically reflect long and complex thought processes—represent a challenging interpretive work-out for the first-time reader and yield little to he or she who seeks the brisker gratifications of an action-driven plot. Starting with *Swann in Love* to a large extent allows readers to sidestep those potential barriers. Much of the apparent indirection or circuitousness of Proust's writing in 'Combray' (and elsewhere in the *Search*) comes as a result of his wish to make time—our lived, subjective experience of temporality—the very substance of his art.

---

[2] The seven volumes of the novel are titled *Du côté de chez Swann* (*Swann's Way*); *A l'ombre des jeunes filles en fleurs* (*In the Shadow of Young Girls in Flower*); *Le Côté de Guermantes* (*The Guermantes Way*); *Sodome et Gomorrhe* (*Sodom and Gomorrah*); *La Prisonnière* (*The Captive*); *Albertine disparue* (*The Fugitive*); and *Le Temps retrouvé* (*Time Regained*). In 1984 a stand-alone edition of *Swann in Love* was published by Vintage Books, with a preface by the film-maker Volker Schlöndorff, as a tie-in with the release of his film adaptation of *Swann in Love*, starring Jeremy Irons and Ornella Muti, but it is no longer in print.

The multifaceted nature of Proust's writing, its imbrications, its coils and loops, can put off those experiencing it for the first time, but these qualities do not represent indulgent or arbitrary obscurantism. Rather, it is through syntax, word choice, imagery, and even punctuation that Proust seeks to approximate the non-linear, non-neat-and-tidy ways in which we experience temporality. The famously challenging, destabilizing opening pages of 'Combray' derive their complexity from the fact that in those pages we are witness to the narrator-protagonist of this vast novel trying to establish not only where in time and space he finds himself but also *who* he is. Such philosophical enquiry is not wholly foreign to the pages of *Swann in Love*, but this latter's status as a love story told essentially in the third person makes it more conventional and approachable in terms of its narrative structure. Its thematic preoccupations, however, are cut from very much the same cloth as the rest of the *Search*, which makes *Swann in Love* an excellent introduction to Proust's novel as a whole. In concentrated form we find the exploration of how social context colours the way individuals interact (often to great comic effect), how they relate to works of art, how infatuation leads to what we call love, and how this can spill over into jealousy. It is a study in desire, an examination of how the pursuit of pleasure inevitably brings with it some measure of suffering. It also returns repeatedly to the question of truth in human relations and how capable we are of telling lies (even, or especially, to ourselves) when it suits us, yet we cower and crumble when we discover (or simply suspect) that our beloved might have lied to us. In all of this *Swann in Love* anticipates the larger movements of Proust's novel, outlined below.

Lessons in Love

Proust's *Search* provides an expansive account of French life in the *fin de siècle* period. Its themes and preoccupations—time and memory, art and aesthetics, perception and sensation, desire and pleasure, sexuality, love, jealousy, mortality, loss—are largely revealed in *Swann's Way* before fuller exposition and exploration in later volumes. In this way 'Combray' functions as an operatic overture does, introducing the core cast of characters, the key themes and motifs of the work. The centrality of time and memory to the development of the novel is given prominence early on in the renowned 'madeleine scene', familiar even to those who have not read any Proust. In this scene, the protagonist, with a sudden and quite unanticipated rush of happiness, recalls a whole swathe of childhood experience at Combray that he thought he had forgotten for ever. The vivid involuntary memory comes back to him as an adult as a result of tasting a spoonful of some madeleine cake dissolved in lime-blossom tea: the taste sensation recalls his experience of tasting the same concoction during his childhood and effectively rekindles in the adult the little boy he once was, giving him the impression of existing at one and the same time in the present and the past. The experience of course is fleeting, but its import is fundamental to the protagonist. Such moments intimate a continuity of the self through time and counter for him the prevailing gloomy sense he had hitherto had of consisting of a succession of fragmented, discontinuous selves. *Swann in Love* has at its core a similar experience of involuntary memory, though rather than being associated with joy and exhilaration as it is for the protagonist in 'Combray', for Swann it is an experience that teaches him lessons about love that are far harder to swallow than a spoonful of cake crumbs dissolved in tea. The seeds of Swann's love for Odette are sown when he unexpectedly hears in her presence a piece of music he had listened to once before. The unanticipated pleasure and contentment derived from hearing anew the sonata for piano and violin by the (fictional) composer Vinteuil becomes associated with the relationship that subsequently develops between Swann and Odette: they come to think of it as the 'anthem of their love'. In the latter stages of *Swann in Love*, having all but separated from Odette and purposefully avoided the sonata, Swann hears it once more and finds himself involuntarily confronting his feelings for the woman he cannot but associate with a particular 'little phrase' from that sonata. The little phrase, fleeting and condensed as it may be, contains by turns the tenderness of Klimt's *Kiss* and the aching turmoil of Munch's *Scream*.[3]

---

[3] Gustav Klimt (1862–1918) and Edvard Munch (1863–1944) were both contemporaries of Proust, though it seems he did not encounter their work. Munch's *The Scream* was painted in 1893, during approximately the period dealt with in *Swann in Love*; Klimt's *The Kiss* dates from 1907–8, the year that *In Search of Lost Time* began to take shape in Proust's notebooks. The Chilean film-maker Raoul Ruiz directed films relating to both Proust and Klimt: his fascinating, surrealistic *Le Temps retrouvé* (*Time Regained*) appeared in 1999, whilst his biopic *Klimt* appeared in 2006. John Malkovich, who plays the Baron de Charlus in *Time Regained*, also plays the title role in *Klimt*.

While the opening section of *Swann's Way* presents the rural, slow-paced, often quaint, familial setting of Combray, *Swann in Love* announces the more dynamic societal world of Paris that will be the setting for much of the remainder of the *Search*. Love is undoubtedly an important theme in 'Combray' but the focus here is principally on the protagonist's childhood love for his mother, whose attention and embrace at bedtime he was on occasion forced to forgo as a result of the presence of a dinner-guest who kept his mother from him. That guest, 'the unwitting author of all my sadness' ('l'auteur inconscient de mes tristesses'), as the narrator puts it, was Charles Swann.[4] In *Swann in Love*, where we travel back to Swann's younger years, before his marriage, we find that he was already the author of a good deal of sadness of his own.[5] But the pattern of suffering in love that we encounter in *Swann in Love*, which takes a series of forms—from infatuation, blinkeredness, and possessiveness to creeping suspicion and crushing jealousy—recurs not only in the narrator's later relationship with Albertine (see below) but also in the relations of, for example, Robert de Saint-Loup and his mistress Rachel or the Baron de Charlus and the violinist Charlie Morel. Human desire, by Proust's account, whether directed toward the same or the opposite sex, tends sooner or later to lead individuals to behave in ways that are damaging to themselves and hurtful to those they love.

The Art of Love

Works of art—and not just Vinteuil's sonata—punctuate Swann's trajectory in *Swann in Love*. A simple glance through the notes appended to this edition will make it clear that while artistic references of all sorts abound, two main periods stand out as the most frequently occurring; the first is the nineteenth century, which is to say the period contemporary to the novella. *Swann in Love* can be read as a commentary on the fascinating coexistence of various cultures—high-, middle-, and low-brow—in the Paris of the Belle Epoque. A marked conflict of taste exists between Swann, who moves in sophisticated circles and attended the École du Louvre (the establishment

---

[4] *Du côté de chez Swann* in *A la recherche du temps perdu*, ed. Jean-Yves Tadié, 4 vols (Paris: Gallimard, 1987–9), i. 43. My translation.

[5] Swann eventually marries Odette. This detail is occluded from *Swann in Love*, yet it is revealed to readers of *Swann's Way* in 'Combray', where Swann's marriage is mentioned as a point of controversy and local gossip.

that produces museum conservators trained in subjects such as art history and archaeology), and the bourgeois of the Verdurin circle, especially Odette, whose tastes are, in the main, diametrically opposed to his own. The second period is, broadly speaking, the Renaissance: time and again in these pages we find allusions to artists from the fifteenth to seventeenth centuries, to Botticelli and to Michelangelo, to Mantegna, Rembrandt, and Vermeer. The eyes through which Swann sees the world are those of a connoisseur (perhaps a dilettante) but not the eyes of an artist—for these we must turn to Proust's fictional artists, those who, as the *Search* progresses, serve in a variety of ways as tutelary figures to the protagonist: the composer Vinteuil, the painter Elstir, and the writer Bergotte.

Swann's points of reference are the old masters; Odette's are twee, popular numbers from the theatre and vaudeville, the very mention of which would normally cause Swann to recoil in discomfort. Curiously, though, it is his learning and culture that lead him, in part, to fall for Odette. The enchantment of the little phrase from Vinteuil is part of the spell, but another aspect is Swann's tendency to find in visual art substitutes or replacements for the figures he encounters in real life. In the footmen on the stairs of Madame de Saint-Euverte's residence, for example, Swann sees figures from Mantegna and Dürer, and in the kitchen-maid at Combray he sees an embodiment of Giotto's 'Charity' (1304–6) from the Scrovegni Chapel in Padua. However, his most enduring artistic substitution comes with Odette. What captures his imagination is the resemblance she bears to the figure of Jethro's daughter, Zipporah, as depicted, famously, in Botticelli's fresco of 'Scenes from the Life of Moses' (1481–2). Swann is quickly in thrall to the idea that Odette is an embodiment of an ideal of beauty and grace otherwise only accessible via a reproduction in a book or, at best, by craning one's neck and squinting up from some twenty metres below in the Sistine Chapel itself. His admiration for art blinkers him to the actual failings of the flesh-and-blood Odette and clouds his awareness of their incompatibilities as a couple. And so it is that their 'love', as Proust presents it, gathers strength and its hold over Swann: since his imagination is captured by the emotive power of Vinteuil's music and the entrancing quality of Botticelli's Zipporah, his rational judgement is suppressed or ignored. Love, in Proust's vision of things, is a contrary force and as *Swann in Love* unfolds it becomes more and more clear that rather than being soul-mates

somehow cosmically destined to share a life together, as a conventionally romantic love story might have it, Swann and Odette are in fact
bonded by his idolatrous relation to art.[6]

What brings an additional dimension to the story is Swann's awareness of his self-deception. While he experiences the predictable sentiments of one who is 'falling in love', before long he recognizes his
infatuation for what it is, sees through the veil he had cast over the
vulgarities and improprieties of the Verdurins, and is disabused of his
illusions, yet he is unable to break away from Odette. This process is
most evident, perhaps, if we examine two accounts of Swann's interior
monologue, the first an encomium and the second a furious rant.
In the grip of his infatuation, Swann persuades himself that the
Verdurin salon consists of 'charming people'. 'That's the kind of life
one should lead!', he says to himself (p. 58). But soon, hostile towards
his connections beyond their intimate circle and keen to ingratiate
Odette with the less threatening and more malleable Forcheville, the
Verdurins turn against Swann. His exclusion from a trip to Chatou is
the embittering final straw that prompts a seething tirade. They are
'at the bottom of the social ladder, the last circle of Dante' and, he
concludes, 'it was high time I stopped demeaning myself by mixing
with those vile, dreadful people' (p. 95). Despite this pendulum swing
and the force of his realization, Swann does not turn his back on
Odette, but—if anything—redoubles his efforts to keep apprised of
her whereabouts. The damage, however, is done, and it is the vocabulary of illness, of pain, torture, and suffering that comes to dominate
in the second half of the novella: although Swann realizes that he has
deluded himself, the attachment he has to Odette leaves him all but
powerless to slough it off. Possessiveness, and the morale-sapping,
appetite-suppressing, sleep-depriving actions and preoccupations
that jealousy fuels, affect Swann to his very core. To witness him fran-
tically scouring the boulevards for Odette, or peering feverishly up at
her window from outside in the street, late at night, is to witness the
grip in which he is held by his infatuation. The threat of Forcheville
and the claims of an anonymous letter are but two aspects of Swann's

---

[6] Swann's tendency towards mediated forms of desire or, to put it another way, his
habit of investing in interposed, substitute objects is memorably epitomized in his allusion to their love-making as 'do a cattleya', in reference to the orchids Odette wore in her
corsage when they consummated their relationship.

struggle. Beyond the real-life rival there looms a host of imagined lovers, trysts and assignations, and as Swann's scholarly inquisitiveness is channelled into his enquiries about Odette's fidelity, her evasiveness and partial revelations (often of details Swann had never previously suspected) only augment his turmoil. Suspicions—that Odette might have previously been a kept woman, that she might have been seeing Forcheville more than she had let on, that she might have had lesbian relationships—consume Swann's mental energy, yet the intractability of what he seeks, the fact that a full and comprehensive knowledge of her past and her present is impossible, keeps him inexorably in pursuit of an unreachable goal.

Culture and Society

To read *Swann in Love* as a love story, as we have seen, involves coming up against Proust's gloomy, not to say pessimistic, view of human relations. It should be noted, however, that Proust's presentation of sexual identity and preference as quantities that shift and vary throughout a person's life and according to circumstance was extremely radical in its time. Both Odette and Albertine have affairs with lovers of both sexes and Swann's fears about Odette's lesbian affairs adumbrate those that preoccupy the protagonist to the point of obsession in his relations with Albertine. In *In the Shadow of Young Girls in Flower*, even during the earliest stages of his relationship with Albertine, he expresses suspicions about her intimacy with the other girls at Balbec. He pries, he questions, he insinuates, just as Swann had before him. Later in the novel it is the belief that he has 'proof' of her lesbian past in a remark she makes about a close friendship with the composer Vinteuil's daughter, who was known to be a lesbian, that prompts the protagonist to move Albertine into his Paris apartment where he hopes he can prevent her from further indulging such proclivities. In *The Captive*, we find that the narrator's mind, even more inquisitive than Swann's, proves to be a yet richer source of hypothetical situations in which his beloved may or may not have deceived him or betrayed him with other young women, or with men. And the fear of otherness—in this case, the straight man's fear of lesbian betrayal—is illustrative of the socio-cultural climate at the time of which Proust writes.

On the basis of *Swann in Love*, one might not initially consider

Swann himself to be an individual with whom one would associate alterity or outsider status: he is an associate of the Prince of Wales, a close friend of the President of the Republic, a member of the exclusive Jockey Club. Yet for all these seemingly unequivocal marks of being an elite 'insider' (the status, indeed, that keeps the Verdurins, as aspiring bourgeois, from ever fully accepting him), in late nineteenth-century France, one detail of Swann's identity indelibly marks him out from those with whom he associates: his Jewishness. Swann's origins as the son of a Jewish stockbroker, about which readers learn in 'Combray', differentiate him from his blue-blooded friends and associates. The shifting attitudes towards him and his family (and towards other Jewish characters) as the Dreyfus Affair unfolds are explored by Proust in particular in *The Guermantes Way* and in *Sodom and Gomorrah*, where the plight of Jews in contemporary society is compared at length with that of another persecuted minority group: homosexuals.[7] Social acceptance—being 'in' or 'out', fashionable or behind the times, up-to-date or out-of-touch—is a major theme of *Swann in Love*, which is, after all, more than a 'mere' love story. It offers a snapshot of various strata of French society at the *fin de siècle*; the contemporary artistic allusions that underpin the novella point towards this, as suggested above, but a range of other elements in the narrative are also revealing of the societal backdrop of 1880s Paris.[8]

---

[7] The Dreyfus Affair grew out of the case of Alfred Dreyfus, a Jewish Captain in the French army who in 1894 was convicted of treason for allegedly selling secrets to the Germans. Dreyfus was publicly degraded then deported and held in solitary confinement in dreadful conditions on Devil's Island (off the coast of French Guiana). The case stirred powerful and widespread anti-Semitism in France throughout the 1890s. Public pressure, including the campaigning of the novelist Émile Zola (1840–1902), his emphatic public letter 'J'accuse!' (1898), and the 'Manifesto of the Intellectuals', a petition on which Proust's signature appears, led to Dreyfus's retrial. Despite the weight of the case against the army, for their framing of Dreyfus and the various cover-ups that had ensued, Dreyfus, farcically, was found guilty a second time. He was eventually pardoned in 1899 and reinstated in the army, but the divisions the affair had caused ran deep. For an incisive account of the role of the affair in Proust's novel see Edward J. Hughes, 'The Dreyfus Affair', in Adam Watt, ed., *Marcel Proust in Context* (Cambridge: Cambridge University Press, 2013), 167–73; for a readable and authoritative historical account of the affair, see Ruth Harris, *The Man on Devil's Island: Alfred Dreyfus and the Affair that Divided France* (London: Allen Lane, 2010).

[8] It is unusual, in discussion of Proust's novel, to be able to identify with certainty the period of a given episode, for reasons outlined above in relation to the novel's shifting narrative perspectives. The autonomy of *Swann in Love* as a retrospective account of a single set of events makes it a case apart. Indeed, there are more explicit references to concrete dates and events in these pages than anywhere else in the *Search*. Swann, for

The opening of the novella submerges us without preamble in the resolutely bourgeois salon of Monsieur and Madame Verdurin. By contrast to the Guermantes who trace their noble line back centuries, into the very pages of French history, Madame Verdurin, we are told, 'came from a respectable, extremely wealthy, and utterly undistinguished family' (p. 3). Proust's novel is structured throughout with parallelisms, mirrorings, and echoes, and within *Swann in Love* we find an illuminating structural parallel between the bourgeois salon of the Verdurins and the aristocratic Saint-Euverte salon at which Swann suffers his final realizations about the state of his relationship with Odette towards the end of the novella. What Proust presents here are two worlds that exist in parallel. Swann is an extreme rarity, as an individual who shuttles between the two. Whilst each social class outwardly condemns the other as variously vulgar, tawdry, lacking in taste, dull and unthinkably boring, we glimpse how the attraction of the unknown creates an allure around the aristocratic milieux in the eyes of the bourgeois and how the aristocrats themselves seem desperate to hold on to a world that is increasingly under threat of extinction. Proust uses the two salons to hold up a range of characters to satirical scrutiny, and neither side, bourgeois or aristocratic, is portrayed in a particularly endearing light. A notable contrast is that a good number of the guests at the Verdurin salon have occupations: Cottard is a doctor, Monsieur 'Biche' a painter, Brichot an academic at the Sorbonne, and Saniette an archivist. As such they have a degree of anchorage in the world beyond the drawing-room and dining table that is rather more substantive than that of the aristocrats who mingle *chez* Saint-Euverte. Swann, although loosely engaged in writing a study of the Dutch artist Vermeer (1632–75), is essentially a man of leisure, someone used to having the means to satisfy his desires as whim may take him, yet he has a familiarity with the world outside that of the upper crust because he does not see social standing as a barrier to possible sexual gratification and accordingly pursues young girls of the working class as readily as he does women of noble birth. Proust sensitizes us to the class divides in French society whilst at the same time alerting us to the foibles and insecurities that are common to all human subjects, regardless of heredity or income. *Chez* Verdurin,

example, is said to be a regular diner with Président Grévy: Jules Grévy's presidential term ran from 1879 to 1887.

Doctor Cottard is perpetually fearful of having misunderstood a coded reference or blundered over a question of etiquette and so constantly churns out puns, clichés, and non-sequiturs in the hope of keeping face, whilst the painter revels in vulgarity, knowing that his status as an artist in such surroundings grants him immunity from criticism. Meanwhile, in the Saint-Euverte salon we find minor aristocrats eager to ensure that others are aware of their more distinguished connections and, just as Madame Verdurin perpetually overemphasizes how moved she is by the works of art she encounters, we find a competitive edge to the way Madame de Saint-Euverte's guests record their appreciation of the music being played. In short, we see variations on effectively the same anxieties and the same compensatory, defensive responses to them. The two salons are arenas for the observation of human interaction—it is not by chance that the novelist encountered at Madame de Saint-Euverte's indicates that he is there 'as an observer' (p. 130)—and Proust's astonishing ear for argot and tell-tale class-marked uses of language, as well as his eye for the physical tics and twitches that mark us out individually and as groups within groups, provide much of the liveliness and energy of these scenes.

Swann is unique in his participation in both salons, but another element also straddles the divide and this, for Swann, spells disaster: it is the piece of music that is played, Vinteuil's sonata for piano and violin. When Swann and the Princesse des Laumes meet at Madame de Saint-Euverte's salon their conversation is a joy to encounter: it is easy-going and understated, much is unsaid, insinuated. The wit, humour, and mutual understanding of two old friends, meeting in territory familiar to them both, are captured wonderfully, and strike a marked contrast to Swann's more reserved interactions with the Verdurin set. His spark and verve are quickly extinguished, however, once the strains of Vinteuil's sonata reach his discerning ears. Hearing the sonata once again brings about the involuntary memory of happier times with Odette but also brings with it the realization that the relationship has left him 'a wretched figure' he struggles even to recognize (p. 149).

Marcel Proust—A Life of Writing

Proust is best known for his vast novel-cycle *In Search of Lost Time*. It was not his only work, however. Proust is also the author of a substantial body of journalistic writings, reviews and essays on

literary and artistic topics which illuminate his age and provide a rich
sense of how his personal aesthetics developed between his years as
a precocious *lycée* student in Paris in the 1880s and the later period,
from 1908 to 1922, in which he devoted (and ultimately sacrificed) his
life to the composition and publication of his novel. Early attempts at
finding a voice and a vehicle for it can be most profitably read and
studied. In 1896 he produced a volume of mannered prose sketches
and somewhat derivative poems, many of them previously published
in newspapers and journals, entitled *Pleasures and Days* (*Les Plaisirs
et les jours*), which gave him a reputation as a lightweight society
writer, dilettantish and lacking direction. Determined to prove himself, yet uncertain of the best route to take, he subsequently channelled his creative efforts into four partially overlapping projects.
First he produced over fifteen hundred pages of manuscript notes
towards a third-person narrative that never quite coalesced into
a coherent, structured novel. Begun in 1895, these notes—above all
concerned with the thoughts, impressions, and perceptions of a young
man by the name of Jean Santeuil—were abandoned by 1899. They
were posthumously ordered, edited, and published as *Jean Santeuil*
in 1952. Although it contains a good many elements that would be
recycled or incorporated in one way or another into *In Search of Lost
Time*, *Jean Santeuil* is a long way from being an 'early novel'. We
might think of it as a set of stepping-stones at best. Secondly, between
1899 and 1906 Proust devoted his time not to the production of fiction (the *Jean Santeuil* notes had left him at something of an impasse)
but to the work of translation. In an idiosyncratic yet effective way,
Proust worked with his mother and Marie Nordlinger, the English-
speaking cousin of his friend Reynaldo Hahn, to produce French
versions of two works by the English critic, artist, social thinker, and
art historian John Ruskin (1819–1900). Proust's heavily annotated
translation of *The Bible of Amiens* appeared in 1904, followed by his
version of *Sesame and Lilies* in 1906, to which is appended an important
prefatory essay, subsequently widely republished as 'Days of Reading'.[9]
This essay in particular was a chance for Proust to explore ideas about

---

[9] *The Bible of Amiens* (1882) is Ruskin's study of the development of Christianity in
France, with a focus on Amiens and its cathedral, originally constructed in the thirteenth
century. *Sesame and Lilies* (1865) brings together two lectures Ruskin gave which treat the
education, duties, and comportment of men and women.

art, memory, and the nature of subjective experience that would feed into the pages of 'Combray' (and other parts of the *Search*). Ruskin provided lasting lessons in aesthetics, in architectural and art history, and in the less concrete but equally pertinent matter of how as individuals we relate to place and space. Proust is a writer greatly sensitive to the world around him, both its natural and built environments, and Ruskin played a major role in developing that sensitivity. The practice of translation, however, in the end left Proust unfulfilled—this was not 'real' writing, but drudgery in the service of others. His father and mother had died in 1903 and 1906 respectively; now he was alone (his brother had married and started a family), his fortieth birthday was on the horizon, and he had precious few accomplishments to speak of.

The turning point came for Proust during 1908–9 when he embarked on two broadly concurrent undertakings. Following reports of the extraordinary 'Lemoine Affair'—the tale of a crooked engineer who succeeded, for a time, in swindling the De Beers diamond company out of almost two million francs with the claim that he had mastered a method of manufacturing diamonds—Proust wrote a series of quite brilliant pastiches of well-known writers in the French tradition, based on these outlandish events. He wrote accounts of the affair in the style of (among others) the great nineteenth-century novelists Balzac and Flaubert, as well as the Goncourt brothers, the prolific critic Emile Faguet, and the historian Jules Michelet.[10] The process of identifying and reproducing the salient traits of style of revered authors was a sort of 'literary criticism in action' for Proust whilst also, crucially, serving as 'a matter of hygiene . . . necessary to purge oneself of the most natural vice of idolatry and imitation'.[11] Proust realized that by actively reproducing the writing style of others, he could avoid the risk of unconsciously doing so when producing his own work. He was thus able to arrive at the voice that speaks to us from the pages of *In Search of Lost Time*, but this would only emerge from a final transitional project that was begun at the same time Proust was crafting his pastiches.

[10] For an incisive and illuminating account of these texts and their relation to Proust's later writing, see Hannah Freed-Thall, ' "Prestige of a Momentary Diamond": Economies of Distinction in Proust', *New Literary History* 43.1 (2012), 159–78.

[11] See *Correspondance de Marcel Proust*, ed. Philip Kolb, 21 vols (Paris: Plon, 1970–93), viii. 61 and xviii. 380.

In 1908, he started working on a book-project we now know as *Against Sainte-Beuve* (*Contre Sainte-Beuve*, posthumously published in 1954), which was ultimately abandoned in favour of the novel that grew out of these notes. *Against Sainte-Beuve* can be read as one might walk around an artist's studio or workshop, examining sketches and maquettes, rough drawings and studies that show the tentative, combinatory steps that precede and foreshadow a masterpiece. Here we can see Proust trying his hand at a variety of approaches to the writerly vocation. Proust started with the idea of a critical essay taking issue with the methods of Charles-Augustin Sainte-Beuve (1804–69), the most influential French literary critic of the nineteenth century. His intention was to write a fictional dialogue between himself and his mother, who would come to his bedside and listen to his account of plans for an article challenging Sainte-Beuve's view that the merits of a given literary work are determined by the moral qualities of the writer who produced it. Proust's view—that a work of art should be judged on its own terms, regardless of the qualities of its creator— prefigures the aesthetic lessons learned in the *Search* by the novel's narrator-protagonist, as well as later twentieth-century literary theoretical writing concerning 'the death of the author' and the autonomy of the work of art. This dialogue-cum-essay, however, grew quickly beyond its anticipated dimensions and in one of Proust's notebooks from this time, known as the *Carnet de 1908*, it is possible to trace the fervent, dynamic, multi-directional movements of his thinking: here we find, intermingled with notes relating to potential developments of the essay on Sainte-Beuve, fictional fragments—sketches of scenarios and characters—as well as reading notes and scribbled lists of topics for exploration, and possible structural forms for his narrative. Gradually, in this and a succession of other *carnets* (notebooks) and *cahiers* (school jotters that Proust bought cheaply in large quantities), between 1908 and 1912 a first-person voice and a novelistic structure emerged that would, in time, become *A la recherche du temps perdu*.

Composition and Structure of In Search of Lost Time

Proust's novel is the story, told in the first person, of how an individual comes to recognize that he is ready and able to fulfil his vocation as a writer. His life is not especially eventful, but the society in which he moves, the relationships he forms, and the struggles he endures with his health serve, for most of his life, to prevent him from getting down to work. The complexity—and astonishing accomplishment—of the novel is in the telling, in the non-linear structure of the narrative, in the variability in perspective of the narrative voice that leads us through the tale and the multiple speeds at which it moves. An event or a fleeting impression is dwelt on for pages, whilst months, even years, can pass in a parenthesis. At times we hear the voice of the youthful protagonist, close to the action of which he is part, at others we are in the company of a more worldly, adult narrator looking back on the events of his life. This plurality of perspective and approach is mirrored in the composition history of the work, which rapidly and untidily grew well beyond its original anticipated parameters.

The novel's seven volumes did not materialize, of course, all at once. Proust began with *Swann's Way*, which appeared in 1913, but the second volume published, *In the Shadow of Young Girls in Flower* (1919), was not the second to be written. Proust began by writing 'Combray', the opening section of the first volume, more or less as we have it, and then wrote what we now know as the closing section of the final volume, *Time Regained*. These book-ends were in place by 1910–11 and the writing of the latter sections of the first volume and what would become the third volume, *The Guermantes Way*, followed in 1911–12. Prior to this Proust had envisaged a novel in two parts, the volumes entitled *Le Temps perdu* and *Le Temps retrouvé* (*Time Lost* and *Time Regained*), but as the first volume grew, for practical reasons a certain amount of material had to be excised and placed at the beginning of a second volume. With the publication of *Swann's Way* in 1913 a three-volume structure was therefore anticipated: the second would be *The Guermantes Way* and the last *Time Regained*. The planned overarching title at this stage was *Les Intermittences du cœur* (*The Intermittencies of the Heart*). Proust's writing, however, never tended toward concentration: proliferation, rather, is the watchword of his creative process and in 1914 the material of that envisaged second volume was in fact separated out, spliced with new drafts and expansions, to form the basis of *In the Shadow of Young Girls in Flower* and *The Guermantes Way*.

Two major events of 1914—one personal, one geopolitical—had further and fundamental impact on the development of Proust's novel. The outbreak of war meant the suspension of the publication of Proust's work, though ill health meant he was not called up for service and was thereby at liberty to continue to develop his novel during the years of the conflict. It is likely that Proust's relationship with a young man seventeen years his junior, Alfred Agostinelli, was a motivating force in his developing the story of the protagonist's relationship with a girl named Albertine, encountered among a group of young friends in the fictional resort town of Balbec. Agostinelli was a 19-year-old taxi driver when Proust first met him during his vacation in the Normandy seaside town of Cabourg in the summer of 1907. They saw each other regularly—Proust spent the summer in Cabourg every year from 1907 to 1914—and eventually, in the spring of 1913, Proust installed Agostinelli in his Paris apartment, ostensibly to serve as a secretary. When, unannounced, Agostinelli fled Paris in December 1913 for Monte Carlo, Proust was distraught and went to great lengths (in vain) to secure his return. Using money Proust had given him, Agostinelli registered at a flying school under the assumed name of 'Marcel Swann'. When news reached him that Agostinelli had drowned after crashing his plane into the sea off Antibes in May 1914, Proust was devastated. These events contributed to the shaping of two volumes of *In Search of Lost Time* that were drafted during the war years: *The Captive*, which tells of the narrator's fraught existence with Albertine in Paris, and *The Fugitive*, which deals with her flight and accidental death in a horse-riding accident. The story of the narrator's relationship with Albertine begins in *In the Shadow of Young Girls in Flower*, which became the *Search*'s second volume, published to significant acclaim—and the award of the Goncourt Prize—in 1919. *The Guermantes Way*, which offers an anatomy of Parisian high-society life in the Belle Epoque, followed in two instalments in 1920 and 1921, with the *Search*'s fourth volume, *Sodom and Gomorrah*, the heart of its radical exploration of the various shadings of human sexuality and also largely the product of the war years, appearing in two instalments in 1921 and 1922, the year of Proust's death. *The Captive* and *The Fugitive*, sometimes known as the 'Albertine cycle', were published posthumously, in 1923 and 1925 respectively, their editing (and that of *Time Regained*) completed by Proust's brother Robert and his editor Gaston Gallimard. Finally, repeatedly revised, expanded, and adjusted by Proust up to the end of his life, so as to take into account the developments of the intervening volumes unforeseen when it was first drafted in 1910–11, and dealing in significant measure with the effects of the war on life in Paris, *Time Regained* eventually appeared in 1927.[12]

Critical Reception

The reception of *Swann in Love* is very much a part of the reception first of *Swann's Way* and then of the *Search* more generally, and it should be noted that discussion of the reception of Proust's work is complicated by the extended period over which it was published (1913–27) and the great socio-cultural changes that took place during that period.[13] With a handful of exceptions (including essays by Samuel Beckett and Walter Benjamin, for example—see Select Bibliography for details), it was not until the middle years of the twentieth century that *In Search of Lost Time* as a whole began to receive serious and wide-ranging critical attention. Early reviews of *Swann's Way* were largely lukewarm: Proust's elaborate syntactical structures and shifting perspectives left many early readers somewhat perplexed. The main breakthrough for Proust and the *Search* came with the renewed impetus and publicity the work received in 1919 with the change of publisher from Grasset to the imprint of the Nouvelle revue française, the publication of *In the Shadow of Young Girls in Flower*, and the award of the Goncourt Prize to this volume. After an opening section set in Paris, Proust's second volume transports its readers to the seaside and immerses us in a bright and enchanting world of sea-spray and sunrises, of adolescent infatuation and the narrator's various, continuing initiations into the domains of society, of love, and of art, away from the confines of family life in Paris and Combray. The idea that, in Proust's novel, the protagonist's journey towards

---

[12] For a concise and authoritative account of these matters, see Nathalie Mauriac Dyer, 'Composition and Publication of *A la recherche du temps perdu*', in Watt, ed., *Marcel Proust in Context*, 34–40. Those interested in the timeline of events that can be construed from a reading of the novel will learn much from Gareth H. Steel's *Chronology and Time in A la recherche du temps perdu* (Geneva: Droz, 1979).

[13] On the early reception of Proust's work, see Anna Magdalena Elsner, 'Critical Reception During Proust's Lifetime', and Vincent Ferré, 'Early Critical Responses, 1922–1950s', in Watt, ed., *Marcel Proust in Context*, 183–90 and 191–8. For a selection of contemporary responses, from reviews of *Pleasures and Days* in the 1890s to the 'Hommage' published after Proust's death by the *Nouvelle revue française* and the earliest critical essays of the 1930s, see Leighton Hodson, ed., *Marcel Proust: The Critical Heritage* (London: Routledge, 1989).

fulfilling his vocation as a writer takes the form of a series of apprenticeships, or processes of learning how to interpret the world around
him in its multitudinous complexity, has been an influential one in
Proust criticism and stems principally from a critical study titled
Proust et les signes (*Proust and Signs*), first published by Gilles Deleuze
in 1964 and reissued, with revisions and additions, in its final form in
1970.[14] Society, love, and art all involve us in emitting or interpreting
signs of various sorts: by Deleuze's reading, then, we can think of the
bulk of *Swann in Love* as revolving round such exchanges, which are
complicated by the fact that in society and in love people are in the
habit of projecting images or emitting messages that are not wholly or
consistently truthful. And art (Deleuze argues) is made up of signs
that do not correlate to material referents in the world, and as such
are a purer, higher order of 'sign' (take, for example, the little phrase
in Vinteuil's sonata, which Swann loads with significance yet which
has no objective existence or referent beyond the fleeting sound signature emitted by the instruments that produce it).

A good deal of critical interest in *Swann in Love* is prompted by the
role of the little phrase of the sonata and, more broadly, with Proust's
handling of music and how this is integrated into his broader thematics of art and memory. The Nobel Prize-winning author Samuel
Beckett (1906–89) was one of Proust's earliest English-language critics. In his short study, first published in 1931, Beckett proposes that
'Swann is the cornerstone of the entire structure', also noting that
'a book could be written on the significance of music in the work of
Proust'.[15] Several studies have indeed since been devoted to the role
of music in Proust's novel, a number of which highlight the ways in
which Swann's experience with Vinteuil's sonata returns for Proust's
protagonist when later (in *The Captive*) he hears—unexpectedly,
just as Swann's hearing of the sonata *chez* Saint-Euverte was
unanticipated—a septet by Vinteuil, the existence of which was previously unknown to him. The same little phrase, which comes to be
cherished by Proust's protagonist and is played to him by Albertine in

[14] Gilles Deleuze, *Proust et les signes*, 4th, revised edition (Paris: Presses universitaires
de France, 1970); *Proust and Signs*, trans. Richard Howard (London: The Athlone Press,
2000). On the criticism of this period, see Thomas Baldwin, 'Mid-Twentieth-Century
Views, 1960s to 1980s', in Watt, ed., *Marcel Proust in Context*, 199–205.

[15] Samuel Beckett, *Proust and Three Dialogues with Georges Duthuit* (London: John
Calder, 1987), 34, 91.

his apartment, emerges in the septet and he has a euphoric involuntary memory experience that proves to him the extraordinary emotive force of which art is capable.[16] Swann's experience of the sonata stops short of aesthetic revelation. To this extent, some critics, such as John Cocking, one of the earliest English-language scholars of Proust's work, have interpreted Swann and Proust's protagonist as, respectively, frustrated and successful versions of essentially the same character.[17] Cocking was also one of the first to highlight the nature of *Swann in Love* as a sort of *mise-en-abyme* narrative: 'We need to have the pattern established for us in a clear-cut way at this stage', writes Cocking, 'so that we can sense the correspondences when Marcel falls in love, expect the pattern to be completed in the same way, and enjoy the surprise and understanding when it reaches a different conclusion.'[18]

In his invaluable critical study, *Proust Among the Stars* (1998), Malcolm Bowie draws our attention in particular to how the narrator's account of Swann's encounter with Vinteuil's sonata *chez* Verdurin does something rather more than describe an auditory experience. He reads the passage as a study in desire: 'Desire belongs to everyone', Bowie writes, 'and finds its opportunities everywhere. When it is not blocked or diverted, it moves in trance like progression from its first stirrings towards its "ineffable" outcome, and beyond into an afterlife of quietened but still intense sensation. Musical structure has become a modelling device for the structure of desire itself.'[19] Bowie thus suggests that Proust invites us to consider the ebb and flow of human desire as resembling the modulations of a piece of music. 'Desire as it pursues and achieves its satisfaction,' Bowie continues, 'and gradually

---

[16] The classic study of the theme is *Proust as Musician* by Jean-Jacques Nattiez, trans. Derrick Puffett (Cambridge: Cambridge University Press, 1989), originally published as *Proust musicien* (Paris: Christian Bourgois, 1984). For an insightful overview, see Julian Johnson, 'Music', in Watt, ed., *Marcel Proust in Context*, 90–6. For an elegant and stimulating piece with particular focus on Vinteuil's sonata and septet, see Alex Ross, 'Imaginary Concerts', *New Yorker*, 24 August 2009. Available online at http://www.newyorker.com/magazine/2009/08/24/imaginary-concerts.

[17] See John Cocking, 'Swann', in *Proust: Collected Essays on the Writer and his Art* (Cambridge: Cambridge University Press, 1982), 64–7. These pages are reprinted from his early short study, *Proust* (London: Bowes and Bowes, 1956).

[18] Cocking, 'Swann', 167. Like Cocking here, some critics refer to the protagonist of Proust's novel as 'Marcel': on two occasions in the *Search* it is indicated that this is (or could be) his name, though these are in *The Captive*, which Proust did not himself finish editing before his death.

[19] Malcolm Bowie, *Proust Among the Stars* (London: HarperCollins, 1998), 217.

descends from that summit towards its own rebirth as desire, has a familiar contour to it, and Proust figures and refigures this in terms that emphasize the generalizable properties of private experiences.'[20] This final observation is apposite for *Swann in Love* but also for the *Search* as a whole: the predominantly first-person focus of the novel does not preclude it from being a remarkable source of insights into human behaviour and interaction more generally. Nevertheless, the focus in Proust's writing on processes of mind, on desire, attraction, truth-telling, jealousy, and suspicion has prompted a significant body of psychoanalytical (or psychoanalytically-informed) criticism. Bowie himself is the author of probably the best single essay in this vein: the chapter 'Proust, jealousy, knowledge' in his comparative study *Freud, Proust and Lacan: Theory as Fiction* (1987) is required reading for anyone interested in these central themes.[21] Similarly influential and insightful is René Girard's classic 1961 study *Mensonge romantique et vérité romanesque* (published in English translation as *Desire, Deceit, and the Novel: Self and Other in Literary Structure*, 1976), which sheds significant light on what Girard identifies as the triangular nature of desiring relations in Proust, as well as on the societal forces that shape them.[22] Additionally, although less immediately accessible in its style, the major study by critic, theorist, and novelist Julia Kristeva, *Le Temps sensible: Proust et l'expérience littéraire*, which appeared in 1994 (*Time and Sense: Proust and the Experience of Literature*, 1996), is worth the effort. Kristeva is also a psychoanalyst and her approach reflects this; she explicitly counters Deleuze's contention about the protagonist's 'apprenticeships' and writes lucidly about Swann's role as precursor and quasi-paternal double of the narrator.[23]

A final area of interest for critics of *Swann in Love* is what we might broadly term sociological and cultural-historical critique. Daniel Karlin's sparkling study *Proust's English* (2005) contains much material relating to *Swann in Love*, especially in the chapter on 'Swann and

---

[20] Ibid.

[21] Malcolm Bowie, *Freud, Proust and Lacan: Theory as Fiction* (Cambridge: Cambridge University Press, 1987), 46–65.

[22] See René Girard, *Mensonge romantique et vérité romanesque* (Paris: Grasset/Fasquell, 1961) and *Desire, Deceit, and the Novel: Self and Other in Literary Structure*, trans. Y. Freccero (Baltimore, MD: Johns Hopkins University Press, 1976).

[23] Julia Kristeva, *Le temps sensible: Proust et l'expérience littéraire* (Paris: Gallimard, 1994); *Time and Sense: Proust and the Experience of Literature*, trans. Ross Guberman (New York: Columbia University Press, 1996).

Odette'.[24] Karlin contextualizes Odette's penchant for Anglicism within the history of Anglo-French relations and late nineteenth-century culture, whilst demonstrating how it feeds into the novel's broader thematics of social interaction and acceptance, sexuality and aesthetics. The book-jacket of Karlin's study bears a reproduction of James Tissot's famous painting *Le balcon du Cercle de la rue Royale* (*The Balcony of the Rue Royale Circle*, 1868), a work depicting a dozen members of a highly exclusive private club, including, on the right-hand side of the canvas, Charles Haas (1833–1902), who was an acquaintance of Proust's and a model for Charles Swann. Haas was Jewish, wealthy, idle, intelligent, and, as well as belonging to the *Cercle de la rue Royale* he was (like Swann) a member of the similarly exclusive Jockey Club.[25] The opulence on show in Tissot's painting—the sheen of top hats, the glimmer of polished shoes, the plumply upholstered furniture, the poise, comfort, and assurance in leisure of its subjects—captures one of the social worlds of *Swann in Love*. Proust's sensitivity to the coexistence of multiple strata in society and to what happens when they intermingle is at the heart of Edward Hughes's superb study *Proust, Class, and Nation* (2011). Readers will learn much from Hughes's chapter on 'Taste in *Un amour de Swann*', in which he argues that the novella 'delivers [. . .] a form of social psychoanalysis to which sociology approximates especially in its analysis of taste'.[26] Indeed, Hughes relates the themes of class and taste (artistic and otherwise) to the preoccupations with national identity, Judaism, and societal flux that subtend so much of *In Search of Lost Time*, as the following remark makes clear: 'whether we stress Swann's paternalistic will to exert cultural influence over his inferiors or the reader's sense that the Narrator wishes to deflate the pomposity

---

[24] Daniel Karlin, *Proust's English* (New York: Oxford University Press, 2005), 71–115.

[25] Proust most likely had another contemporary additionally in mind when constructing the character of Swann: Charles Ephrussi (1849–1905), who was also Jewish, and very well-connected in the worlds of art and high society. Ephrussi was an art historian and critic who gave Proust access to the archives of the *Gazette des beaux-arts*, where he was able to consult reproductions of many of the artworks mentioned in *In Search of Lost Time*. Public interest in Ephrussi was recently stirred by Edmund de Waal's fascinating family memoir, which focuses on a collection of netsuke first owned by Charles Ephrussi: see *The Hare with Amber Eyes: A Hidden Inheritance* (London: Chatto & Windus, 2010).

[26] Edward J. Hughes, ' "Tout est affaire d'époque, de classe": Taste in *Un amour de Swann*', in *Proust, Class, and Nation* (Oxford: Oxford University Press, 2011), 85–110 (p. 85).

of Swann's claims, the story of an unhappy love in *Un amour de Swann* is simultaneously conveyed as the record of a culture war.'[27]

* * *

It has long been a commonplace of Proust criticism to compare *In Search of Lost Time* to the great epics of the European tradition, from Dante's *Divine Comedy* and Cervantes' *Don Quixote* to Robert Musil's *The Man Without Qualities*. Now, with Karl Ove Knausgård's six-volume autobiographical cycle *My Struggle*, critics are looking back to Proust as the Ur-model of the form. Reading *Swann in Love*, however, goes some way to counter this tendency to equate Proust only with what the French call works of *longue haleine* (not long-winded, but rather those requiring significant time and effort). *Swann in Love* is a short fiction that should be considered alongside other bewitching masterpieces of the form, from Henry James's *Daisy Miller* (1878) to Georges Rodenbach's *Bruges-la-morte* (1892), Thomas Mann's *Death in Venice* (1912), Raymond Radiguet's *The Devil in the Flesh* (1923), and even Nabokov's *Lolita* (1955). It is a concentrated masterpiece that deserves acknowledgement as such and one which, of course, can set readers on to a path of much more extended exploration and discovery.

[27] Ibid. 103.

TRANSLATOR'S NOTE

IN a short story entitled 'The Walk', Lydia Davis writes of a translator and a critic who happen to be together in Oxford, having been invited to take part in a conference on translation at the University. There is a certain tension between the two because the critic has previously written negatively about the translator's work. The translator-narrator, referring to the critic, with whom she goes on a walk around the town, remarks:

He felt that she kept too close to the original text. He preferred the studied cadences of an earlier version and had said so in person and in print. She felt that he admired lyricism and empty rhetorical flourishes at the expense of accuracy and faithfulness to the style of the original, which was far plainer and clearer, she said, than the flowery and obfuscating earlier version.[1]

Davis is alluding to a review by André Aciman[2] of her own translation of *Du côté de chez Swann* (*The Way by Swann's*) for the Penguin edition of Proust, while the 'earlier version' is that of C. K. Scott Moncrieff, published between 1922 and 1930, and subsequently revised by Terence Kilmartin and D. J. Enright (see Select Bibliography: Proust in English). I invoke Davis's story not to adjudicate between her and Aciman, but to bring into focus questions of style that confront anyone attempting to translate Proust. Moreover, I would echo, loudly, the words of Mark Treharne, translator of *Le Côté de Guermantes* (*The Guermantes Way*) for the Penguin edition, when he says in his Translator's Introduction: 'I have worked very much in the shadow of these previous translators and with much gratitude towards them.'

For fifty years, Moncrieff's translation *was* Proust for English-speaking readers unable to read him in the original. This translation was not simply majestic in its scale but was in many ways admirable in its realization. Moncrieff had an exquisite ear for the cadences of Proust's prose, and a considerable talent for elegant phraseology. He was prone, however, to tamper with the text, through embellishment or the gratuitous heightening of language; and his translation also

[1] *The Collected Stories of Lydia Davis* (New York: Farrar, Straus and Giroux, 'Picador', 2009), 575–87 (p. 576).
[2] 'Proust's Way?', *New York Review of Books*, 1 December 2005.

contained numerous little errors and misapprehensions and the occasional howler. The reservation most commonly voiced about his translation is that it falsified Proust's tone. He tended to make Proust sound 'flowery' and precious, whereas, as Davis rightly stresses, Proust's style, though marked by syntactic complexity, is not in the least affected or self-consciously ornate. His prose is rigorous, concentrated, exact. Kilmartin made hundreds of small, deft changes (including occasional syntactic adjustments) to Moncrieff, making his prose overall plainer and more accurate, though his revised edition remains fundamentally Moncrieff's. Davis's translation is impressive in its exactitude; but her determination to stay as close as possible to the original, not only in terms of diction but also in the retention of the precise order of elements in a sentence, runs the risk of compromising her ability to write idiomatic English. 'Accuracy' and 'faithfulness' are not quite the same.

The aim of the present edition is to introduce Proust to a new and wider audience by offering, in a manageable compass, a well-crafted example of his key themes and signature style. That *Proustian* style is largely identified with his famously long sentences, with their 'coiling elaboration'.[3] As they uncoil, the sentences express the rhythms of a sensibility, the directions and indirections of desire, the complication and conflicts of a mind—Swann's—in the grip of doubts and uncertainties, obsessions and fantasies. I have tried to capture the intricate harmonies of those sentences, which combine syntactic complexity with complete clarity. Grand rhythm and aphoristic concentration often work together. Proust's sentences are elaborately constructed, but they have a beautiful precision and rhythmic balance: a musicality that becomes particularly apparent when the text is read aloud.

I have tried to maintain the full range of Proust's tones and registers, and the shifts between them; and to catch as much as possible of his humour. Proust is not only a great prose stylist but also a great comic writer. His comedy is various: the out-and-out comedy of characters like the buffoon Cottard (with the consequent need to catch such characters' particular idioms of speech—to mimic Proust's mimicry, so to speak); the high comedy of the great set-scenes; the narrator's

---

[3] Richard Howard, 'Intermittencies of the Heart', in *The Proust Project*, ed. André Aciman (New York: Farrar, Straus and Giroux, 2004), 98.

wry wit; and the irony that informs the portrayal of Swann's tormented feelings as well as the social pretensions of his circle. It is important to capture the 'double-think' subtleties of Swann's interior monologue expressed in free indirect style: to capture, as one of the anonymous readers of an early sample translation nicely put it, 'the veneer of genteel intellectualism over Swann's frustrated lust, and the algebra of sentiments and calculated motives [which comes across] as representing the way the character is thinking (rather than, in reality, the way the narrator is constructing his thoughts with his omniscience and literary artifice)'.

Style is vision. In general terms, I would characterize the art of translation as a particular, and particularly intense, form of critical reading and creative writing, involving a multiplicity of exact choices about voice, tone, register, rhythm, syntax, echoes, sounds, connotations—the colour, texture, and music of words: all those factors that make up 'style' and reflect the marriage between style and meaning. I agree very much with Christopher Prendergast's statement that 'the kinds of judgments and decisions bound up with literary translation make it one of the higher forms of criticism'.[4]

I wish to record my gratitude to a number of friends and colleagues who, very generously, read my translation and offered useful comments: Valerie Minogue, Adam Watt, Judith Luna, Alexandre Pateau, and Guillaume Gourdon. My thanks, too, to the Fondation Ledig-Rowohlt for granting me a residency at its wonderful writers' colony in Lavigny, Switzerland, where I had a book-lined (not cork-lined) room in which to complete this translation. Finally, I would like to dedicate my translation to the memory of my mother, Ida Nelson, who taught me more about language and its uses than she ever knew.

B.N.

---

[4] Quoted by Boyd Tonkin in 'Christopher Prendergast: "Proust is an invitation to slow down" ', *The Independent*, 12 October 2002.

SELECT BIBLIOGRAPHY

Un amour de Swann was first published as part of *Du côté de chez Swann* by Grasset in 1913. The authoritative scholarly edition of Proust's complete novel is the second 'Pléiade' text, edited by Jean-Yves Tadié: *A la recherche du temps perdu*, 4 vols, 'Bibliothèque de la Pléiade' (Paris: Gallimard, 1987–9). *Un amour de Swann* is found in the first volume, pp. 185–375. The text of the Pléiade edition, without the notes and critical apparatus, is available in a single, hefty paperback: *A la recherche du temps perdu*, edited by Jean-Yves Tadié, 'Collection Quarto' (Paris: Gallimard, 1999). *Du côté de chez Swann* and *Un amour de Swann* are available in many paperback editions in French: for the latter, published with notes and a 'dossier' of critical material, see *Un amour de Swann*, edited and annotated by Mireille Naturel (Paris: Flammarion, 2002).

Proust in English

The original English translation of *A la recherche du temps perdu*, by C. K. Scott Moncrieff (for all but the last volume), has been twice revised. First it was reworked by Terence Kilmartin, in the light of the first scholarly 'Pléiade' edition of the French text (1954); then Kilmartin's version was revisited and tweaked by D. J. Enright who in turn benefited from the second, much more comprehensive 'Pléiade' edition (1987–9). The 'final' Scott Moncrieff–Kilmartin–Enright version, still widely available today, was published by Vintage Classics in 1992 under the title *In Search of Lost Time*, eschewing Moncrieff's original title *Remembrance of Things Past*, which was a borrowing from Shakespeare's Sonnet 30. The various editions of the Scott Moncrieff translation have served generations of readers and there is undoubtedly a reassuring continuity to the work. It can be faulted, however, for being at times over-elaborate, embellished, or flowery in a way that is not in keeping with Proust's writing and that can skew the impression of the writer's voice for readers without French. William C. Carter, the eminent Proust scholar and author of an authoritative English-language biography of the writer, is currently addressing this issue by producing a comprehensively revised edition of the first translation of the novel with Yale University Press. To date, *Swann's Way* and *In the Shadow of Young Girls in Flower* have appeared. This edition has the benefit of Carter's extensive notes to the text, providing an English-language reading edition that comes close to the scholarly presentation of the French Pléiade text, though without the reproduction of drafts and variants. Finally, readers may consult the most recent complete translation of the novel, which was published in the UK in 2002 under the general editorship of Christopher Prendergast. Each of the seven volumes of the novel in this, the 'Penguin Proust', is translated by a different individual and as a result there is a degree of unevenness as one moves from volume to volume.

Works by Proust in English Translation

In Search of Lost Time, 6 vols, trans. C. K. Scott Moncrieff (except for *Time Regained*, trans. Andreas Mayor and Terence Kilmartin), revised by Terence Kilmartin and D. J. Enright (London: Vintage, 2000–2).

In Search of Lost Time, trans. C. K. Scott Moncrieff, edited and annotated by William C. Carter (New Haven and London: Yale University Press, 2013–).

In Search of Lost Time, ed. Christopher Prendergast, trans. Lydia Davis, James Grieve, Mark Treharne, John Sturrock, Carol Clark, Peter Collier, and Ian Patterson, 6 vols (London: Allen Lane/Penguin, 2002).

Swann's Way, ed. Susanna Lee, 'Norton Critical Edition' (New York and London: W. W. Norton and Company, 2014).

Against Sainte-Beuve and Other Essays, trans. John Sturrock (Harmondsworth: Penguin, 1988).

Jean Santeuil, trans. Gerard Hopkins (New York and London: Weidenfeld & Nicolson, 1955).

Pleasures and Days, trans. Andrew Brown (London: Hesperus, 2004).

Selected Letters, ed. Philip Kolb, trans. Ralph Manheim, Terence Kilmartin, and Joanna Kilmartin, 4 vols (New York and London: Doubleday/Collins/HarperCollins, 1983–2000).

Biographies of Proust in English

Albaret, Céleste, *Monsieur Proust*, trans. Barbara Bray (New York: New York Review of Books, 2003 [1976]).

Carter, William C., *Marcel Proust: A Life* (New Haven and London: Yale University Press, 2000; revised edition with new preface, 2013).

Carter, William C., *Proust in Love* (New Haven and London: Yale University Press, 2006).

Tadié, Jean-Yves, *Marcel Proust: A Biography*, trans. Euan Cameron (London: 2000 [1996]).

Watt, Adam, *Marcel Proust*, 'Critical Lives' (London: Reaktion, 2013).

White, Edmund, *Proust* (London: Weidenfeld & Nicolson, 1999).

Studies in English of Proust and his World

Bales, Richard, ed., *The Cambridge Companion to Proust* (Cambridge: Cambridge University Press, 2001), esp. Cynthia Gamble, 'From *Belle Epoque* to First World War: the Social Panorama', 7–24.

Beckett, Samuel, *Proust and Three Dialogues with Georges Duthuit* (London, 1987 [1931]).

Benjamin, Walter, 'The Image of Proust', in *Illuminations*, trans. Harry Zohn, ed. Hannah Arendt (London: Pimlico, 1999 [1970]), 197–210.

Bernard, Anne-Marie, ed., *The World of Proust as Seen by Paul Nadar*, trans. Susan Wise (Cambridge, MA, and London: MIT Press, 2002 [1999]).

Bowie, Malcolm, *Freud, Proust and Lacan: Theory as Fiction* (Cambridge: Cambridge University Press, 1987).

Bowie, Malcolm, *Proust Among the Stars* (London: HarperCollins, 1998).

Compagnon, Antoine, *Proust Between Two Centuries*, trans. Richard Goodkin (New York: Columbia University Press, 1992 [1989]).

Ellison, David, *A Reader's Guide to Proust's* In Search of Lost Time (Cambridge: Cambridge University Press, 2010).

Girard, René, *Desire, Deceit, and the Novel: Self and Other in Literary Structure*, trans. Y. Freccero (Baltimore, MD: Johns Hopkins University Press, 1976).

Hodson, Leighton, ed., *Marcel Proust: The Critical Heritage* (London: Routledge, 1989).

Hughes, Edward, *Proust, Class, and Nation* (Oxford: Oxford University Press, 2011).

Kern, Stephen, *The Culture of Time and Space: 1880–1918* (Cambridge, MA, and London: Harvard University Press, 2003 [1983]).

Watt, Adam, *The Cambridge Introduction to Marcel Proust* (Cambridge: Cambridge University Press, 2011).

Watt, Adam, ed., *Marcel Proust in Context* (Cambridge: Cambridge University Press, 2013).

Works in English relating to Swann in Love

Bersani, Leo, 'Social Contexts: Observation and Invention', in *Marcel Proust: Fictions of Life and Art* (Oxford and New York: Oxford University Press, 2013 [1965]), 139–98.

Bowie, Malcolm, 'Proust, Jealousy, Knowledge', in *Freud, Proust and Lacan: Theory as Fiction* (Cambridge: Cambridge University Press, 1987), 46–65.

Cocking, John, 'Swann', in *Proust: Collected Essays on the Writer and his Art* (Cambridge: Cambridge University Press, 1982), 64–7.

Deleuze, Gilles, *Proust and Signs*, trans. Richard Howard (London: The Athlone Press, 2000 [1964/1970]).

Hughes, Edward J., ' "Tout est affaire d'époque, de classe": Taste in *Un amour de Swann*', in *Proust, Class, and Nation* (Oxford: Oxford University Press, 2011), 85–110.

Karlin, Daniel, 'Swann and Odette', in *Proust's English* (New York: Oxford University Press, 2005), 71–115.

Nattiez, Jean-Jacques, *Proust as Musician*, trans. Derrick Puffett (Cambridge: Cambridge University Press, 1989 [1984]).

Watt, Adam, 'Lessons in Reading', in *Reading in Proust's* A la recherche: *le délire de la lecture* (Oxford: Oxford University Press, 2009), 73–9.

Watt, Adam, ed., *Swann at 100 / Swann à 100 ans* (= *Marcel Proust Aujourd'hui* 12 [2015]). Ten of the fifteen articles published here, commemorating the centenary of *Swann's Way*, are in English.

A CHRONOLOGY OF MARCEL PROUST

1871 (10 July) Marcel Proust is born to Jeanne Proust née Weil and Dr Adrien Proust in the village of Auteuil, to the west of Paris. His mother is a non-practising Jew, his father a non-practising Catholic. He is very weak in infancy.

1872 The Proust family moves to an apartment on the Boulevard Malesherbes in the 8th arrondissement of Paris.

1873 (24 May) Birth of Robert Proust, Marcel's brother.

1878–86 Family vacations at Illiers in the Eure-et-Loir (the village is renamed Illiers-Combray in 1971, commemorating Proust's novel and the centenary of Proust's birth).

1881 Proust's first, and near fatal, asthma attack. Respiratory and other health problems will henceforth be a permanent part of his life.

1882–9 Proust attends the Lycée Fontanes (renamed Condorcet in 1883); attendance poor due to ill health, but various friendships formed.

1889 Proust turns 18. His final year of *lycée*. Inauguration of the Eiffel Tower as the entrance arch to the World's Fair.

1890 Enrols at the Faculty of Law and the School of Political Science.

1891 Journalism appears in *Le Mensuel*. Thomas Hardy, *Tess of the D'Urbervilles*.

1893 Publications in the important journal *La Revue blanche*. Completes *Licence en droit*.

1894 President Carnot assassinated in Lyon by an anarchist. (Dec.) Court martial judges Captain Albert Dreyfus guilty.

1895 Completes *Licence ès lettres*. Unpaid position at the Bibliothèque mazarine. Scarcely attends due to 'ill health'. Stays in Brittany with Reynaldo Hahn. Begins notes towards *Jean Santeuil*. Trial of Oscar Wilde for gross indecency.

1896 (Mar.) Publication of *Les Plaisirs et les jours*.

1897 Duels with journalist Jean Lorrain over Lorrain's public insinuations of Proust's homosexual relation with Lucien Daudet. Neither combatant is injured. Henry James, *What Maisie Knew*.

1898 (13 Jan.) Zola's 'J'accuse!' in *L'Aurore*. Later in the year Proust attends Émile Zola's trial.

1899 *Jean Santeuil* abandoned. Proust starts work on a translation of John

Ruskin's *The Bible of Amiens*. Sigmund Freud, *Die Traudeutung* (*The Interpretation of Dreams*). Joseph Conrad, *Heart of Darkness*.

1900 Ruskin's death. Proust publishes a series of articles on Ruskin. Travels to Venice with his mother and friends in April; returns to Venice, alone, in October.

1902 Travels to Belgium and Holland with Hahn, visits Bruges and Amsterdam amongst other places. Sees Vermeer's *View of Delft* and many old Dutch masters.

1903 (Feb.) Marriage of Robert Proust. Society pieces published in *Le Figaro*. (Nov.) Sudden death of Proust's father.

1904 *La Bible d'Amiens* published. Translation of Ruskin's *Sesame and Lilies* is begun. Society journalism continues.

1905 (June) Proust's important essay on reading, the preface to *Sésame et les lys*, is published. (July) French government passes a law separating the Church from the State. Madame Proust is taken ill in Évian and rushed back to Paris by Robert. (26 Sept.) Death of Madame Proust. (Dec.) Having promised his mother he would do so before her death, Proust checks In to the clinic of Dr Paul Sollier, an experimental psychologist and ex-pupil of Jean-Martin Charcot at the Salpêtrière hospital in Paris. His psychotherapeutic treatment lasts until late January.

1906 Dreyfus reinstated in the army. *Sésame et les lys* is published. Proust resolves to move into what was his great-uncle Georges Weil's Paris residence, 102 Boulevard Haussmann.

1907 Pablo Picasso's *Demoiselles d'Avignon* completed in Paris. Various articles and stories published. Summer in Cabourg on the Normandy coast. Proust meets Alfred Agostinelli, a young taxi-driver. Proust will return to Cabourg every year between 1907 and 1914.

1908 Proust plans a project 'Contre Sainte-Beuve' ('Against Sainte-Beuve'), part critical essay, part dialogue. Features of what will become *In Search of Lost Time* take shape. Pastiches appear in *Le Figaro*. Gustav Klimt exhibits *Der Kuss* (*The Kiss*) for the first time.

1909 *Contre Sainte-Beuve* amounts to around 400 pages; publishers show no interest. F. T. Marinetti's first *Manifesto of Futurism* in Paris; Gustav Mahler's *Symphony No. 9*.

1910–11 Proust develops the core sequences of his novel that will become *Swann's Way*, *Time Regained*, part of *The Guermantes Way* and, latterly, parts of *In the Shadow of Young Girls in Flower*.

1912–13 Successive rejections from publishers.

1913 In the spring, Agostinelli moves into Proust's apartment as a secretary. *Swann's Way* is accepted for publication at the author's expense by

Grasset. Igor Stravinsky's *Rite of Spring*, D. H. Lawrence's *Sons and Lovers*, Marcel Duchamp's *Bicycle Wheel*. (14 Nov.) Publication of *Swann's Way*.

1914 (May) Agostinelli dies, drowned in the Mediterranean as a result of a flying accident. (Aug.) French forces mobilized. Printing presses cease activity during the war. James Joyce, *Dubliners*.

1915 Proust develops *Sodom and Gomorrah* and the 'Albertine cycle': *The Captive* and *The Fugitive*.

1916 Negotiations with the *Nouvelle revue française* (NRF), who wish to take over publication of Proust's novel from Grasset. (May) Proust reports suffering a 70-hour period of insomnia. (July) First Dada manifesto proclaimed in Zurich.

1917 (Feb. and Oct.) Revolution in Russia. (18 May) In Paris, Proust attends the première of *Parade*, performed by the Ballets Russes, with a scenario by Jean Cocteau, score by Erik Satie, set and costumes by Picasso, and programme notes by Guillaume Apollinaire.

1918 Proust's fragile health becomes a near-constant preoccupation as he devotes longer and longer hours to correcting his novel.

1919 (June) NRF reissues *Swann's Way*, publishes *Pastiches et mélanges* (selected journalism) and *In the Shadow of Young Girls in Flower*. Proust has to move house, twice, eventually settling at 44 Rue Hamelin in October. (Dec.) *In the Shadow of Young Girls in Flower* awarded the Goncourt Prize.

1920 André Breton employed by Gallimard as proof-reader for *The Guermantes Way*. (May) Breton and Philippe Soupault's *Les Champs magnétiques* (*The Magnetic Fields*), the first work of surrealist (or proto-surrealist) 'automatic writing'. (Oct.) First instalment of *The Guermantes Way* published.

1921 (May) Proust sees Vermeer's *View of Delft* once more, at an exhibition at the Jeu de Paume museum in Paris. Second instalment of *The Guermantes Way* published in tandem with the first part of *Sodom and Gomorrah*.

1922 Increasing doses of self-medication. (Feb.) Joyce's *Ulysses* published in Paris. (Apr.) Second instalment of *Sodom and Gomorrah* published. (Oct.) T. S. Eliot's *The Waste Land* appears in *The Criterion*. (18 Nov.) Proust dies after developing pneumonia. Gaston Gallimard and Robert Proust undertake to publish the remaining volumes of the *Recherche*.

1923 Publication of *La Prisonnière*.

1925 Publication of *Albertine disparue*; Virginia Woolf, *Mrs Dalloway*.

1927 Publication of *Le Temps retrouvé*.

SWANN IN LOVE

To belong to the 'little set', the 'little circle', the 'little clan' of the Verdurins, one condition was sufficient but necessary: tacit adherence to a Credo one of whose articles was that the young pianist who was Madame Verdurin's protégé that year and of whom she would say 'It shouldn't be allowed to play Wagner as well as that!' was 'streets ahead' of both Planté and Rubinstein and that Dr Cottard was a better diagnostician than Potain.* Any 'new recruit' who could not be persuaded by the Verdurins that the evenings people spent in houses other than theirs were as dull as ditchwater was immediately banished. Since the women were in this respect more rebellious than the men, more reluctant to give up their interest in society and their desire to find out for themselves how entertaining the other salons might be, and since the Verdurins felt that this spirit of enquiry and this demon of frivolity might become contagious, and fatal to the orthodoxy of their little church, they had been led to expel, one after another, all those of the 'faithful' who were of the female sex.

Apart from the doctor's young wife, they were reduced almost exclusively that year (even though Madame Verdurin herself was a virtuous woman and came from a respectable, extremely wealthy, and utterly undistinguished family, with which she had gradually and deliberately lost contact) to a person almost of the *demi monde*, Madame de Crécy,* whom Madame Verdurin affectionately called by her first name, Odette, and declared to be 'a darling', and to the pianist's aunt, who must once have worked as a concierge; both of them were unworldly people who, in their naivety, had been so easily deluded into believing that the Princesse de Sagan and the Duchesse de Guermantes were obliged to pay certain poor souls in order to have anyone at all at their dinner-parties, that if someone had offered to get them invited to the homes of either of these great ladies, the former concierge and the *cocotte* would disdainfully have declined.

The Verdurins never invited one to dinner; one always had one's 'place laid'. There was no fixed programme for the evening's entertainment. The young pianist would play, but only if he 'felt like it', because they never forced anyone to do anything, and, as Monsieur Verdurin would say: 'We're all friends here, long live friendship!' If the pianist wanted to play the ride of the *Valkyrie* or the prelude to

Tristan,* Madame Verdurin would object, not because she disliked those pieces but, on the contrary, because they affected her too much: 'So you want me to have one of my migraines? You know perfectly well the same thing happens every time he plays that! I know what I'm in for! Tomorrow, when I want to get up—Goodbye to that! Out of the question!' If he did not play, they would chat, and one of their friends, usually their favourite painter that year, would 'launch', as Monsieur Verdurin put it, 'into one of his silly stories that would make them all split their sides', especially Madame Verdurin, who was so apt to take literally the figurative expressions for the emotions she felt that on one occasion Dr Cottard (a junior doctor at the time) had had to reset her jaw after she dislocated it by laughing too much.

Black tie was forbidden because one was 'among friends' and also because one did not want to be like the 'bores' whom they avoided like the plague and invited only to the grander soirées, which were held as rarely as possible and only if it might amuse the painter or make the musician better known. The rest of the time they were happy to play charades and have supper in fancy dress, but only among themselves, not allowing any outsiders to mingle with the 'little clan'.

But as the 'special friends' began to occupy an increasingly prominent place in Madame Verdurin's life, the bores, the outcasts, became anything and anybody that kept her friends away from her, anything that occasionally prevented them from being free—the mother of one, the professional occupations of another, the country house or ill-health of a third. If Dr Cottard felt he should leave straight after dinner to make another visit to a patient who was seriously ill, Madame Verdurin would say: 'Who knows, it might be better for him if you don't go and disturb him this evening; if you don't, he'll have a good night's rest; you'll go round early tomorrow morning and find him as right as rain.' By the beginning of December it would make her quite ill to think that the 'faithful' would 'let her down' on Christmas Day and the 1st of January. The pianist's aunt insisted that on New Year's Day he come to dinner with the family at her mother's house:

'It's not as if your mother might die,' cried Madame Verdurin bitterly, 'if you don't go and have dinner with her on New Year's Day, the way they do *in the provinces*!'

Her anxieties would return during Holy Week: 'Doctor, you're a man of science and a free-thinker, I assume you'll be coming on Good Friday just like any other day?' she said confidently to Cottard the first year, as if there could be no doubt as to his answer. But she trembled as she waited for it, for if he did not come, she might find herself alone.

'I'll come on Good Friday . . . to say goodbye, because we're going to spend the Easter holiday in Auvergne.'

'In Auvergne! You'll be eaten alive by fleas and vermin! It will serve you right!' And she added, after a pause: 'If only you'd told us, we would have tried to organize a party; we could all have gone together in comfort.'

Similarly, if one of the 'faithful' had a friend or if one of the lady members had a beau who occasionally might make them 'otherwise engaged', the Verdurins, who were not upset by a woman having a lover provided that she had him at their house, loved him in their midst, and did not prefer his company to theirs, would say: 'Well, bring your friend along.' And they would take him on for a trial period, to see if he was capable of keeping no secrets from Madame Verdurin, if he was worthy of being enrolled in the 'little clan'. If he was not, the member of the 'faithful' who had introduced him would be taken aside and very kindly advised to break with his friend or his mistress. But if everything proved satisfactory, the newcomer would in his turn become one of the 'faithful'. So when, that year, the *demi-mondaine* told Monsieur Verdurin that she had made the acquaintance of a charming man, Monsieur Swann, and intimated that he would very much like to be invited to their house, Monsieur Verdurin transmitted the request to his wife there and then. (He never formed an opinion about anything until she had formed hers, his particular role being to carry out her wishes, as well as the wishes of the 'faithful' in general, with great skill and ingenuity.)

'Madame de Crécy has a request. She would like to introduce one of her friends to you, a Monsieur Swann. What do you think?'

'Well, how could anyone refuse anything to such an angel of perfection? You be quiet, nobody asked for your opinion. I'm telling you you're an angel of perfection.'

'If you say so,' replied Odette in a bantering tone, and then added: 'You know I'm not *fishing for compliments*.'*

'All right, then! Bring your friend along, if he's nice.'

The 'little clan' had absolutely nothing in common with the circles in which Swann moved, and true socialites would have felt there was little point in his enjoying his exceptional position in society merely to end up with an introduction to the Verdurins. But Swann was so fond of women that once he had got to know more or less every lady of the aristocracy and they had nothing more to teach him, he had come to see the naturalization papers,* almost a patent of nobility, bestowed upon him by the Faubourg Saint-Germain as no more than a sort of negotiable bond, a letter of credit with no value in itself but which enabled him to create an immediate position of prestige in some provincial backwater or some obscure Parisian circle where the daughter of the local squire or town clerk had taken his fancy. For at such times desire or love would revive in him a feeling of vanity which, though he was now entirely free of it in his everyday life, was no doubt what had originally inclined him towards the career as a man of fashion in which he had wasted his intellectual gifts on frivolous pleasures and used his erudition in matters of art merely to advise society ladies on the paintings they should buy and how they should decorate their houses; and it was this vanity that made him want to shine, in the eyes of any new lady friend with whom he was infatuated, with an elegance which the name Swann did not in itself confer. This desire was especially strong if the new lady friend was of humble background. Just as it is not to other intelligent men that a man of intelligence will be afraid of appearing stupid, so it is not by a great lord but by a country bumpkin that a man of fashion will fear that his distinction will go unrecognized. From time immemorial, three-quarters of all the mental ingenuity and lies told out of vanity by people who merely demean themselves thereby, have been aimed at inferiors. And so Swann, who could be natural and casual with a duchess, would tremble for fear of being scorned, and immediately put on airs in the presence of a chambermaid.

He was not like so many people who, from laziness or a resigned sense of the obligation entailed by their exalted social position to remain moored forever in the same place, abstain from the pleasures life offers them outside the worldly situation in which they remain confined until the day they die, and are content, in the end, to describe as pleasures, once they have become used to them, and for want of anything better, the mediocre distractions, the just bearable tedium, it offers. Swann did not try to convince himself that the women with whom he spent his time were attractive, but tried instead to spend his time with women he had already found attractive. And these were often women whose beauty was of a somewhat vulgar kind, since the physical qualities he looked for without realizing it were the exact opposite of those he admired in the women sculpted or painted by his favourite artists. Soulfulness and melancholy froze his senses, but he was instantly aroused at the sight of flesh that was pink, healthy, and abundant.

If on his travels he met a family with whom it would have been more elegant for a gentleman not to wish to seek acquaintance, but which counted among its members a woman who seemed to be adorned with a charm not previously encountered, to remain aloof and seek to deny the desire she had inspired, to substitute a different pleasure for the pleasure he might have known with her by writing to one of his former mistresses to invite her to join him, would have seemed to him as cowardly an abdication in the face of life, as stupid a renunciation of a new form of happiness as if, instead of exploring the country round about, he had shut himself up in his hotel room and looked at postcards of Paris. He did not lock himself away in the edifice of his relationships, but had converted it, in order to be able to erect it again on a new spot wherever he encountered a woman he found attractive, into one of those collapsible tents of the kind explorers carry with them. As for what was not portable or exchangeable for some new pleasure, he would have given it away, however enviable it might appear to other people. How many times had his credit with a duchess who for years had been wanting to please him in some way, without finding any opportunity to do so, been squandered in one fell swoop by an ill-advised telegram asking to put him in touch immediately, by return cable, with one of her stewards whose daughter had caught his eye in the country, just as a starving man might swap a diamond for a crust of bread. Indeed, he had even laughed at his behaviour afterwards, for there was in him, albeit redeemed by rare moments of consideration for others, a certain churlishness. Moreover, he was one of those men of intelligence who, having led a life of idleness, seek consolation and perhaps an excuse in the idea that their idleness offers their intelligence objects just as worthy of interest as those offered by art or scholarship, that 'Life' contains situations that are more interesting, more novelistic than any novel. This, at least, was what he maintained; and he had no difficulty in convincing even the most refined of his society friends, in particular the Baron de Charlus, whom he liked to amuse with accounts of the racy adventures he had had, such as his encounter with a woman on a train whom he had taken back to his house and discovered to be the sister of a reigning monarch who at that time held in his hands all the tangled threads of European politics, with which Swann was thus kept well informed in the most delightful manner, or when, through a complex set of circumstances, the choice about to be made by the conclave determined whether or not he would be able to sleep with a kitchen maid.

And it was not only the brilliant phalanx of virtuous dowagers, generals, and academicians to whom he was particularly close that Swann forced with such cynicism to act as his go-betweens. All his friends were used to receiving periodic letters in which a word of recommendation or introduction was asked of them with a diplomatic skill which, persisting as it did through his successive love affairs and varying pretexts, revealed, more clearly than any bungling would have done, a permanent characteristic and an identical quest. Many years later, when I began to take an interest* in his character because of the ways it resembled my own, but in completely different respects, I often asked to hear how, whenever he wrote to my grandfather (who was not my grandfather yet, for it was at about the time of my birth that Swann's great love affair began, and for a long time these practices of his were interrupted), the latter, recognizing his friend's handwriting on the envelope, would exclaim: 'Here's Swann again, asking for something. On guard!' And, either from distrust or from the unconscious spirit of devilry that makes us offer something only to those who have no desire for it, my grandparents would flatly refuse even his most easily satisfied requests, such as an introduction to a girl who dined with them every Sunday, which meant that whenever Swann broached the subject they had to pretend they had stopped seeing her, although they would be wondering throughout the whole week who on earth they could invite to dinner with her, and often ended up with no one, because they did not want to ask the one person who would have been delighted to come.

Sometimes a particular couple, friends of my grandparents who had been complaining that they never saw anything of Swann, would announce to them with satisfaction and possibly a desire to make them envious, that he had become utterly charming towards them and was constantly at their house. My grandfather did not want to spoil their pleasure but would look at my grandmother and hum the tune of:

> Quel est donc ce mystère?
> Je n'y puis rien comprendre.*

Or:

> Vision fugitive . . .*

Or:

> Dans ces affaires
> Le mieux est de ne rien voir.*

A few months later, if my grandfather asked Swann's new friend: 'And Swann? Do you still see a lot of him?', the other person's face would fall: 'Never mention that man's name to me again!'

'But I thought you were such good friends . . .'

For several months, Swann had been on similarly close terms with some cousins of my grandmother, dining at their house nearly every day. Suddenly, without warning, he stopped coming. They thought he was ill, and my grandmother's cousin was about to send someone round to ask after him when she found in the pantry a letter in his hand, which the cook had left by accident in the accounts book. In it he told the woman that he was leaving Paris and would not be able to see her again. She had been his mistress and when he broke off with her she was the only person he thought he needed to tell.

If, however, his mistress of the moment was a woman of rank or at least one whose background was not too humble nor her reputation too dubious to prevent him from taking her into the world of polite society, then for her sake he would return to it, but only to the particular sphere in which she moved or into which he had drawn her. 'No use expecting Swann to drop by this evening,' people would say. 'Remember—it's his American's night at the Opera.' He would make sure she was invited to the most exclusive salons, where he was always welcome, where he dined weekly or played poker; every evening, when a slight frizz had been added to the brush of his red hair, tempering with a certain softness the sparkle of his green eyes, he would choose a flower for his buttonhole and go off to join his mistress for dinner at the house of one or other of the women of his circle; then, thinking of the admiration and affection soon to be lavished upon him, in the presence of the woman he loved, by all these fashionable people for whom he could do no wrong and whom he would meet again there, he rediscovered the charm of that worldly life, to which he had grown indifferent but whose very substance, penetrated and coloured by the warmth of a newly inserted flame which now played on it, seemed to him precious and beautiful, since he had incorporated into it a new love.

But, in contrast to each of these love affairs, or each of these flirtations, which had been the more or less complete fulfilment of a dream inspired by the sight of a face or a body which Swann had spontaneously, without any kind of effort, found attractive, when he was introduced to Odette de Crécy one evening at the theatre by an old friend of his who had spoken of her as a ravishing creature with whom he might perhaps come to a pleasant arrangement, but had made her out to be a more difficult proposition than she actually was in order to appear to have done him a bigger favour by introducing her to him, she had struck Swann as being not without beauty, certainly, but as having a kind of beauty that left him indifferent, that aroused in him no feeling of desire, even gave him a sort of physical repulsion, one of those women such as everyone has known, different for each of us, who are the opposite of the type our senses crave. She had too sharp a profile to appeal to him, her skin too delicate, her cheekbones too prominent, her features too drawn. Her eyes were lovely, but so large that they drooped under their own weight, straining the rest of her face and making her always look as if she were ill or in a bad mood. Some time after this introduction at the theatre, she had written to ask if she could see his art collections, which interested her very much because although she was 'an ignoramus', she 'liked pretty things'; it seemed to her, she said, that she would understand him better once she had seen him in his *home*, where she imagined him 'so relaxed and comfortable with his tea and his books', though she had not hidden her surprise that he lived in a part of town that must be so depressing and 'was so un-*smart* for a man who was so very *smart* himself'. And when he had allowed her to come, she had told him as she left how sorry she was to have spent such a short time in a house she had been so glad to visit, speaking of him as though he meant more to her than the other people she knew, and seeming to establish between their two selves a sort of romantic bond that had made him smile. But Swann was already approaching the age of disillusion when one knows how to content oneself with being in love for the sake of being in love without requiring too much reciprocity, when that meeting of hearts, though it is no longer as in early youth the goal towards which love inevitably tends, nevertheless remains a part of it by an association of ideas so strong that it may become the cause of love if it manifests itself first. In his younger days, a man dreams of winning the heart of the woman he loves; later, the feeling that he possesses a woman's heart may be enough to make him fall in love with her. And so, at an age when it would seem—since what one seeks above all in love is subjective pleasure—that one's appreciation of the beauty of a woman should play the largest part in it, love may come into being, love of the most physical kind, without there having been any initial desire. At this stage of life, one has already been a victim of love several times; it no longer evolves by itself in accordance with its own mysterious and immutable laws, to the astonishment of our passive hearts. We come to its aid, we distort it with memory or suggestion; recognizing one of its symptoms, we remember and recreate the rest. Since we know its melody, engraved on our hearts in its entirety, we do not need a woman to remind us how it begins—filled with the admiration which beauty inspires—in order to recall how it goes on. And if she starts in the middle—where the two hearts come together, where it sings of living only for each other we are familiar enough with the music to be able to join our partner straightaway in the passage where she awaits us.

Odette de Crécy went to see Swann again, then visited him more and more often; and no doubt each visit revived his feeling of disappointment at seeing that face whose details he had half forgotten in the meantime and which he had not recalled as being either so expressive or, despite her youth, so faded; he regretted, as she chatted with him, that her considerable beauty was not of the sort he would instinctively have preferred. It must be said that Odette's face seemed thinner and sharper than it was because her forehead and the upper parts of her cheeks, those smooth and flatter surfaces, were covered by the masses of hair which women favoured at the time—drawn forward in a fringe, crimped up, or falling in loose ringlets over the ears; and as for her figure, which was most shapely, it was difficult to see it as a coherent whole (because of the fashions of the period, and despite the fact that she was one of the best-dressed women in Paris), the bodice jutting out as if over an imaginary stomach and ending in a sharp point, and the double skirts and bustles swelling like a balloon underneath, making a woman look as if she were composed of different parts that had been badly fitted together; so variously, according to the vagaries of their design or the consistency of their material, did the flounces, the pleats, and the bodice follow the line that led to the bows, the puffs of lace, the fringes of dangling jet beads, or guided them along the corset, but never related in any way to the living body, which, depending on whether the architecture of all these frills and furbelows corresponded to her own shape, or was too thoroughly different, found itself either fiercely gripped or completely lost from sight.

But when Odette had left, Swann would smile as he thought of how she had said that time would hang heavily until he allowed her to come back again; he would recall the anxious, shy way in which she had once begged him that it should not be too long, and the look in her eyes at that moment, fastened on him in fearful entreaty, which made her appear so touching under the bunch of artificial pansies pinned to the front of her round white straw hat with its black velvet ribbons. 'And what about you?' she had said. 'Couldn't you come and have tea at my house one day?' He had pleaded pressure of work, an unfinished essay—which, in reality, he had abandoned years earlier—on Vermeer of Delft.* 'I know I'm useless, a pathetic little creature like me, compared with all you great scholars,' she had replied. 'I'd be like the frog before the Areopagus.* But I really would love to learn, to know things, be initiated. What fun it must be to study all those books and bury your head in old papers!' She had added this last comment with the self-satisfied air an elegant lady has when she declares that she likes nothing better than getting her hands dirty doing some messy job, like 'lending a hand in the kitchen'. 'You'll laugh at me, but that painter who keeps you from seeing me' (she meant Vermeer)—'I've never heard of him. Is he still alive? Can I see any of his work in Paris, so that I can have an idea of what it is you like and try to work out what's going on inside that great head of yours that works so hard, in that mind I always feel is so busy with its thoughts, so that I could say: "Yes, that's what he's thinking about." How wonderful it would be to share in your work!' He had regretfully refused, citing his fear of new friendships, for what he had called, out of gallantry, his fear of being hurt. 'You're afraid of affection? How strange; that's all I ever look for, I'd give my life to find it,' she had said, in a tone of such unaffected conviction that he had been quite moved. 'You must have been hurt by some woman. And you think all

other women are like her. She can't have understood you; you're such
an exceptional person. That's what I liked about you straightaway,
I felt you weren't like anyone else.'

'And you too,' he had said to her, 'I know very well what women are
like, you must be busy with all sorts of things, you can't have much
time for yourself.'

'But I never have anything to do! I'm always free, I'll always be free
for you. At whatever time of the day or night that might be convenient
for you to see me, send for me and I'll be only too happy to come. Will
you do that? Do you know what would be nice? If I arranged an introduction to Madame Verdurin, whose house I go to every evening.
Imagine if we met there and I thought it was partly for my sake that
you had come!'

And doubtless, as he recalled their conversations thus, as he thought
of her thus when he was alone, he was combining her image with
those of many other women in his romantic daydreams; but if, due
to some circumstance or other (or even not, since a circumstance
that presents itself at the moment when a state of mind, hitherto
latent, makes itself felt, may have had no influence on it at all), the
image of Odette de Crécy came to absorb all these daydreams, if they
were no longer separable from the memory of her, then the imperfec-
tions of her body would no longer have any importance, nor would
the question of her body being more or less to his taste than any other
body, since, now that it had become the body of the woman he loved,
it would henceforth be the only one capable of filling him with joy
or misery.

It so happened that my grandfather had known—which was more
than could be said of any of their current friends—the family of these
Verdurins. But he had lost touch completely with 'young Verdurin', as
he called him, whom he regarded, more or less, as having fallen—
though without losing his grip on his millions—among bohemians
and riff-raff. One day he received a letter from Swann asking if he
could put him in touch with the Verdurins: 'On guard! On guard!' my
grandfather had exclaimed. 'I'm not a bit surprised, it's just where
Swann was bound to end up. A nice lot! I can't do what he asks
because, for one thing, I no longer know the gentleman in question.
And for another, there must be some woman involved, and I never get
mixed up in that sort of thing. Well, well! It'll be interesting to see
what happens if Swann falls in with the young Verdurins.'

And so, my grandfather having declined Swann's request, it was Odette herself who had taken him to the Verdurins'.

On the day when Swann made his first appearance, the Verdurins had had to dinner Dr and Madame Cottard, the young pianist and his aunt, and the painter then in favour, and these were joined later in the evening by several other members of the 'faithful'.

Dr Cottard was never quite sure of the tone he should adopt in response to anyone who addressed him, whether his interlocutor wanted to make a joke or was serious. And so, as a precautionary measure, he would add to each of his facial expressions the offer of a conditional and tentative smile whose anticipatory subtlety would exculpate him from the charge of simple-mindedness, if the remark made to him turned out to have been facetious. But since he also had to take the opposite possibility into account, and could not dare to allow this smile to settle clearly on his face, one saw floating over his features a perpetual uncertainty in which could be read the question he never dared to ask: 'Do you really mean that?' He was no more confident of how to behave in the street, or even in life generally, than in a drawing-room, and he might be seen greeting passers-by, carriages, or events with a cunning smile that precluded any attribution of impropriety to his attitude, since it demonstrated that if it turned out to be unsuitable, he was well aware of it, and if he had adopted that attitude, it was simply as a joke.

On all points, however, on which a direct question seemed to him permissible, the doctor did not fail to attempt to reduce the field of his doubts and complete his education.

And so, acting on the advice given him by a wise mother on his leaving the provinces for Paris, he never let pass an unfamiliar figure of speech or proper name without trying to secure the fullest information about them.

As regards figures of speech, his thirst for knowledge was insatiable, because, sometimes supposing them to have a more precise meaning than they actually have, he wanted to know exactly what people meant when they used those he heard most often: the bloom of youth, blue blood, a fast life, the moment of truth, elegance personified, to give carte blanche, to be struck dumb, etc., and in what particular circumstances he himself could introduce them into his conversation. Failing these, he would fall back on a number of puns he had memorized. As for new names of people mentioned in his presence, he contented himself merely with repeating them in an interrogative tone, which he thought sufficient to elicit explanations without his appearing to ask for them.

Since he completely lacked the critical faculty which he thought he exercised in all things, the refinement of manners that consists in telling a person whom you are doing a favour that you are greatly obliged to them, without expecting them to believe you, was wasted on the doctor, who took everything literally. Blind though Madame Verdurin was to his faults, and though she continued to find him most clever, she had in the end become irritated to see that, when she invited him to share a stage-box for a performance by Sarah Bernhardt,* saying to him, to be especially gracious: 'It was so kind of you to come, Doctor, since I'm sure you've already heard Sarah Bernhardt many times before, and we may also be too close to the stage', Dr Cottard, who had entered the box with a half-smile hovering between appearance and disappearance until someone authoritative informed him of the quality of the performance, replied: 'It's true that we're much too close and one is beginning to get a little tired of Sarah Bernhardt. But you said you would like me to come. And your wish is my command. I'm only too happy to do you this little favour. There's nothing I wouldn't do for you, you're so kind!' And he added (in vain hope of comment): 'Sarah Bernhardt—she's what they call "the Golden Voice", isn't she? And the reviewers often write that she "sets the stage on fire". That's an odd expression, isn't it?'

'You know,' Madame Verdurin had said to her husband, 'I think we're on the wrong track when, out of modesty, we make light of the presents we give the Doctor. He's a man of science, he has no truck with practical matters, he has no idea of the value of things, he relies completely on what we tell him.'

'I hadn't dared to say anything, but I had noticed,' replied Monsieur Verdurin. And the following New Year's Day, instead of sending Dr Cottard a three-thousand-franc ruby and saying it was just a trifle, Monsieur Verdurin bought an artificial stone for three hundred, while giving the impression that it would be hard to find one as beautiful.

When Madame Verdurin had announced that Monsieur Swann would be joining them that evening, the doctor had exclaimed in a tone coarsened by surprise, 'Swann?'—for the most trivial piece of news always took especially by surprise this man who thought himself always prepared for everything. And seeing that no one answered him, he roared: 'Swann? Who's this Swann?', his attack of anxiety suddenly subsiding when Madame Verdurin said: 'Oh, it's the friend Odette told us about.'

'Ah, I see. That's all right then,' replied the doctor, relieved. As for the painter, he was delighted by Swann's appearance at Madame Verdurin's, because he assumed he was in love with Odette and he liked to see himself as a match-maker. 'I absolutely love arranging marriages,' he confided in Dr Cottard's ear. 'I've already arranged quite a few—even between women!'

By telling the Verdurins that Swann was very '*smart*', Odette had made them fear that he might be a 'bore'. However, he made an excellent impression, of which one of the indirect causes, though they did not know it, was his belonging to the fashionable world. In fact, he enjoyed over men who have never mixed in high society, even men of intelligence, one of the advantages of those who have had some experience of it, which is that they no longer see it transfigured by the desire or the horror it inspires in their imagination, but consider it of no importance. Their amiability, unconnected with snobbery or any fear of seeming too amiable, reflects their independence, showing the ease and grace of movement of gymnasts whose supple limbs perform exactly the movements they want, without any indiscreet or awkward assistance from the rest of the body. The simple, elementary gymnastics of a man of the world extending a gracious hand to the unknown young man who is being introduced to him, or bowing discreetly to the ambassador to whom he himself is being introduced, had eventually been absorbed, without his being aware of it, into Swann's whole social manner, so that towards people socially inferior to him, like the Verdurins and their friends, he displayed an instinctive warm attentiveness, and made friendly overtures, which, they felt, a 'bore' would never have done. He had a moment of coldness only with Cottard: seeing the doctor wink at him and smile ambiguously before they had spoken to each other (a particular performance that Cottard called 'Let's see what happens'), Swann thought the doctor probably remembered him from a chance encounter in some house of ill repute, though he frequented such places very rarely and had never indulged in that form of dissipation. Finding the allusion in bad taste, especially in front of Odette, who might form a bad impression of him because of it, he assumed an icy manner. But on learning that the lady standing near him was Madame Cottard, he thought that so young a husband would not have tried to allude to entertainments of that sort in the presence of his wife; and he stopped reading into the doctor's knowing look the meaning he had suspected. The painter straightaway invited Swann to visit his studio with Odette; Swann thought how pleasant he was. 'Perhaps you will be more highly favoured than me,' Madame Verdurin said in a tone of mock resentment. 'Perhaps he'll show you his portrait of Cottard' (which she had commissioned from the painter). 'Don't forget, Monsieur Biche,' she reminded the painter, for whom it was a time-honoured joke to address him as 'Monsieur', 'to capture that lovely, attractive, shrewd, and amusing look in his eyes. You know that what I want most is his smile; that's what I asked you for—a portrait of his smile.' And since this phrase struck her as especially noteworthy, she repeated it very loudly to make sure it would be heard by a large number of guests, some of whom, on a vague pretext, she had induced to come closer before she uttered it again. Swann asked to be introduced to everyone, even to an old friend of the Verdurins, Saniette, whose shyness, simplicity, and good nature had lost him all the esteem he had enjoyed because of his skill as a palaeographer, his large fortune, and the distinguished family he came from. When he talked, he made a kind of burbling sound—an effect people found delightful because they felt it betrayed not so much an impediment of speech as a quality of soul, a vestige as it were of the childhood innocence he had never lost. Each consonant he could not pronounce seemed a further expression of the hardness of which he was incapable. In asking to be introduced to Monsieur Saniette, Swann appeared to Madame Verdurin to be reversing roles (to the extent that, in response, she insisted on the difference: 'Monsieur Swann, would you be so kind as to allow me to introduce our friend Saniette?'), whereas in Saniette it aroused warm feelings towards Swann, which the Verdurins, however, never revealed to him, as they found Saniette rather irritating and had no desire to provide him with new friends. But, on the other hand, they were very touched by Swann's immediate request to be introduced to the pianist's aunt. She was wearing a black dress, as always, because she thought that women always looked well in black and that nothing could be more distinguished, but her face was extremely red, as it always was after she had eaten. She bowed respectfully to Swann, but straightened up majestically. Since she was entirely uneducated and was afraid of making mistakes of grammar, she deliberately pronounced words in an indistinct manner, thinking that if she made a blunder it would be so blurred by imprecision that no one could be certain whether she had made it or not; the result was that her conversation was reduced to a series of vague croakings from which emerged now and then the few words and phrases of which she was fully confident. Swann felt he could poke a little fun at her as he talked with Monsieur Verdurin, but the latter was quite offended.

'She's a splendid woman,' he replied. 'I grant you she's not brilliant; but I assure you she's very pleasant company when you talk to her on your own.'

'I don't doubt it,' Swann hastened to concede, and added: 'I just meant she doesn't strike one as "distinguished" ' (giving special stress to the adjective) 'and actually that's a compliment!'

'Well,' said Monsieur Verdurin, 'this will surprise you: she writes delightfully. You've never heard her nephew play? He's marvellous, isn't he, Doctor? Would you like me to ask him to play something, Monsieur Swann?'

'Oh, that would be a joy . . .', Swann started to say, when he was interrupted in a facetious manner by the doctor. Having once heard it said that over-emphasis in conversation and the use of formal expressions were out of date, the doctor thought, whenever he heard a solemn word used seriously (as Swann had just used the word 'joy'), that the speaker was guilty of pomposity. And if, in addition, the word happened to occur in what he called an old cliché, however much it might be in common usage, he would assume that the sentence of which he had heard the opening words was ridiculous and would complete it ironically with the platitude he seemed to be accusing the speaker of intending to use, though it had never entered the latter's head.

'A joy for ever!' he cried mischievously, throwing up his arms for effect.

Monsieur Verdurin could not help laughing.

'What are those good folk laughing about over there?' called Madame Verdurin. 'You seem to be having a jolly time in your little corner.' Then she added, in a tone of mock-childish chagrin: 'Don't imagine I'm enjoying myself over here, sitting in disgrace all by myself!'

Madame Verdurin was sitting on a high Swedish chair of waxed pine, which she had been given by a violinist from that country and which she kept in her drawing-room, though in shape it was rather

like a kitchen stool and was quite out of keeping with her beautiful
antique furniture; but she made a point of displaying the gifts which
the 'faithful' would give her from time to time, so that the givers
would have the pleasure of recognizing them when they came to the
house. She tried to persuade them to give her only flowers and sweets,
which are at least perishable; but she was not successful, and the
house therefore contained a whole collection of footwarmers, cushions, clocks, screens, barometers, and vases, in a constant accumulation of the useless and ill-assorted.

From her lofty perch she would participate energetically in the
conversation of the 'faithful', and would delight in their banter, but
ever since the accident to her jaw, she had stopped making the effort
to explode with laughter and contented herself instead with a kind of
dumb-show that signified, without tiring her or exposing her to danger, that she was laughing to the point of tears. At the slightest hint of
a joke being cracked by one of the 'faithful' at the expense of a 'bore'
or a former member of her circle who had been relegated to the camp
of the 'bores'—and to the absolute despair of Monsieur Verdurin,
who for so long had made himself out to be as affable as his wife, but
who now, since his laughter was real, would quickly get out of breath
and had thus been outdistanced and defeated by her trick of feigned,
incessant hilarity—she would utter a little cry, screw up her bird-like
eyes, already slightly clouded by leucoma, and suddenly, as if she had
only just had time to block out some indecent sight or parry a fatal
blow, buried her face in her hands, which covered it completely and
hid it from view, would seem to be doing her utmost to suppress, to
annihilate, a fit of laughter which, had she given in to it, would have
made her faint. So there she sat, dizzy with the gaiety of the 'faithful',
drunk with good fellowship, gossip, and sycophancy, clinging to her
perch like a bird whose biscuit has been soaked in mulled wine, sob-
bing with affability.

Meanwhile, Monsieur Verdurin, after asking Swann's permission
to light his pipe ('we don't stand on ceremony here, we're among
friends'), went over to ask the young musician to sit at the piano.

'I say, leave him alone! He didn't come here to be pestered like
that!' exclaimed Madame Verdurin. 'I won't have him tormented!'

'But why do you think it might bother him?' said Monsieur Verdurin.
'I dare say Monsieur Swann doesn't know the Sonata in F sharp
we've discovered. He'll play the piano arrangement for us.'

'Oh, no! Not my sonata!' cried Madame Verdurin. 'I don't want to cry
and get a head cold and neuralgia, like last time. No thank you, I don't
want to go through that again! It's all right for the rest of you, it's obvious that you're not the ones who will have to stay in bed for a week!'

This little scene, which was re-enacted each time the pianist sat
down to play, never failed to delight her friends as much as if they
were seeing it for the first time, for they took it as proof of the enchanting originality of the 'Patronne' and of her sensitivity to music. Those
standing near her would gesture to those farther away, smoking or
playing cards, to come closer, since something was happening, saying
'Pay attention! Pay attention!' as they do in the Reichstag at interesting moments. And the following day they would commiserate with
those who had been unable to attend, reporting that the performance
had been even more entertaining than usual.

'Well, all right then,' said Monsieur Verdurin. 'He can just play the
andante.'

'Just the *andante*! You can't be serious!' exclaimed Madame Verdurin.
'It's precisely the *andante* that breaks me up. Just listen to the Patron!
He's priceless! It's as if he said: "It's the Ninth, we'll just listen to the
finale", or "It's the *Meistersingers*,* we'll leave after the overture." '

The doctor, however, urged Madame Verdurin to let the pianist play,
not because he thought the distressing effect the music had on her
was feigned—he recognized in it certain neurasthenic symptoms*—
but because he shared the habit, common to many doctors, of immediately reducing the severity of their prescriptions as soon as it strikes
them that something more important is involved, such as some fashionable gathering they are attending, and at which the presence of
the person they are advising to forget at once their dyspepsia or flu
is essential.

'You won't be ill this time, you'll see,' he said, trying to hypnotize
her with his gaze. 'And if you are ill, we'll look after you.'

'Really?' replied Madame Verdurin, as if the prospect of such
a favour left her no choice but to capitulate. Perhaps, too, by repeatedly saying she would be ill, there were moments when she forgot it
was only a lie, and she actually assumed the disposition of an invalid.
And invalids, tired of always having to make the infrequency of their
attacks dependent on their prudence, like to believe they can do with
impunity whatever gives them pleasure but is usually bad for them, as
long as they put themselves in the hands of a person of authority who,

without obliging them to make the slightest effort, by uttering a word or dispensing a pill, will get them back on their feet.

Odette had gone to sit on a tapestry-covered couch near the piano. 'You see, I've got my own little spot,' she said to Madame Verdurin.

The latter, seeing Swann sitting by himself on a chair, made him get up: 'You don't look comfortable there. Go and sit next to Odette. You can make room for Monsieur Swann, can't you, Odette?'

'What lovely Beauvais,'* said Swann before he sat down, trying to be pleasant.

'Ah! I'm glad you appreciate my couch,' replied Madame Verdurin. 'But I must tell you, if you think you'll ever see another one as beautiful, you're quite mistaken. They've never made anything quite like it. And these little chairs are marvellous too. You can have a look at them in a moment. The emblem on each bronze moulding corresponds to the subject on the upholstery; there's a lot to enjoy, you know, if you want to study them. Even the little friezes round the edges—look at them, look at the little vine on the red background in the Bear and the Grapes. It's so well drawn. Don't you think so? They really knew about drawing! Don't the grapes make your mouth water? My husband claims I don't like fruit because I eat less than he does. But the fact is I'm greedier than any of you, but I don't need to put them in my mouth because I can feed on them with my eyes. What are you all laughing at? Ask the doctor, he'll tell you that those grapes act on me like a real purgative. Some people go to Fontainebleau for their cure; I stay here for my own little Beauvais cure. Now, Monsieur Swann, you mustn't leave without feeling the little bronze mouldings on the backs. The patina is so soft, isn't it? No, no, with your whole hand—feel them properly.'

'Ah, if Madame Verdurin is going to start fondling her bronzes, we won't have any music tonight,' said the painter.

'You be quiet, you're being naughty! Anyway,' she said, turning to Swann, 'we women are forbidden pleasures far less voluptuous than this. But nothing fleshly can compare with it! When Monsieur Verdurin paid me the compliment of being jealous—come on, at least be polite about it, don't say you were never jealous . . .'

'But I didn't say a word! Doctor, you're my witness: did I say anything?'

Swann carried on feeling the bronzes to be polite, not daring to stop right away.

'Come along, you can stroke them later; now you're the one who's going to be stroked. Your ears are, at least; I think you'll like it; here's the young man who'll be doing it for you.'

When the pianist had finished playing, Swann was even more affable towards him than anyone else in the room. This is why:

The year before, at a soirée, he had heard a piece of music played on piano and violin. At first, he had enjoyed only the physical quality of the sounds produced by the instruments. And then he had felt a great pleasure when, beneath the delicate line of the violin, slender but persistent, compact and commanding, he had suddenly seen, struggling to rise in a sort of liquid swell, the solid mass of the piano-part, multiform but indivisible, smooth yet tumultuous, like the deep blue restlessness of the waves when charmed and softened by moonlight. But at a certain moment, though unable to distinguish any clear outline of what he found so pleasing, or even find words to describe it, suddenly entranced, he had tried to hold on to the fleeting phrase or harmony—he did not know which—that had just been played and had expanded his soul, as the fragrance of certain roses floating in the moist evening air has the power to dilate our nostrils. Perhaps it was his ignorance of music that had given him so confused an impression, the kind of impression that may, however, be the only one that is purely musical, immaterial, entirely original, irreducible to any other order of impressions. An impression of this kind, that vanishes in an instant, is, so to speak, *sine materia*.* No doubt the notes we hear at such moments tend already, according to their pitch and frequency, to spread out before our eyes over surfaces of varying dimensions, to trace arabesques, to give us sensations of breadth or tenuousness, stability or caprice. But the notes vanish before these sensations have developed sufficiently to avoid submersion by those already evoked by the succeeding or even the simultaneous notes. And this impression would continue to envelop with its liquidity and softness the motifs that momentarily emerge, scarcely discernible, then immediately fall away and disappear, leaving only the particular pleasure they give, impossible to describe or recall or name, ineffable—were it not for memory, which, like a labourer trying to build firm foundations amid the waves, constructs facsimiles of these fleeting phrases, enabling us to compare them to those that follow and to appreciate the difference between them. Thus, scarcely had Swann's feeling of delight faded away than his memory provided him with an immediate transcription, sketchy and provisional, admittedly, but at which he could glance while the music continued, so that when the same impression suddenly recurred, it was no longer impossible to grasp. He could picture to himself its extent, the symmetries of its arrangement, its notation, its expressive value; he had before him something which was no longer pure music, but a design, an architecture or thought that makes it possible to recall the actual music. This time he had distinguished quite clearly one phrase as it rose above the waves of sound. It had suggested at once sensual pleasures he had never imagined before hearing it, which he felt he could never experience except through that phrase; and it had filled him with a new and strange kind of love.

With its slow rhythm, it led him first in one direction, then another, then yet another, towards a state of happiness that was noble, unintelligible, and precise. Then all at once, having reached a certain point from which he was preparing to follow it, after a momentary pause it abruptly changed direction, and with a new, more rapid movement, subtle, melancholy, persistent, and gentle, it carried him along with it towards new vistas. Then it disappeared. He passionately wanted to see it again a third time. And it did reappear, but did not speak to him any more clearly, and the sensual pleasure it produced even seemed less profound. But when he had returned home he felt a need for it, he was like a man into whose life a woman, glimpsed for a moment passing by, has brought the image of a new kind of beauty that enriches his own sensibility, though he does not know whether he will ever be able to see again this woman he already loves, without even knowing her name.

Indeed, it seemed for a moment that this love for a phrase of music would open up for Swann the possibility of a kind of rejuvenation. He had long since abandoned any attempt to devote his life to an ideal goal, limiting it to the pursuit of everyday satisfactions, and he had come to believe, without ever admitting it to himself in so many words, that this would not change for as long as he lived; worse still, since his mind was empty of lofty ideas, he no longer believed in, though he could not entirely deny, their existence. Thus he had developed the habit of taking refuge in trivial thoughts, which enabled him to ignore the really important things in life. Just as he did not ask himself if he would have done better not to go into society, but on the other hand had no doubt that if he had accepted an invitation he ought to turn up and that if he did not pay a call afterwards he must at least leave his visiting-card, so in his conversation he took care never to express with any warmth his own real opinion about anything, but simply to offer factual information which had a certain value in itself and enabled him to reveal nothing of his own assessment of the matter. He was extremely precise when it came to a recipe, the date of a painter's birth or death, and the titles of his works. Occasionally, despite everything, he would forget himself and express an opinion about a work or someone's outlook on life, but then he would give his remarks an ironic tone, as if he did not entirely mean what he was saying. But now, like certain valetudinarians in whom, suddenly, a change of surroundings, or diet, or sometimes a spontaneous and mysterious organic development, seems to bring about such a sudden improvement in their health that they begin to envisage the unhoped-for possibility of belatedly starting a completely new life, Swann found in himself, in the memory of the phrase he had heard, in certain other sonatas he had asked people to play for him to see if he might discover his phrase in them, the presence of one of those invisible realities in which he no longer believed and to which, as if the music had had a sort of compelling influence on the moral aridity from which he suffered, he felt once more the desire, and almost the strength, to devote his life. But, since he had not managed to find out who had written the work he had heard, he had not been able to acquire a copy and had eventually forgotten it. During the week after the soirée, he had bumped into several people who had also been there and he had asked them about the recital; but some had arrived after the music or left before; some had indeed been there while it was performed but had gone into another room to talk, and those who had stayed to listen could tell him no more than the others. As for the hosts, they knew it was a recent work which the musicians they had hired had asked to play; but since the performers had gone on tour, Swann was unable to discover anything further. Many of his friends were musicians, but though he could recall the special, indescribable pleasure the little phrase had given him, and could actually see the shape of it in his mind's eye, he was incapable of singing it for them. So he stopped thinking about it.

But that evening, at Madame Verdurin's, the young pianist had hardly been playing for more than a few minutes when suddenly, after a high note held through two whole bars, he sensed it approaching, escaping from underneath that sonority, sustained and extended like a curtain of sound veiling the mystery of its incubation, and he recognized the secret and various murmurings of the airy fragrance of the phrase he loved. It was so distinctive, its charm was so unique, so inimitable, that Swann felt as though he had met in a friend's drawing-room a woman he had admired in the street and despaired of ever seeing again. Finally, it receded, still diligent and purposeful, through all the ramifications of its fragrance, leaving on Swann's face the reflection of its smile. But now he could ask the name of this stranger (they told him it was the *andante* from the *Sonata for violin and piano* by Vinteuil);* now he possessed it, could have it in his house as often as he liked, could try to learn its language and its secret.

And so, when the pianist had finished, Swann went over and thanked him with a warmth that Madame Verdurin found most gratifying.

'He's a charmer, isn't he?' she said to Swann. 'He's really got the hang of that sonata, the little devil. You didn't know the piano could do all that, did you? My word, it's everything—except a piano! I'm amazed every time; I think I'm hearing an orchestra. Though it's better than an orchestra, more complete.'

The young pianist bowed, and with a smile, emphasizing his words as if he were uttering a witticism, said: 'You're very kind.'

And while Madame Verdurin was saying to her husband: 'Go and get him some orangeade, he deserves it', Swann was describing to Odette how he had fallen in love with that little phrase. When Madame Verdurin called over, 'Well now, Odette, it looks as if someone is saying nice things to you', Odette replied: 'Yes, very nice', and Swann found her ingenuousness delightful. Meanwhile, he had been asking people about Vinteuil and his work, the period of his life when he had composed the sonata, and, the thing he wanted to know most of all, the meaning the little phrase could have had for him.

But all these people who professed to admire the composer (when Swann said that his sonata was truly beautiful, Madame Verdurin exclaimed: 'It most certainly is! No one dares admit they don't know Vinteuil's sonata, not to know it is simply not allowed', and the painter added: 'Oh, yes! It's a really great piece of work, isn't it? It may not be what you call "mainstream" or "popular", but it makes a huge impression on us artists'), these people seemed never to have wondered about these questions, for they were incapable of answering them.

In fact, one or two particular comments Swann made about his favourite phrase prompted Madame Verdurin to say: 'Well, that's funny! I never paid much attention; you know, I've never been one for splitting hairs or discussing fine points; we don't waste time nit-picking in this house, it's not our style.' Dr Cottard gazed at her in speechless admiration, with the zeal of a student, as she revelled in an endless flow of clichés. Both he and his wife, however, with a kind of common sense that is characteristic of people of humble background, were careful never to offer an opinion or to pretend to admire a piece of music which, once they were back in the privacy of their own home, they admitted to each other they did not understand any more than they understood the painting of 'Monsieur Biche'. Since the public's notions of the charm and beauty and forms of the natural world are derived only from the stereotypes of an art gradually assimilated, and since original artists start by rejecting those stereotypes, Monsieur and Madame Cottard, typical in this respect of the public, found neither in Vinteuil's sonata nor in the painter's portraits what for them constituted harmony in music or beauty in painting. It seemed to them, when the pianist played the sonata, that he was hitting on the keyboard random notes that bore no relation to the forms of music they were used to, and that the painter was simply throwing colour at random on to his canvases. When they were able to recognize a human form in one of the paintings, they found it clumsy and vulgarized (that is to say, lacking the elegance of the school of painting through which they viewed all living creatures, even those they saw passing by in the street), and devoid of truth, as if Monsieur Biche did not know that shoulders have a particular shape or that women do not have purple hair.

However, when the 'faithful' had dispersed, the doctor thought he had a good opportunity, and while Madame Verdurin was saying a further word about Vinteuil's sonata, he, like a novice swimmer throwing himself into the water when there are not too many onlookers, exclaimed with sudden resolution: 'Yes, he's what you call a musician *di primo cartello*!'*

Swann learned only that the recent appearance of Vinteuil's sonata had greatly impressed a certain avant-garde school of musicians, but that it was still completely unknown to the general public.

'Actually, I know someone called Vinteuil,' said Swann, thinking of the piano teacher who had taught my grandmother's sisters.

'Perhaps it's him,' exclaimed Madame Verdurin.

'Oh, no!' replied Swann, laughing. 'If you had ever set eyes on him, you wouldn't think that for a second.'

'Then to ask the question is to answer it?' said the doctor.

'But he could be a relative,' Swann went on. 'That would be rather sad, but of course a genius can have a silly old fool as a cousin. If that were the case, I confess I would accept any torture to get the old fool to introduce me to the composer of that sonata: starting with the torture of the old fool's company, which would be awful.'

The painter knew that Vinteuil was very ill at the moment and that Dr Potain was afraid he would not be able to save him.

'What!' cried Madame Verdurin. 'Do people still consult Potain?'

'Now, now, Madame Verdurin!' said Cottard, in a bantering tone. 'You forget that you're talking about one of my colleagues, in fact one of my mentors.'

The painter had heard a rumour that Vinteuil was on the verge of insanity. And he declared that there were signs of it in certain passages of the sonata. This comment did not strike Swann as being in any way absurd; but it disturbed him, for, since a work of pure music contains none of the logical connections whose dislocation in language is an indication of insanity, to read insanity in a sonata seemed to him as mysterious as the idea of insanity in a dog or a horse, though such cases have been known.

'Don't talk to me about your mentors, you know ten times as much as he does,' Madame Verdurin said to Dr Cottard, in the tone of a woman who has the courage of her convictions and stands up to anyone who does not agree with her. 'At least you don't kill your patients!'

'But, Madame, he's a member of the Academy,' replied the doctor ironically. 'If a patient prefers to die at the hand of one of the princes of science . . . It's far more stylish to be able to say: "I'm being treated by Potain."'

'Oh, it's more stylish, is it?' said Madame Verdurin. 'So illness can be a question of style now, can it? I didn't know that . . .' Then, suddenly burying her face in her hands, she exclaimed: 'You're so funny! Silly me, there I was taking you seriously when all the time you were pulling my leg.'

As for Monsieur Verdurin, finding it rather tedious to force a smile over such a trifle, he contented himself with drawing on his pipe and reflecting sadly that, when it came to amiability, he would never be able to compete with his wife.

'You know, we like your friend very much,' said Madame Verdurin to Odette when the latter was bidding her good night. 'He's so unaffected, and very charming; if they're all like that, the friends you'd like to introduce to us, you're very welcome to bring them along.'

Monsieur Verdurin pointed out that Swann had not, however, appreciated the pianist's aunt.

'But the poor man felt a bit out of his element,' answered Madame Verdurin. 'You can't expect him to have caught the tone of the house on his very first visit, like Cottard, who has been one of our little clan for years. The first time doesn't count, but it was useful for getting to know us. Odette, it's agreed that he will join us tomorrow at the Châtelet. Will you pick him up?'

'No, he doesn't want me to.'

'Very well, as you wish. As long as he doesn't let us down at the last minute!'

To Madame Verdurin's great surprise, he never let them down. He would join them wherever they happened to be, sometimes in restaurants on the outskirts of Paris which were relatively unfrequented because the season had not yet started, but more often at the theatre, which Madame Verdurin liked very much. One day at her house, hearing her say how useful it would be to have a special pass for first nights and gala performances, that it had been a great nuisance not to have one on the day of Gambetta's funeral,* Swann, who never talked about his brilliant connections but only about those who were not well regarded, whom he felt it would be insensitive to conceal, and among whom, in the Faubourg Saint-Germain, he had taken to including all his contacts in the world of officialdom, responded: 'Don't worry, leave it to me, you'll have one in time for the new production of *Les Danicheff*.* As it happens, I'm having lunch with the Prefect of Police tomorrow at the Élysée.'

'What? At the Élysée?' cried Dr Cottard, at the top of his voice.

'Yes, where Monsieur Grévy lives,'* replied Swann, a little embarrassed by the effect of his remark.

And the painter said to the doctor by way of a joke: 'Do you have attacks like that very often?'

Usually, once an explanation had been given, Cottard would say: 'Oh, I see! Of course', and would make no further display of emotion.

But this time, Swann's words, instead of having the usual calming effect, raised to fever-pitch his astonishment that a man with whom he was actually dining, who had no official position, nor any particular claim to distinction, was on visiting terms with the Head of State.

'What? Monsieur Grévy? You know Monsieur Grévy?' he said to Swann with the stupid, incredulous look of a sentry outside the Palace being asked by a stranger to be allowed to see the President of the Republic, and who, realizing from these words 'the sort of man he is dealing with', as the newspapers say, assures the poor lunatic that he will be granted an immediate audience and directs him to the special infirmary of the Barracks.

'I know him slightly,' replied Swann, trying to erase what had seemed too dazzling, in the doctor's eyes, about his relations with the President of the Republic. 'We have some friends in common.' (He did not dare say the friend was the Prince of Wales.) 'He invites so many people, you know, and I can assure you his lunches are actually rather tedious; and they're very simple, never more than eight at table.'

Cottard, taking Swann at his word, immediately adopted the view that there was nothing special about an invitation to lunch with the President and that such invitations were freely available to anyone. From then on, he no longer found it surprising that Swann, like so many others, should visit the Élysée, and he even felt a little sorry for him for having to attend lunches which Swann himself admitted were a bore.

'Oh, I see! Of course,' he said, sounding like a suspicious customs officer who, after hearing your explanations, stamps your passport and lets you go through without opening your luggage.

'Yes, I can well believe that those lunches are awfully dull, it's very noble of you to go to them,' said Madame Verdurin, for whom the President of the Republic was a bore to be especially dreaded, in that he had at his disposal means of seduction, and compulsion, which, if employed upon the 'faithful', would be capable of making them desert her. 'They say he's as deaf as a post and eats with his fingers.'

'In that case, it definitely can't be much fun for you to go there,' said the doctor with a note of commiseration in his voice; and then, recalling Swann's mention of eight guests at a time, he asked quickly, less out of idle curiosity than with a linguist's zeal: 'Are they what you would call "private" luncheon-parties?'

But the prestige of the President in the eyes of the doctor ultimately prevailed over both the modesty of Swann and the malevolence of Madame Verdurin, and every time he sat down to dinner with the Verdurins Cottard would ask anxiously: 'Will we be seeing Monsieur Swann this evening? He's a personal friend of Monsieur Grévy. Does that mean he's what they call a *gentleman*?' He even went so far as to offer Swann an invitation-card to the Dental Exhibition.

'This will let you in, and anyone you might like to take with you, but dogs are not allowed. I'm just mentioning that because some friends of mine didn't know and they could have kicked themselves afterwards.'

As for Monsieur Verdurin, he noted the distressing effect on his wife of the discovery that Swann had friends in high places but had never mentioned it.

If no arrangement had been made to go out somewhere, it was at the Verdurins' that Swann would join the little clan, but he came only in the evenings and hardly ever agreed to have dinner, in spite of Odette's entreaties.

'We could have dinner on our own, if you'd prefer,' she would say.

'And what about Madame Verdurin?'

'Oh, that wouldn't be a problem. I would just tell her my dress wasn't ready, or my cab was late. One can always think of some excuse.'

'You're very sweet.'

But Swann thought that, if he showed Odette (by agreeing to meet her only after dinner) that there were pleasures he preferred to that of her company, it would be a long time before her interest in him waned. And, in any case, since he much preferred to Odette's type of beauty that of a little working-class girl, as fresh and plump as a rose, with whom he had become smitten, he liked to spend the early part of the evening with her, knowing that he would see Odette later on. It was for these reasons that he never agreed to have Odette pick him up on her way to the Verdurins'. The young girl would wait for him near his house at a street corner his coachman Rémi knew; she would get in beside Swann and remain there in his arms until the carriage drew up outside the Verdurins'. When he walked in, Madame Verdurin would point to the roses he had sent that morning and say: 'You deserve a good scolding', then send him to his place next to Odette, and the pianist would play, just for the two of them, the little phrase by Vinteuil that had become, so to speak, the anthem of their love. He

would begin with the sustained violin tremolos which for several bars
were without accompaniment, occupying the whole foreground, then
all of a sudden they seemed to move aside and, as in those paintings
by Peter De Hooch* that acquire depth from the narrow frame of
a half-open door, in the distance, quite different in colour, in the vel-
vety softness of an intervening light, the little phrase would appear,
dancing, pastoral, interpolated, episodic, belonging to another world.
It rippled past, simple and immortal, distributing on all sides the gifts
of its grace, with the same ineffable smile; but Swann thought he
could detect in it now a certain disenchantment. It seemed to realize
how vain was the happiness to which it showed the way. In its airy
grace there was a suggestion of something over and done with, like
the mood of detachment that follows regret. But this hardly mattered
to him, he considered the phrase less for what it was in itself—in
terms of what it might express for a composer totally unaware of his
existence or that of Odette when he wrote it, and for all those who
would hear it in the centuries to come—than as a token, a memento,
of his love, which even for the Verdurins, even for the young pianist,
would remind them of Odette and himself at the same time, and bind
them together; so much so that he had given up, as Odette capri-
ciously had insisted, the idea of having some other pianist play him
the entire sonata, of which this passage thus remained the only one he
knew. 'Why do you need the rest?' she had said. 'This is *our* piece.'
Indeed, he even found it painful to think, as the little phrase floated
past, so very near and yet so infinitely far away, that although it was
addressed to them it did not know them, and he was almost sorry that
it had a meaning of its own, its own intrinsic and unalterable beauty,
independent of them, just as a gift of jewellery or even letters written
by a woman we love may make us resent the water of the gems or
the words chosen, because they are not created exclusively from the
essence of a passing love affair and a particular person.

It often happened that he stayed so long with the young girl before
going to the Verdurins' that, as soon as the little phrase had been
played by the pianist, Swann would realize that it was almost time for
Odette to go home. He would drive her back as far as the door of her
little house in the Rue La Pérouse, behind the Arc de Triomphe. It
was perhaps because of this, and so as not to monopolize her
favours, that he sacrificed the less necessary pleasure of seeing her
earlier in the evening, of arriving with her at the Verdurins', to the

exercise of this right to leave together, which she recognized as his and to which he attached greater value, since it made him feel that no one else would see her, come between them, or prevent her staying with him in thought, after he had left her.

And so she would go home in Swann's carriage; one night, when she had just stepped down and he was saying he would see her the following day, she ran to pick one of the last remaining chrysanthemums from the little garden in front of the house and gave it to him before he left. He held it pressed to his lips during the drive home, and when after a few days the flower withered, he locked it away with great care in his desk.

But he never went into the house. In fact, he had only set foot in it on two occasions, in the afternoon, in order to participate in that practice which was of such vital importance for her: 'taking tea'. The loneliness and emptiness of the little streets (nearly all of them lined with small adjoining townhouses, their monotony suddenly broken by some sinister-looking single-storey building, the historical testimony and sordid remains of the time when this part of Paris was still in bad repute), the snow still lying in the garden and on the trees, the unkemptness of the season, and the proximity of nature all added an element of mystery to the warmth and the flowers he had found inside.

From the ground floor, raised slightly above street-level, leaving on the left Odette's bedroom, which looked out at the back onto a little parallel street, a straight staircase led up between dark painted walls hung with Oriental draperies, strings of Turkish beads, and a large Japanese lantern suspended from a silken cord (but illuminated with a gas-jet, so as not to deprive visitors of the latest comforts of Western civilization) and brought him to her drawing-room and morning-room. These were entered via a narrow hallway whose wall was chequered by a wooden trellis of the kind you see on garden walls, but gilded, and lined along its entire length by a rectangular box in which bloomed, as in a greenhouse, a row of those large chrysanthemums which were still rare at the time, yet nothing to compare with the ones horticulturalists have since succeeded in producing. Swann was irritated by the fashion for these flowers, which had begun the previous year, but on this occasion he had been pleased to see the gloomy hallway streaked with pink, orange, and white rays by these fragrant but short-lived stars which light up on grey days. Odette had received him in a pink silk dressing-gown, her neck and arms bare. She had made him sit next to her in one of the many mysterious alcoves arranged in the recesses of the room, sheltered by immense palms in china flower-pot holders, or by screens to which she had attached photographs, fans, and ribbons tied in bows. She had said: 'You can't be comfortable like that, wait a minute, I'll fix you up', and with a rather smug little laugh that implied some unique invention of her own, she had installed behind his head and under his feet cushions of Japanese silk which she kneaded and shaped as if she were prodigal of these riches, regardless of their value. But when the valet brought in, one after the other, the many lamps which, nearly all contained in large Chinese vases, burned singly or in pairs, all on different pieces of furniture as though on altars, and which had turned the already almost nocturnal gloom of that late winter afternoon into a more last-ing, more rosy, more human sunset—perhaps making some passing lover stop in the street outside and fall into a reverie at the mystery that was revealed and yet concealed by the glowing panes—she had kept a sharp eye on the servant to see whether he had placed each of them in their designated places. She thought that if even one were put where it ought not to be, the overall effect of her sitting-room would be destroyed, and her portrait, which rested on a sloping easel draped in plush, would be ill-lit. So she paid fervent attention to the man's every clumsy movement and gave him a stern reprimand for having passed too close to a pair of flower stands which she made a point of cleaning herself for fear that they might get damaged and which she now went over to examine, to make sure he had not chipped them. She thought there was something 'quaint' about the shapes of all her Chinese knick-knacks, and also about the orchids, the cattleyas espe-cially, which, with chrysanthemums, were her favourite flowers, because they had the great merit of not looking like flowers, but of seeming to be made of silk or satin. 'This one looks as if it was cut out of the lin-ing of my coat,' she said to Swann, pointing at an orchid, with a sug-gestion of respect in her voice for this very 'chic' flower, this elegant, unexpected sister which nature had given her, so far removed from her on the scale of existence and yet so refined, more deserving than many women of being granted admission to her salon. As she drew his attention, first, to flame-tongued dragons painted on a vase or embroidered on a screen, then to the petals of a bunch of orchids, then to a dromedary of silver inlaid with niello with its eyes encrusted with rubies, standing on the mantelpiece next to a toad carved in jade, she pretended first to be frightened of the dangerous monsters, then to laugh at their comic appearance, blushing at the impropriety of the flowers, and then feeling an irresistible desire to go and kiss the dromedary and the toad—whom she called her 'little darlings'. And these affectations were in sharp contrast to the sincerity of certain of her religious devotions, for instance to Notre-Dame de Laghet,* who, when she was living in Nice, had cured her of a mortal illness, and whose gold medallion she always wore, attributing to it infinite powers. Odette made Swann her special tea, asked him: 'Lemon or cream?' and when he answered 'cream', said with a laugh: 'A *soupçon*!' And when he declared it to be very good, she added: 'You see, I know what you like.' The tea had, in fact, seemed as precious a thing to Swann as it did to her, and love has such a need to find a form of justification, a guarantee that it will last, in pleasures which, without it, would never have become pleasures and which cease to be pleasures when love itself ceases, that when he left her at seven o'clock to go and dress for the evening, during the whole journey home in his carriage, unable to contain the great pleasure the afternoon had given him, he kept repeating to himself: 'How nice it would be to have a little woman like that in whose house one could always be sure to find that rare thing— a good cup of tea.' An hour later, he received a note from Odette and immediately recognized the large handwriting, in which an affectation of British stiffness imposed an appearance of discipline on ill-formed characters that might have suggested to eyes less biased than his own an untidiness of mind, a deficient education, a lack of frankness and resolution. Swann had left his cigarette case at her house. 'If you had left your heart here too, I would not have let you have it back.'

His second visit to her may have been more significant. On his way to the house that day, as always when he was to see her, he pictured her to himself beforehand; and the need he felt, in order to find her face at all pretty, to focus on her fresh, pink cheekbones rather than on the rest of her cheeks, which were so often sallow and drawn, and sometimes marked with little red spots, troubled him in so far as it proved that the ideal is unattainable and happiness limited. He had brought an engraving she wanted to see. She was a little off-colour, and received him in a dressing-gown of mauve crêpe de Chine, pulling the richly embroidered material over her chest like a cloak. As she stood beside him, letting her long hair flow loose down her cheeks, bending one leg rather like a dancer so that she could lean more easily over the engraving, at which she gazed, her head tilted to one side, with those great eyes of hers which seemed so tired and sullen when she was not in good spirits, Swann was struck by her resemblance to the figure of Zipporah, Jethro's daughter, in a fresco at the Sistine Chapel.* He had always derived a peculiar pleasure from discerning in the paintings of the Old Masters not just the general characteristics of the real world around us, but what seems on the contrary the least susceptible of generalization, the individual features of people we know: for example, in a bust of the Doge Loredano by Antonio Rizzo,* he saw the prominent cheekbones, the slanting eyebrows, in fact the spitting image of his coachman Rémi; in the colouring of a Ghirlandaio,* the nose of Monsieur de Palancy; in a portrait by Tintoretto,* the invasion of the fleshy part of the cheek by the side-whiskers, the broken nose, the piercing gaze, the swollen eyelids of Dr du Boulbon. Perhaps because he had always felt a certain regret at having limited his life to the social world and to conversation, he believed that he was granted a kind of indulgent forgiveness by the great artists in the fact that they too had contemplated with pleasure, and incorporated into their work, faces like these, which gave it a special stamp of reality and truth to life, a modern flavour; perhaps, also, he had let himself become so involved in the frivolous ways of society people that he felt a need to find in an old masterpiece these anticipatory and rejuvenating allusions to personalities of the present day. Perhaps, on the other hand, he still had enough of the artist in him to derive pleasure from the ways in which these individual characteristics took on more general significance as soon as he saw them, uprooted and set free, in the resemblance between an older portrait and a modern original which it was not intended to represent. Whatever the reason, and perhaps because the richness of impressions he had been experiencing for some time, though deriving from his love of music, had actually enhanced his enjoyment of painting, he now experienced a greater pleasure—and this was to have a lasting effect on him—at that moment, when he noticed the resemblance between Odette and the Zipporah of Sandro di Mariano, who is better known now by his popular nickname of Botticelli, for that name evokes, not the actual work of the Master but the banal and false idea of it adopted in popular culture. He no longer appraised Odette's face according to the finer or poorer quality of her cheeks and the fleshy softness he assumed he would feel with his lips if he ever dared to kiss her, but as a skein of beautiful, delicate lines that his eyes unravelled, following their curves and windings, connecting the rhythm of her neck to the flow of her hair and the curvature of her eyelids, as if contemplating a portrait of her in which her type became clear and intelligible.

He stood gazing at her; a fragment of the fresco appeared in her face and in her body, and from then on he would always try to rediscover it in her, whether he was with her or was only thinking about her, and although no doubt he valued the Florentine masterpiece not only because he could rediscover it in Odette, her resemblance to it conferred a certain beauty on her too, and made her more precious. Swann was annoyed with himself for having misjudged the value of a creature whom the great Sandro would have found adorable, and was gratified by the fact that his pleasure in seeing Odette had found some justification in his own aesthetic culture. He reflected that by associating the thought of Odette with his dreams of happiness he had not resigned himself to a second-best as imperfect as he had hitherto believed, for she satisfied his most refined artistic tastes. He forgot that this did not make Odette any more the sort of woman he found desirable, since his desires had always run counter to his aesthetic tastes. The phrase 'Florentine work of art' was immensely useful to Swann. It enabled him, like a title, to insert Odette's image into a world of dreams from which, until then, she had been excluded and where she was now invested with a kind of nobility. And while the purely physical view he had had of this woman, by perpetually renewing his doubts about the quality of her face, her body, the whole nature of her beauty, had weakened his love, these doubts were swept aside and his love confirmed now that he could stand on the firm ground of his aesthetic values; while, in addition, the kiss, the physical possession, which would seem natural and unremarkable if granted by a person of flawed beauty, now coming to crown his adoration of a work of art in a gallery, seemed to hold out the promise of supernatural delights.

And whenever he was tempted to regret the fact that for months he had done nothing but see Odette, he told himself that it was not unreasonable to devote a good deal of his time to a priceless work of art, cast for once in a different and especially delightful material, in an exceedingly rare exemplar which he would contemplate at some moments with the humility, spirituality, and disinterestedness of an artist, at others with the pride, egotism, and sensuality of a collector.

He placed on his study table, as if it were a photograph of Odette, a reproduction of Jethro's daughter. He would gaze in admiration at the large eyes, the delicate features with their suggestion of an imperfect complexion, the wonderful locks of hair that fell over the tired cheeks, and, adapting to the idea of a living woman what he had until then found beautiful in aesthetic terms, he translated it into various physical attractions which he was delighted to see combined in a person he might come to possess. Now that he had become acquainted, in the flesh, with the original of Jethro's daughter, the vague feeling of sympathy that draws us to a masterpiece as we look at it became a desire that henceforth stood in for the desire that Odette's body had not at first inspired in him. After he had gazed for a long time at the reproduction of Botticelli, his thoughts would turn to his own Botticelli, even more beautiful in his eyes, and, moving the photograph of Zipporah closer to him, he would imagine that it was Odette he was clasping to his breast.

And yet he strove to think up ways not only of preventing Odette from growing tired of him, but also, sometimes, of preventing himself from becoming tired of her; feeling that Odette, since she had been able to see him frequently, no longer seemed to have much to say to him, made him fear that the rather uninteresting, monotonous, and seemingly immutable behaviour she now adopted when they were together would eventually destroy his romantic hope that one day she would declare her passion, a hope which alone had made him fall in love and remain in love. And so, in an attempt to change Odette's too fixed attitude towards him, of which he was afraid of becoming weary, he would suddenly write her a letter full of feigned disappointment and simulated anger, which he would have delivered to her before dinner. He knew she would be alarmed, and would answer him, and he hoped that, when the fear of losing him tugged at her heart, words would spring forth that she had never yet uttered to him; and indeed, it was in this way that he had obtained the most affectionate letters she had so far written to him, including one, which she had sent round to him at midday from La Maison Dorée* (it was the day of the Paris-Murcia Fête,* held in aid of the victims of the Murcia floods), that began with the words: 'My dear Charles, my hand is shaking so much that I can hardly write', and that he had kept in the same drawer as the withered chrysanthemum. Or, if she had not had time to write to him, when he arrived at the Verdurins' she would run up to him, saying: 'I must talk to you', and he would gaze curiously at the revelation on her face and in her words of what until then she had kept hidden in her heart.

Even as he drew close to the Verdurins' house, when he caught sight of the great lamp-lit windows whose shutters were never closed, he felt quite touched at the thought of the charming creature he would soon see in her full splendour, bathed in the golden light. From time to time the silhouettes of the guests would stand out, slender and black, against the light from the lamps, as if on a screen, like the little pictures fitted at intervals around a translucent lampshade and separated from each other by panels of pure light. He would try to distinguish Odette's silhouette. Then, as soon as he arrived, without his being aware of it, his eyes would shine with such joy that Monsieur Verdurin would say to the painter: 'I think things are warming up.' And for Swann, Odette's presence did indeed give the house something that was lacking in the other houses he frequented: a kind of sensory apparatus, a nervous system that extended throughout every room and produced constant tremors of excitement in his heart.

And so, through its simple, regular functioning as a social organism, the 'little clan' automatically arranged Swann's daily meetings with Odette and enabled him to feign indifference as to whether he saw her or not, and even a desire not to see her, a desire that carried no great risk of being fulfilled, since, whatever he wrote to her during the day, he was bound to see her in the evening and take her home.

Once, however, depressed by the thought of the inevitable ride home together, he had taken his young girl all the way to the Bois so as to delay his appearance at the Verdurins', and he arrived at their house so late that Odette, thinking he was not coming, had already left. When he saw she was no longer in the drawing-room, Swann felt a pang in his heart; he trembled at the thought of being deprived of a pleasure he was now fully appreciating for the first time, since until then he had always had the certainty of its being available whenever he wished, which, as with all pleasures, reduces them and may even prevent us from completely realizing their full extent.

'Did you see his face when he realized she wasn't here?' Monsieur Verdurin said to his wife. 'I think we can say he's hooked.'

'Whose face?' demanded Dr Cottard, who, having left the house to make a brief visit to a patient, had just come back to fetch his wife and did not know whom they were talking about.

'What, didn't you bump into the most handsome of Swanns at the front door . . . ?'

'No. Monsieur Swann was here?'

'Oh, just for a moment. We had a very agitated, very anxious Swann. Odette had already left, you see.'

'You mean there's "hanky panky", she's allowed him to "enter the castle"?' asked the doctor, cautiously testing the meaning of these expressions.

'No, no,' replied Madame Verdurin. 'There's certainly nothing going on, and just between ourselves, I think she's making a big mistake and behaving like an absolute ninny—which is what she is, in fact.'

'Now, now, now,' said Monsieur Verdurin, 'how can you be so sure? We haven't exactly been in a position to see for ourselves, have we?'

'She would have told me,' replied Madame Verdurin haughtily. 'She tells me everything! I've told her, since she's not with anyone else at present, she should sleep with him. She makes out that she can't, that she was really attracted to him, but he's shy with her, which makes her shy with him, and anyway she doesn't love him in that sort of way, for her he's a kind of ideal, she's afraid of spoiling her feelings for him, but how would I know? And yet it would be just what she needs.'

'I beg to differ,' said her husband. 'The gentleman is not quite my cup of tea. I find him rather pretentious.'

Madame Verdurin froze, assumed a blank expression as if she had turned into a statue, a device that enabled her to appear not to have heard that intolerable word 'pretentious', which seemed to imply that a person could be pretentious in relation to them, and therefore 'superior' to them.

'Anyhow, if there's nothing going on, I don't think it's because the fellow believes that she's *virtuous*,' Monsieur Verdurin went on ironically. 'Still, you never know, he does seem to think she's intelligent. I don't know if you heard him holding forth to her the other evening about Vinteuil's sonata; I'm terribly fond of Odette, but to give her lectures on aesthetic theory—really, you'd have to be a complete nincompoop.'

'Come on now, stop saying nasty things about Odette,' said Madame Verdurin, in a 'little girl' voice. 'She's delightful.'

'But she can still be delightful. Nobody's saying nasty things about her, just that she's no genius and no saint. In fact,' he said to the painter, 'are you that keen for her to be virtuous? If she was, we might not find her so delightful.'

On the landing Swann had been stopped by the butler, who had not been there when he arrived and had been asked by Odette—but this was already an hour earlier—to tell him, in case he should still come, that she would probably go and have a cup of chocolate at Prévost's on her way home. Swann set off for Prévost's, but his carriage was forever being held up by other carriages or by people crossing the street, loathsome obstacles he would gladly have knocked out of the way, were it not that being booked by a policeman would have delayed him even more than the passing pedestrians. He counted the minutes as they passed, adding a few seconds to each to be sure he was not making them too short and allowing himself to think that he had a greater chance than he actually had of arriving early and finding Odette still there. And at one point, like a man in a fever who emerges from sleep and becomes aware of the absurdity of the dreams that had been swirling in his mind without his clearly distinguishing himself from them, Swann suddenly realized the strangeness of the thoughts he had been turning over since the moment he was told at the Verdurins' that Odette had already left, the unfamiliar aching of his heart, which he noticed now as if he had just woken up. What! All this agitation because he would not see Odette until tomorrow, precisely what he had wanted, an hour before, as he was being driven to Madame Verdurin's! He was obliged to acknowledge that in this same carriage which was taking him to Prévost's, he was no longer the same man and was no longer alone, that a new person was there with him, attached to him, a part of him, from whom he might not be able to free himself, whom he was going to have to treat with circumspection, as one behaves towards a superior or copes with an illness. And yet from the moment he had begun to feel that a new person had been added to him in this way, his life seemed more interesting. It hardly occurred to him that, even if it took place, this possible meeting at Prévost's (the anticipation of which so devastated, so denuded the moments preceding it that he could not find a single idea or memory with which to offer his mind some rest) would probably, like the others, not amount to much. As on every other evening, once he was with Odette, casting at her changeable face a furtive glance which he would immediately turn away for fear that she would see in his eyes his mounting desire and stop believing in his lack of interest, he would no longer be able to think about her, so busy would he be finding excuses that would enable him not to leave her immediately and yet ensure, without his seeming at all concerned, that he would find her again the next day at the Verdurins': excuses, in other words, that would enable him to prolong for the time being, and to renew for one more day, the disappointment and torment he suffered because of the pointless presence of this woman to whom he had made approaches but never dared to take in his arms.

She was not at Prévost's; and so he resolved to look in every restaurant along the boulevards. To save time, while he looked in some, he sent to the others his coachman Rémi (Rizzo's Doge Loredano), for whom he then waited—having drawn a blank himself—at a prearranged spot. The carriage did not reappear, and Swann imagined the coming moment as one when Rémi would say: 'The lady is there', or when he would say: 'The lady was not in any of the cafés.' And so he saw the remainder of the evening before him, single and yet alternative, preceded either by a meeting with Odette which would put an end to his agony, or by the forced abandonment of his search and acceptance of the need to return home without having seen her.

The coachman returned, but as he pulled up in front of Swann, Swann did not say: 'Did you find the lady?' but: 'Remind me tomorrow to order some more firewood; I think our stocks are running low.' Perhaps he felt that if Rémi had found Odette in one of the cafés, waiting for him, the end of the ill-fated evening would already be cancelled out by the realization, already forming in his mind, of the happy one, and there was no need for him to rush to seize a happiness that had already been captured, was now held in a safe place, and would never be able to escape. But it was also from the force of inertia; his mind lacked the suppleness which some people lack in their bodies, and who, at the moment when they need to avoid a collision, snatch a flame away from their clothing, or perform a sudden movement, take their time, pause for a moment in their present position as if to steady themselves and find their momentum. And no doubt, if the coachman had interrupted him by saying: 'The lady is there', he might well have replied: 'Oh yes, of course! That errand I sent you on! Well, well! Is that so?' and then continued with what he was saying about the firewood in order to hide the state of his emotions and give himself time to get over his anxiety and devote himself to happiness.

But what the coachman came back to tell him was that he had not found her anywhere, and, as a trusted old servant, offered his advice: 'I think all Monsieur can do now is go home.'

But the indifference Swann affected easily enough as long as Rémi could do nothing to change the answer he had brought back fell away when he saw Rémi attempt to make him give up hope and abandon his search.

'Certainly not!' he cried. 'We must find the lady. It's extremely important. If she doesn't see me, she'll be most annoyed, and offended too. It's about a business matter.'

'I don't see how the lady could be offended,' replied Rémi, 'if she was the one who left without waiting for Monsieur, and said she was going to Prévost's, and then wasn't there.'

By now the restaurants were closing. Under the trees along the boulevards, fewer people were wandering along, barely distinguishable in the gathering darkness. Every now and then the shadowy figure of a woman coming up to him, murmuring in his ear, asking him to take her home, would make Swann start. He brushed nervously against all these dim forms as if, among the shades of the dead, in the kingdom of darkness, he were searching for Eurydice.*

Of all the modes by which love comes into being, of all the disseminating agents of this holy evil, one of the most efficacious is this great breath of agitation that sweeps over us from time to time. For then the die is cast, and the person whose company we enjoy at the time is the one we will love. It is not even necessary, until then, that we should have been attracted to that person more than to others, or even to the same extent. All that is required is that our predilection becomes exclusive. And that condition is fulfilled when, at a moment when we are deprived of that person's company, the quest for the pleasures their company gave us is suddenly replaced by an anxious need whose object is that very person, an absurd need which the laws of this world make impossible to satisfy and difficult to cure: the senseless and painful need to possess the person entirely.

Swann asked Rémi to drive him to the few restaurants that were still open. The hypothesis of a happy ending to his search was the only one he had been able to envisage at all calmly; and now he no longer hid his agitation nor the importance he attached to the meeting with Odette; he promised Rémi a reward if they were successful, as though, by inspiring in his coachman a desire to succeed that would reinforce his own, he could make Odette, if she had already gone home to bed, nevertheless appear in one of the boulevard restaurants. He continued as far as the Maison Dorée, looked in twice at Tortoni's, and, still not seeing her, had just come out of the Café Anglais again, looking quite distraught as he strode back to the carriage, which was waiting for him on the corner of the Boulevard des Italiens, when he bumped into someone coming from the opposite direction: it was Odette. She explained later that there had been no room at Prévost's and so had gone to have supper at the Maison Dorée in an alcove where he must not have noticed her, and was just walking back to her carriage.

His appearance was so unexpected that she stepped back in alarm. Swann, for his part, had been rushing all over Paris not because he thought it was possible to find her, but because he could not bear the thought of giving up the attempt. But the happiness which his reason had never stopped telling him would be unattainable, that evening at least, now seemed to him all the more real: for, since he had played no part in its preparation by foreseeing the likely circumstances in which it might be realized, it remained external to him; he did not need to draw upon his mind to give it the quality of truth, it contained its own truth, projecting that truth towards him, a truth whose radiance dispelled like a dream the loneliness he had been dreading, a truth which had now become the basis, the support, for his blissful, unthinking reverie. He was like a traveller arriving at the Mediterranean seaboard on a day of glorious weather, and, no longer certain that the lands he has left behind really exist, lets his eyes be dazzled by the bright reflections from the deep luminous blue of the water, rather than looking at them directly.

He climbed up with her into the carriage that had been waiting for her and told Rémi to follow.

In her hand she was holding a bunch of cattleyas, and Swann could see that, under her lace scarf, she had flowers of the same orchid in her hair, fastened to a plume of swan feathers. Beneath the scarf, she was dressed in flowing black velvet caught up on one side to reveal a broad triangle of undergown in white ribbed silk, and showing a yoke, also of white silk, at the opening of the low-cut bodice adorned with more cattleyas. She had hardly recovered from the shock of bumping into Swann when some obstacle in the street made the horse shy. They were thrown forward in their seats, she cried out, then sat trembling and breathless.

'It's all right,' he said. 'Don't be frightened.' And he put his arm round her shoulder, supporting her body against his. Then he went on: 'Don't speak, just nod or shake your head until you've got your breath back. You won't mind if I straighten the flowers on your bodice? That jolt has knocked them out of place. I wouldn't want you to lose them, so I'll push them back in a little.'

Odette, who was not used to a man making such a fuss over her, said with a smile: 'Oh, I don't mind at all.'

But he, intimidated by her answer, and perhaps also to make his excuse seem sincere, or even beginning to believe that he had meant what he said, exclaimed: 'No, don't talk! You'll get out of breath again, you can just make signs, I'll understand perfectly well. You really don't mind? Look, there's a drop of . . . I think some pollen has got sprinkled over you; can I brush it off with my hand? I'm not pressing too hard, I'm not being too rough? I'm tickling you, perhaps? The thing is, I don't want to touch the velvet, it might get crumpled. But you can see they really had to be fastened, or they would have fallen out; I'll push them back in a little further, like this . . . You're sure you don't mind? And if I sniffed them to see if they really have no scent, would that bother you? I've never smelt one, would you believe? You don't mind? Honestly?'

Smiling, she gave a little shrug, as if to say 'you're quite mad; you can see I like it',

He ran his other hand up Odette's cheek; she gazed at him without blinking, with the grave and languid look of the women of the Florentine master in whose faces he had found a resemblance with hers; her shining eyes, wide and slender like theirs, seemed to brim at the edge of her lids and to be on the point of welling out like two tears. She tilted her head to one side, as Botticelli's women all do, in the pagan scenes as well as in the religious paintings. And in an attitude that was no doubt habitual, which she knew was appropriate to moments like this and which she made sure she would not forget to adopt, she seemed to need all her strength to hold her face back, as if some invisible force was drawing it to Swann's. And it was Swann who, for a moment, held her face away from his in his hands, before she let it fall, as though in spite of herself, onto his lips. He had wanted to give his mind time to catch up with him, to recognize the dream it had cherished for so long and to be present at its realization, like a relative invited to share in the success of a child of whom she has always been very fond. Perhaps, too, Swann was also gazing at Odette's face with the eyes of a man who looks intensely at a landscape he is about to leave for ever, as if to carry it away with him, for it was a face he was seeing for the last time: Odette as she was before he slept with her, or even kissed her.

But he was so timid with her that, after ending the evening in her bed, having begun by rearranging her cattleyas, whether from fear of offending her or of appearing in retrospect to have lied, or because he lacked the boldness to formulate a more pressing requirement than the flower-arranging (which he could always resort to again, since it had not annoyed Odette the first time), in the days that followed he used the same stratagem. If she was wearing cattleyas on her bodice, he would say: 'What a shame, the cattleyas don't need to be straightened this evening, they haven't been disarranged as they were the other evening; this one, though, doesn't look very straight. May I see if they have a stronger scent than the others?' Or, if she had none: 'Oh! No cattleyas this evening! That means I won't be able to indulge in my flower-arranging.' So that for some time there was no change to the sequence he had followed that first evening, starting with his touching Odette's bosom with his fingers and lips, and their love-play still began this way each time; and long afterwards, when the flower-arranging (or the ritual pretence of flower-arranging) had long since fallen into disuse, the metaphor 'do a cattleya', having become a term they used without thinking to refer to the act of physical possession—in which, in fact, one possesses nothing—lived on in their language, commemorating the forgotten custom from which it sprang. And perhaps this particular way of saying 'to make love' did not mean exactly the same thing as its synonyms. Even if we feel blasé about women, seeing in the sexual enjoyment of many different ones the same, predictable experience, we can still discover a new kind of pleasure if the women involved are (or are thought to be) difficult enough to oblige us to make it spring from some unexpected incident in our relations with them, as had been for Swann the original arranging of the cattleyas. He tremblingly hoped, that evening (but Odette, he thought, if she was taken in by his stratagem, could not guess his intention), that it was possession of this woman that would emerge from the large purple petals; and the pleasure he felt already and that Odette was tolerating, he thought, only because she had not recognized it, seemed to him, because of that—as it might have seemed to the first man when he tasted it among the flowers of the earthly paradise—a pleasure which had not existed until then, which he was now seeking to create, a pleasure—as indicated by the special name he gave it—entirely new and individual.

Now, every evening, when he took her home, he had to go in, and often she would come back out in a dressing-gown and walk with him to his carriage, and kiss him in full view of the coachman, saying: 'Why should I care what people think?' On evenings when he did not go to the Verdurins' (which happened occasionally now that he had other ways of seeing her), or on the increasingly rare evenings he spent in fashionable company, she would ask him to drop in on his way home, whatever the hour. It was spring, a crisp and frosty spring. On leaving a party, he would climb into his victoria,* spread a rug over his knees, tell the friends who were leaving at the same time and had asked him to join them, that he could not, that he was not going their way, and the coachman would set off at a fast trot, knowing exactly where to go. They were surprised at Swann's behaviour, and indeed he was a changed man. No one ever received a letter from him now asking for an introduction to some woman. He no longer paid any attention to women and avoided places where one might normally meet them. In a restaurant, or in the country, his attitude was the opposite of the one by which, only recently, people would have recognized him, and which had seemed that it would always and inevitably be his. Once a passion takes hold of us, it manifests itself as a temporary, different personality that takes the place of our normal personality and obliterates the signs, invariable until then, by which it expressed itself! What was invariable now, however, was that wherever Swann might be, he never failed to go and see Odette afterwards. The distance that separated him from her he inevitably covered as though it were the rapid and irresistible slope of his very life. In truth, when he had stayed out late at some social gathering, he would often have preferred to go straight home without making that long trip, and not see her until the next day; but the very fact of taking the trouble to call in to see her at an unusual hour, of imagining, after he took leave of his friends, that they would be saying to one another: 'He's very devoted, there must be some woman who makes him go and see her at any time of day or night', made him feel that he was leading the kind of life led by men who conduct love affairs, and in whom the sacrifice they make of their comfort and other interests to a dream of sensual pleasure generates a sort of inner charm. Then, without his realizing it, the certainty that she was waiting for him, that she was not somewhere else with other people, that he would not return home without seeing her, cancelled out the anguish, now forgotten but always ready to be reawakened, he had felt on the evening when Odette had left the Verdurins' before his arrival, an anguish of which the present assuagement was so pleasant that it could be called happiness. Perhaps it was to that anguish that he owed the importance Odette had assumed for him. Other people usually mean so little to us that when we invest one of them with such potential for causing us suffering or happiness, that person seems to belong to another world, takes on an aura of poetry, transforms our life into a sort of emotional field in which he or she will be closer or less close to us. Swann found it impossible to think calmly about what Odette might mean to him in the years to come. Sometimes, as he sat in his victoria on those lovely cold nights, he would see the brilliant moon spreading its light between his eyes and the deserted streets, and would think of that other face, bright and tinged with pink like the moon's, which, one day, had risen in his mind and, since then, had shed upon the world the mysterious light in which he saw it bathed. If he reached Odette's house after the time when she sent her servants to bed, rather than ring the bell at the gate of her little front garden, he would go round into the other street, over which, on the ground floor, among the identical but unlit windows of the adjoining houses, shone the solitary lighted window of her bedroom. He would tap on the pane, and she, thus alerted, would respond and go and wait for him on the other side, at the front door. He would find several of her favourite pieces open on the piano: the *Valse des Roses* or *Pauvre Fou* by Tagliafico* (which, she had written in her will, was to be played at her funeral); he would ask her to play instead the little phrase from Vinteuil's sonata, even though she played very badly, but the most lasting impression we have of a piece of music is often one that rises above a series of wrong notes struck by clumsy fingers on an out-of-tune piano. For Swann the little phrase continued to be associated with his love for Odette. He was well aware that this love was something that did not correspond to anything beyond itself, observable by others; and he realized that Odette's qualities were not such as to justify the value he placed on the time he spent in her company. And often, when his mind was governed by intelligence alone, he would feel a desire to stop sacrificing so many of his intellectual or social interests to this imaginary pleasure. But the little phrase, as soon as he heard it, was able to open up within him the space it needed, rearranging the shape of his inner self; a margin was left for a pleasure which, similarly, did not correspond to any external object, and yet, instead of being purely individual, like his enjoyment of his love for Odette, assumed for Swann a reality superior to that of concrete things. The little phrase aroused in him a yearning for an unknown delight, but gave him nothing precise with which to assuage it. The result was that those parts of Swann's inner self from which the little phrase had erased all concern for material interests, those human considerations that affect all men, had been left vacant and blank, and in them he was free to inscribe the name of Odette. Also, in so far as Odette's affection appeared somewhat weak and disappointing, the little phrase supplemented it, strengthened it with its own mysterious essence. To see Swann's face as he listened to the phrase, one would have thought that he was inhaling an anaesthetic that would enable him to breathe more freely. And the pleasure the music gave him, which was soon to become a form of addiction, did indeed resemble at such moments the pleasure he would have derived from trying out various perfumes, or entering into contact with a world for which we men are not made, which seems formless to us because our eyes cannot see it, meaningless because it eludes our understanding, which we can only grasp through one sense alone. What deep repose, what mysterious renewal for Swann—whose eyes, for all their subtle appreciation of painting, and whose mind, for all its shrewd observation of manners, were indelibly marked by the barrenness of his life—to feel himself transformed into a creature alien to humanity, blind and deprived of any intellectual faculty, almost a fantastic unicorn, a chimerical creature conscious of the world only through its sense of hearing. And since he nevertheless persisted in trying to find in the little phrase a meaning which his intellect could not plumb, what strange intoxication he felt as he divested his innermost self of all the help reason might provide and made it move alone through the corridor, the dark filter, of sound! He was beginning to become aware of how much suffering, perhaps even some secret and unappeased sorrow, lay hidden in that sweet phrase, but he could not feel that suffering. What did it matter that it told him love is fragile, for his own love was so strong! He played with the sadness of it as he felt it pass over him, but he experienced it as a caress that only deepened and sweetened his sense of his own happiness. He would make Odette play it ten times, even twenty times, insisting that as she played she should not stop kissing him. Each kiss calls forth another. Ah, in those first days of love, kisses come so naturally! So closely, in their profusion, do they crowd together that it would be as hard for lovers to count the kisses they exchange in an hour as to count the flowers in a meadow in the month of May. Then she would make as if to stop, saying: 'How do you expect me to play if you keep holding me? I can't do everything at once. Make up your mind what you want—am I to play the phrase or am I to play at kissing you?' He would get annoyed, but she would burst out laughing, laughter that was then transformed into a shower of kisses. Or she would look at him sulkily, and once again he would see a face worthy of figuring in Botticelli's *Life of Moses*; he would place her in it, positioning her head at the required angle; then, once he had painted her in fifteenth-century tempera, on the walls of the Sistine Chapel, the idea that she was actually still there, by the piano, in the present moment, willing to be embraced and possessed, the idea of her physical existence and life would so intoxicate him that, his eyes wild and his jaws tensed as if ready to devour her, he would fall upon his Botticelli virgin and start pinching her cheeks. Then, when he had left her, not without going back in to kiss her once more because he had forgotten to fix in his memory some detail of her fragrance or her features, as he returned home in his victoria he would bless Odette for granting him these daily visits, which he felt could not give her any great pleasure, but which, by protecting him from jealousy—by removing any possibility of his suffering again from the malady that had taken hold of him on the evening when he had failed to find her at the Verdurins'—would help him to arrive, without having any more of those crises of which the first had been so painful that it must be the last, at the end of this strange period of his life, of these hours that were almost enchanted, like those in which he drove through Paris by moonlight. And, noticing during his homeward journey that the moon had changed its position in relation to him and was now almost touching the horizon, he would think that his love, too, was subject to immutable natural laws, and wonder whether this period he had entered would last much longer, whether, quite soon, in his mind's eye, he would no longer see that beloved face except as occupying a distant and diminished position, and on the point of ceasing to shed on him the radiance of its charm. For Swann, now that he was in love, was again finding in the things around him a certain charm, as at the time when, in his adolescence, he had seen himself as an artist; but it was no longer the same charm, for now their charm was conferred by Odette alone. He felt the inspirations of his youth, which had been dissipated by a life of frivolity, reawakening within him, but they all bore the mark, the reflection, of a particular person; and during the long hours which he now found a delicate pleasure in spending at home, alone with his convalescent soul, slowly he became himself again, but owned by another.

He went to her house only in the evenings, and he was as ignorant of how she spent her time during the day as he was about her past life, so much so that he lacked even that small, initial clue which, by enabling us to imagine what we do not know, makes us want to know it. So he never wondered what she might be doing, nor what sort of life she had led. He merely smiled to himself at the thought that, a few years earlier, when he did not know her, someone had mentioned to him a woman who, if he remembered correctly, could only have been Odette, as being a courtesan, a kept woman, one of those women to whom he still attributed, since he had spent very little time in their company, the wilful, fundamentally perverse character with which they had for so long been endowed by the imagination of certain novelists. He told himself that as often as not one has only to take the opposite view of the reputation the world has formed of someone in order to judge that person accurately, and when he compared the character of such a woman with that of Odette, so kind, so artless, so idealistic, and so nearly incapable of not telling the truth that, after he begged her one day, so that he could dine with her alone, to send the Verdurins a note saying she was unwell, the next day he had seen her blushing and stammering as she stood face to face with Madame Verdurin, who was asking her if she felt better, showing on her face, despite himself, how upsetting, how painful it was for her to tell a lie, and, as in her answer she multiplied the fictitious details of her alleged indisposition of the day before, seeming to be asking forgiveness, by her supplicating looks and distressed voice, for the falseness of her words.

There were some days, however, though they were rare, when she came to see him in the afternoon, interrupting his musings or the essay on Vermeer to which he had recently returned. His servant would come to tell him that Madame de Crécy was in the morning-room. He would go and join her, and when he opened the door, as soon as she saw him, a smile would spread across her rosy face, changing the shape of her mouth, the look in her eyes, the moulding of her cheeks. When he was alone again, he would see that smile, and also the smile of the day before, and another with which she had greeted him on a previous occasion, and the one with which she had responded, in the carriage, when he asked her if she minded his rearranging her cattleyas; and Odette's life at all other times, since he knew nothing about it, appeared to him, with its neutral and colourless background, like those sheets of sketches by Watteau* upon which one sees, here, there, in every corner, from every angle, drawn in three colours on the buff paper, an infinite number of smiles. But sometimes, in a corner of that life which Swann saw as completely blank, even if his mind told him it was not, because he could not imagine it, some friend, who, suspecting that they were in love, would not have dared to tell him anything about her that was of the slightest importance, would describe how he had glimpsed Odette that very morning walking up the Rue Abbattuci, wearing a little cape trimmed with skunk, a Rembrandt hat, and a bunch of violets in her bodice. This simple sketch was very disturbing to Swann because it suddenly made him realize that Odette had a life that did not entirely belong to him; he wanted to know whom she had intended to please with that outfit, which he had never seen her wear; and he promised himself that he would ask her where she had been going at that moment, as if the whole colourless life of his mistress—almost non-existent, since it was invisible to him—now consisted of just one thing apart from all those smiles she gave him: her walking along a street wearing a Rembrandt hat, with a bunch of violets in her bodice.

Except when he asked her for Vinteuil's little phrase instead of *La Valse des Roses*, Swann did not try to make her play things that were to his taste alone, or, any more in music than in literature, to correct her bad taste. He was well aware that she was not intelligent. When she said she would love him to tell her about the great poets, she had imagined that she would immediately get to know heroic and romantic verse in the style of the Vicomte de Borelli,* but even more touching. As for Vermeer of Delft, she asked Swann if the painter had suffered over a woman, if it was a woman who had inspired him, and when he told her that nobody knew, she lost interest in the man. She often said: 'Poetry, of course—there would be nothing nicer if it was all true, if poets really believed everything they say. But very often those people are even more calculating than anyone else. I know what I'm talking about, because I had a friend who was in love with a poet of sorts. In his poetry all he talked about was love, the sky, and the stars. And she was really taken in! He did her out of more than three hundred thousand francs.' If Swann then tried to make her understand something about beauty in art, or how to appreciate poetry and painting, after a short while she would stop listening and say: 'Oh! I never imagined it was like that.' And he felt that her disappointment was so great that he preferred to lie and tell her that what he had said was nothing, that he had just scratched the surface, that he did not have time to go into things properly, that there was much more to it. 'More?' she would say sharply. 'What, exactly? Tell me!' But he would not continue, knowing that it would all sound very uninteresting to her, different from what she was hoping for, less sensational and less touching, and fearing that, disillusioned with art, she might at the same time be disillusioned with love.

And in fact she now found Swann less impressive, intellectually, than she had believed. 'You're always so reserved, I can't make you out.' She was much more impressed by his indifference to money, his kindness to everyone, his tact. And it often happens, in fact, to greater men than Swann, to a scientist or an artist, when he is not misunderstood by those around him, that the feeling on their part which proves that they have been convinced of the superiority of his intellect is not their admiration for his ideas, which are beyond them, but their respect for his kindness. What also inspired her with respect was Swann's position in society, though she had no desire that he should try to secure invitations for herself. Perhaps she felt that any such attempt was bound to fail, or was even afraid that the mere mention of her name would prompt dreadful revelations about her. In any case, she had made him promise never to speak of her to others. The reason why she did not want to go into society, she had told him, was a quarrel she had once had with a friend who had avenged herself by speaking ill of her. 'But surely,' Swann objected, 'your friend didn't know everybody in society.' 'Well, yes,' she replied, 'but these things get around; you know how cruel people can be.' Swann could make no sense of this story, but he knew very well that sayings such as 'People can be so cruel' and 'There's no smoke without fire' are generally accepted as true; there must be cases to which they were applicable. Was Odette's one of them? He wondered about it, but not for long, because he was subject to the same mental torpor that had afflicted his father whenever he was faced with a difficult problem. In any event, that social world that so frightened Odette did not, perhaps, inspire her with any great longings, since it was too far removed from the world she knew for her to have any clear picture of it. However, while she had retained in some respects a genuine simplicity (one of the friendships she kept up, for example, was with a little dressmaker, now retired, whose steep, dark, foul-smelling staircase she climbed almost every day), she had a craving to be 'chic', but did not conceive of it in the same way as society people. For them, being 'chic' is something that emanates from a small number of individuals who project it quite far—but more and more faintly the further one is from their most intimate associates—through the circle of their friends or friends of their friends, whose names form a sort of directory. Society people know this directory by heart, they have in these matters an erudition from which they have extracted a type of taste, or tact, so that if Swann, for example, read in a newspaper the names of the people who were present at a dinner-party, he could immediately tell, without having to draw on his knowledge of society, precisely how 'chic' the dinner-party was, just as a literary person, by reading a single sentence, can judge exactly the merit of its author. But Odette was one of those people (extremely numerous, whatever society people may think, and to be found in all classes of society) who do not share these notions, but imagine a quite different kind of 'chic', that assumes different guises according to the circle to which they themselves belong, but has the special characteristic—whether the version Odette dreamed of or that revered by Madame Cottard—of being directly accessible to everyone. The other, the 'chic' of society people, is indeed accessible too, but only after a certain lapse of time. Odette would say of someone: 'He only goes to smart places.'

And if Swann asked her what she meant by that, she would answer almost with contempt: 'I mean smart places! For heaven's sake, if you need to be told, at your age, what the smart places are, you can't be helped! For example, the Avenue de l'Impératrice on Sunday mornings, around the lake at five o'clock, the Éden Théâtre on Thursdays, the Hippodrome* on Fridays, the balls . . .'

'But which balls?'

'The balls people give in Paris! The smart ones, I mean. Herbinger, for instance, you know the one I mean, the one who works for a stock-jobber. You must know who I mean, he's one of the best-known men in Paris, that tall fair-haired young man who's such a snob, always has a flower in his button-hole, a parting at the back, and a light-coloured overcoat; he's always with that old frump he takes to all the first-nights. Well, he gave a ball the other night, and all the smart people in Paris were there. I would have loved to go! But you had to show your invitation at the door, and I couldn't get one. But actually, I'm just as glad I didn't go, I would have been trampled underfoot, and I wouldn't have seen a thing. It's all about being able to say you were at Herbinger's ball. And you know how I like to show off! But in any case, you can bet that out of a hundred girls who say they were there, at least half of them are lying . . . But I'm surprised you weren't there, a real "swell" like you.'

Swann made no attempt, however, to induce her to modify her conception of what was 'chic'; thinking that his own was no more authentic, that it was just as foolish and frivolous, he saw no point in educating his mistress about it, with the result that after a few months she took no interest in the people whose houses he frequented, except in so far as they were able to provide enclosure passes for race-meetings or tickets for first-nights. She wanted him to cultivate useful connections of that kind, but otherwise she was inclined to think that there was nothing very smart about them, having seen the Marquise de Villeparisis go past in the street wearing a black woollen dress and a bonnet tied under her chin.

'But, *darling*, she looks like an usherette or an old concierge! And she's a marquise! I'm no marquise, but you'd have to pay me a lot of money to be seen in a get-up like that!'

And she could not understand why Swann lived in the house on the Quai d'Orléans, which, though she did not dare to tell him, she considered unworthy of him.

It was true that she liked to think of herself as a lover of 'antiques' and would assume a rapturous and knowing air when she described how she adored to spend a whole day looking for 'knick-knacks', hunting for 'bric-à-brac' and 'period things'. Although it was a sort of point of honour she insisted on maintaining, as if in deference to some old family precept, that she should never answer questions or 'account for' how she spent her days, she once mentioned to Swann a friend who had invited her to her house, where she found everything in 'period style'. But Swann could not get her to say what the period was. After a little reflection, however, she replied that it was 'medieval'. By this she meant that the rooms had wood panelling. Some time after that, she mentioned her friend again, and added, in the hesitant tone and with the knowing air one adopts when referring to a person one has met at dinner the evening before and of whom one has never heard until then, but whom one's hosts seem to consider so celebrated that one hopes that the person one is talking to will know who is meant: 'She's got a dining-room that's . . . eighteenth-century!' Personally, she had thought it hideous, very bare, as though the house was unfinished; women looked hideous in it too, and the style would never catch on. She mentioned it again, a third time, and showed Swann the address of the man who had designed the drawing-room, and whom she wanted to send for, when she had enough money, to see if he could design one for her too, not the same, of course, but the kind she dreamed of having but which unfortunately her little house was not large enough to accommodate, with tall dressers, Renaissance furniture, and fireplaces like the ones in the chateau at Blois. On this occasion, she let slip what she thought of Swann's abode on the Quai d'Orléans; for he had criticized her friend for indulging, not in Louis XVI (which, he said, even though it was quite out of fashion these days, could be made to look attractive), but in fake antique: 'You wouldn't want her to live like you, with a lot of broken furniture and threadbare carpets, would you!' she said, her bourgeois respect for appearances getting the better, once more, of her *cocotte*'s dilettantism.

People who liked looking for knick-knacks, who loved poetry, who despised crass calculations involving money, and dreamed of honour and love, she saw as an elite class of humanity, superior to all the rest. There was no need actually to have those tastes, as long as one proclaimed them; when a man had confessed to her at a dinner-party that he liked to wander about and get his hands dirty in curiosity shops, that he would never be appreciated in this commercial age, because he did not care about its concerns, and that because of this he belonged to another age altogether, she would say on returning home: 'He's such an adorable creature, so sensitive! I had no idea!' and she would conceive for him there and then a deep bond of friendship. But on the other hand, men who, like Swann, had those tastes, but did not talk about them, left her cold. She had to admit, of course, that Swann was not interested in money, but she would add sulkily: 'But with him, it's not the same thing'; and, in fact, what appealed to her imagination was not the practice of disinterestedness, but its vocabulary.

Feeling that, often, he could not give her in real life the pleasures of which she dreamed, he tried at least to ensure that she would be happy in his company, tried not to question the vulgar ideas, the bad taste which she displayed in all things, and which he loved, moreover, like everything that came from her, which enchanted him even, for they were so many characteristic features by which the essence of this woman revealed itself to him. And so, when she looked happy because she was going to see *La Reine Topaze,** or when her expression became serious, worried, or petulant because she was afraid of missing the flower-show, or simply of being late for tea, with muffins and toast, at the tea-rooms in the Rue Royale, where she believed that regular attendance was indispensable for the establishment of a woman's reputation for elegance, Swann, enchanted as we all are by the naturalness of a child or the verisimilitude of a portrait so lifelike that it seems about to speak, felt so strongly his mistress's soul rising to the surface of her face that he could not resist going over to touch it with his lips. 'Ah! So little Odette wants to be taken to the flower-show, she wants to show herself off. Well, then, we'll take her, because her wish is our command.' As Swann's eyesight was rather poor, he had to resign himself to wearing spectacles for working at home, and to adopting a monocle, which was less disfiguring, for going out in society. The first time she saw him with one in his eye, she was beside herself with delight: 'I must say that, for a man, it's terribly *chic*! It really suits you! You look like a real *gentleman*.' And she added, with a hint of regret: 'All you need now is a title!' He was happy that Odette was like this, just as, if he had been in love with a Breton woman, he would have enjoyed seeing her in a coif and hearing her say she believed in ghosts. Until then, like many men whose taste for the arts develops independently of their sensuality, an odd discrepancy had existed between the satisfactions he would accord to each, for he enjoyed the seductions of ever more refined works of art in the company of ever more vulgar women, taking a little servant-girl to a private box for a production of a decadent play he wanted to see, or to an exhibition of Impressionist painting, convinced, moreover, that a cultivated society woman would not have understood them any better but would not have been able to stay quiet so nicely. Now, however, ever since he had fallen in love with Odette, to share her feelings, to be at one with her in spirit, was such a pleasant endeavour that he tried to find enjoyment in the things she liked, and the pleasure he felt, not only in imitating her habits but also in adopting her opinions, was all the greater, since they had no roots in his own intelligence, because they reminded him only of his love for her, which was why he had preferred them to his own. If he went to more than one performance of *Serge Panine*,* if he looked for opportunities to see Olivier Métra* conduct, it was for the pleasure of being initiated into Odette's whole way of seeing things, of feeling that he had an equal share in all her tastes. This charm, which the things and places she liked possessed, of bringing him closer to her, seemed to him more mysterious than the charm intrinsic to things and places that were of greater beauty but did not remind him of her. Furthermore, since he had allowed the intellectual beliefs of his youth to weaken, and since, without his being aware of it, they had been eroded by his man-of-the-world scepticism, he thought (or at least he had thought thus for so long that he went on saying it) that the things we admire have no absolute value in themselves, but depend entirely on the period in which one lives, the social class to which one belongs, and changing fashions, the most vulgar of which are equal to those that are regarded as the most refined. And just as he considered that the importance Odette attached to being invited to the opening of a painting exhibition was not in itself more ridiculous than the pleasure he used to take in lunching at the home of the Prince of Wales, so he did not think that the admiration she professed for Monte Carlo or the Righi was more unreasonable than his own liking for Holland, which she imagined to be ugly, or for Versailles, which she found dreary. And so he denied himself the pleasure of visiting those places, delighting instead in the thought that it was for her sake, that he wanted to feel things and love things only with her.

Like everything else that formed part of Odette's environment, and was no more, in a sense, than the means whereby he could see and talk to her, he enjoyed the company of the Verdurins. At their house, since at the heart of all the entertainments, meals, music, games, fancy-dress suppers, excursions to the country and the theatre, even the occasional soirées they put on for the 'bores', there was the presence of Odette, the sight of Odette, conversation with Odette, a priceless gift bestowed upon Swann by the Verdurins' invitations, he was happier among the 'little clan' than anywhere else, and tried to find real qualities in it, imagining that by so doing he would, from choice, be part of it for the rest of his life. Not daring to tell himself, lest he should not believe it, that he would always love Odette, at least in supposing that he would go on visiting the Verdurins for ever (a proposition that, a priori, raised fewer objections of principle on the part of his intelligence), he could see himself in the future continuing to see Odette every evening; this did not, perhaps, amount to quite the same thing as loving her for ever, but for the moment, while he loved her, to feel that he would not stop seeing her one day was all he asked. 'What charming people,' he would say to himself. 'That's the kind of life one should lead! How much more intelligent, more artistic, they are than the people one knows! How genuine, despite some silly little excesses, is Madame Verdurin's love of painting and music, what a passion for works of art, what keenness to encourage artists! Her ideas about society people are not quite right; but then, the ideas society people have about artistic circles are even more wrong! Perhaps I'm not very demanding in terms of intelligent conversation, but I'm perfectly happy with Cottard, despite his awful puns. And as for the painter, he can be dreadfully pretentious when he tries to make an impression on people, but on the other hand he has one of the best minds I've ever come across. The main thing, though, is how free one feels there, one can do as one pleases without any kind of constraint or fuss. So much good humour flows every day through that drawing-room! Apart from a few rare exceptions, I will most certainly never go anywhere else. It's where I will feel more and more at home and want to live my life.'

And since the qualities he believed to be intrinsic to the Verdurins were merely the reflection of the pleasures he enjoyed in their house because of his love for Odette, those qualities became more serious, more profound, more vital, when those pleasures were too. Because Madame Verdurin sometimes gave Swann the only thing that could constitute happiness for him; because, one evening when he felt anxious on seeing Odette talking rather more to one of the guests than to any of the others, and when, irritated with her, he did not want to take the initiative of asking her if she would be coming home with him, Madame Verdurin brought him peace and joy by saying, unprompted: 'Odette, you'll see Monsieur Swann home, won't you?'; because, when the summer holidays were approaching, and he had been wondering

whether Odette might go away somewhere without him, whether he
would still be able to see her every day, Madame Verdurin had invited
them both to spend the summer at her house in the country—Swann,
unconsciously allowing gratitude and self-interest to infiltrate his intelligence and influence his ideas, went so far as to proclaim that Madame
Verdurin was the noblest of souls. If one of his old classmates from
the École du Louvre* happened to mention a number of delightful or
eminent people, he would reply: 'I prefer the Verdurins a hundred
times over.' And then, with a solemnity that was new to him, he would
declare: 'They are magnanimous people, and magnanimity is, in the
end, the only thing that is really important, that confers distinction
here on earth. You see, there are only two kinds of people: those who
are magnanimous, and the rest; and I have reached an age when one
has to choose, to decide once and for all whom one is going to like and
dislike, to stick with the people one likes, and, to make up for the time
wasted with the others, never leave them again for as long as one lives.
And so,' he went on, with the little thrill one feels when, even without
quite realizing it, one says something not because it is true but because
one enjoys saying it and listens to one's own voice as if it is someone
else's, 'the die is cast, I have chosen to love only magnanimous souls,
and to live henceforth only in the company of magnanimous people.
You ask me whether Madame Verdurin is really intelligent. I can
assure you she has shown a nobility of spirit, a loftiness of soul which,
you know, no one could possibly attain without an equal loftiness of
mind. There is no doubt that she has a highly intelligent understanding of the arts. But that may not be her most admirable quality; every
little action, ingeniously and exquisitely kind, that she has performed
for me, every thoughtful attention, every little gesture, so natural yet
so sublime, reveals a more profound understanding of existence than
any philosophical treatise.'

He might have reminded himself, however, that there were some
old friends of his parents who were just as simple as the Verdurins, or
friends of his youth just as fond of art, that he knew other big-hearted
people, but whom, since he had opted for simplicity, the arts, and
magnanimity, he had stopped seeing altogether. But these people did
not know Odette, and, if they had known her, would never have thought
of introducing her to him.

And so, in the whole Verdurin circle, there was probably not a single one of the 'faithful' who was as fond of them, or thought he was as

fond of them, as Swann. Yet, when Monsieur Verdurin had said he did not care much for Swann, he was not only expressing his own sentiments but also guessing those of his wife. Doubtless Swann's affection for Odette was too exclusive and he had neglected to make Madame Verdurin his regular confidante: doubtless the very discretion with which he had availed himself of the Verdurins' hospitality, often refraining from coming to dinner for a reason they never suspected and in place of which they saw a desire not to decline an invitation to the house of some 'bores', and doubtless, too, despite all the precautions he had taken to keep it from them, their gradual discovery of his brilliant position in society—all this contributed to their irritation with him. But the real, deeper reason for it lay elsewhere. It was that they had very quickly sensed in him an impenetrable, private space, where he continued to maintain silently to himself that the Princesse de Sagan was not grotesque and that Cottard's jokes were not amusing; in short, though he never once dropped his affability or rebelled against their dogmas, they felt it was impossible to impose them upon him and fully convert him to them, an impossibility such as they had never encountered in anyone else. They would have forgiven him for associating with bores (to whom, in fact, in his heart of hearts, he infinitely preferred the Verdurins and the whole of the little clan) if only he had been willing to set a good example by renouncing them in the presence of the 'faithful'. But this was an abjuration which they realized they would never be able to get out of him.

How different he was from a 'newcomer' Odette had asked them to invite, although she had met him only a few times, and in whom they were already investing great hopes: the Comte de Forcheville! (It turned out that he was Saniette's brother-in-law, which filled the 'faithful' with amazement: the old palaeographer had such a humble manner that they had always supposed him to be socially inferior to themselves, and did not expect to learn that he came from a wealthy and relatively aristocratic family.) Of course, Forcheville was a tremendous snob, whereas Swann was not; of course, he would never dream of placing the Verdurins' circle above all others, as Swann did. But he did not have the natural refinement that prevented Swann from being party to the more obviously false criticisms Madame Verdurin made of people he knew. As for the vulgar and pretentious tirades the painter would launch into on certain days, and the commercial traveller jokes Cottard ventured, for which Swann, who liked both men, could easily find excuses without having the heart or the hypocrisy to applaud them, Forcheville by contrast was of an intellectual calibre that allowed him to be dumbfounded, awestruck by the first (though he failed to understand a word) and to delight in the second. And indeed the first dinner at the Verdurins' at which Forcheville was present threw into sharp relief all these differences, brought out his qualities, and precipitated Swann's fall from grace.

At this dinner there was, apart from the regulars, a professor from the Sorbonne, a certain Brichot, who had met Monsieur and Madame Verdurin at a spa somewhere and who, if his university duties and scholarly pursuits had not left him little free time, would gladly have come to the house more often. For he had the kind of curiosity and superstition about life which, when combined with a certain scepticism towards the object of their studies, gives some intelligent men in any profession, doctors who do not believe in medicine, schoolteachers who do not believe in Latin compositions, a reputation for having broad, brilliant, and even superior minds. He made a point, at Madame Verdurin's, of seeking the most topical examples when he spoke about philosophy or history, mainly because he thought that such subjects were no more than a preparation for life, and imagined that he was seeing practised in the little clan what he had previously encountered only in books, and perhaps also because, having had instilled into him in his younger days, and having unconsciously preserved, a respect for certain subjects, he believed he was casting aside his scholarly self by taking conversational liberties with them, although, in fact, this seemed daring to him only because he remained a scholar.

At the beginning of the meal, when Monsieur de Forcheville, seated to the right of Madame Verdurin, who for the benefit of the 'newcomer' had taken great pains over her appearance, said to her: 'It's very unusual, that white dress!', the doctor, who could not take his eyes off him, so curious was he to know what kind of man a 'de', as he termed it, would be, and was waiting for an opportunity to attract his attention and engage him in conversation, seized on the word '*blanche*' and, without raising his eyes from his plate, said: 'Blanche? Blanche de Castille?',* then, without moving his head, looked furtively to right and left, smiling uncertainly. Whereas Swann, with his pained and pointless effort to smile, showed how stupid he found this pun, Forcheville had shown not only that he appreciated the subtlety of Cottard's wit but also that he was a man of the world who knew how

to moderate his mirth, which had already greatly pleased Madame
Verdurin by its spontaneity.

'What do you make of a scientist like that?' she asked Forcheville.
'It's impossible to have a serious conversation with him, even for two
minutes.' And she added, turning to the doctor: 'Is that the sort of
thing you say to people at your hospital? If so, it must be a very
entertaining place! I can see I must get myself admitted as a patient!'

'I believe I heard the doctor talking about that old harridan,
Blanche de Castille, if I may be so bold as to put it that way. Is that not
so, Madame?' Brichot asked Madame Verdurin, who, swooning with
laughter, her eyes closed, buried her face in her hands, through which
muffled squeals could be heard. 'Good heavens, Madame,' continued
Brichot, 'I would not wish to alarm the respectful souls, if there are
any, round this table, *sub rosa* . . . And I realize, of course, that our
ineffable republic, Athenian as it most decidedly is, might wish to pay
homage to that obscurantist Capetian lady as the first of our police
chiefs with a real grip on things. Yes, indeed, my dear host, yes indeed,
yes indeed!' he went on in his sonorous voice, articulating each syllable,
in response to an objection by Monsieur Verdurin. 'The *Chronique de
Saint-Denis*, an impeccably reliable source, leaves us in no doubt
about the matter. There could have been no better choice of patron
saint by a secularizing proletariat than that mother of a saint (whom,
by the way, she led a dog's life, as we know from Suger and other Saint
Bernards);* for with her no one failed to get what was coming to him.'

'Who is that gentleman?' Forcheville asked Madame Verdurin.
'He sounds most impressive.'

'What, you don't know the famous Brichot? He's a celebrity
throughout the whole of Europe.'

'Ah! So that's Bréchiot!' cried Forcheville, who had not quite
caught the name. 'You must tell me all about him!' he added, staring
goggle-eyed at the great celebrity. 'It's always interesting to have
dinner with famous men. I must say, you certainly treat your guests
to very select dinner-companions. There's never a dull moment in
your house.'

'Oh, you know, the main thing,' Madame Verdurin said modestly,
'is that they feel at home here. They can say whatever they like, and
the conversation goes off like fireworks. Brichot, this evening, is quite
off form: you know, I've seen him be absolutely dazzling here in my
house; you feel you should go down on your knees before him. But at

other people's houses he's just not the same, he has no wit at all, you have to drag the words out of him, he's actually boring.'

'How odd!' said Forcheville, surprised.

Brichot's brand of wit would have been considered pure stupidity by the people among whom Swann had spent his youth, even though compatible with genuine intelligence. And the intelligence of the Professor, which was lively and well nourished, would probably have been envied by many of the society people Swann considered witty. But those people had so thoroughly inculcated in him their own likes and dislikes, at least in all matters to do with social life, including even the ancillary part of it which should, strictly speaking, be a matter of intelligence—namely, conversation—that Swann could not help but find Brichot's jokes pedantic, vulgar, and nauseatingly crude. Moreover, accustomed as he was to people with good manners, he was shocked by the brusque military tone adopted by the jingoistic academic towards anyone he happened to address. But the main reason for his attitude may have been that, that evening in particular, he had lost some of his indulgence towards Madame Verdurin on seeing how friendly she was to this man Forcheville whom Odette, unaccountably, had brought along. Somewhat embarrassed vis-à-vis Swann, she had asked him on her arrival: 'What do you think of my guest?'

And he, realizing for the first time that Forcheville, whom he had known for years, might be attractive to women and was quite a handsome man, had replied: 'Revolting!' It certainly did not occur to him to be jealous of Odette, but he did not feel quite as happy as usual, and when Brichot, having begun to tell the story of Blanche de Castille's mother, who 'had been with Henry Plantagenet for years before she married him', tried to get Swann to ask him what happened next by saying: 'Isn't that right, Monsieur Swann?' in the sergeant-majorish tone some people adopt to make themselves understood by a peasant or to put heart into a trooper, Swann spoiled Brichot's effect, and thus infuriated the hostess, by asking to be excused for having so little interest in Blanche de Castille, but there was something he wanted to ask the painter. The latter, in fact, had gone that afternoon to an exhibition by an artist, a friend of Madame Verdurin's who had recently died, and Swann wanted to find out from him (for he respected his judgement) if there was really anything more in these last works than the virtuosity that people had found so astonishing in his earlier works.

'In that respect it was extraordinary, but it did not seem to me to be the kind of art you might call "elevated",' Swann said with a smile.

'Elevated . . . to the level of an institution,' interjected Cottard, raising his arms with mock solemnity. The whole table burst out laughing.

'You see?' said Madame Verdurin to Forcheville. 'You just can't be serious with him. When you least expect it, he comes out with one of his pieces of nonsense.'

But she noticed that Swann was the only one who had not laughed. For one thing, he was not pleased that Cottard had made fun of him in front of Forcheville. And then the painter, instead of answering him properly, which he probably would have done if he had been alone with him, preferred to show off to the other guests by treating them to a little speech about the skill of the deceased master.

'I went up very close to one of the paintings to see how it was done. I stuck my nose right into it. Well, it was amazing! I couldn't for the life of me tell whether it was done with glue, or rubies, or soap, or bronze, or sunshine, or poo!'

'And one makes twelve!' cried the doctor, but too late for anyone to understand his interjection.

'It looks as if it was made out of just anything,' continued the painter. 'There's no way you can work out what the trick is, any more than you can with *The Night Watch* or *The Regentesses*, and the brush-work is even better than Rembrandt or Hals.* It's got everything. No, really, everything! I swear.'

And just as singers who have reached the highest note they can produce continue in a falsetto, very softly, he went on in a murmur, laughing, as if the painting had been preposterously beautiful: 'It smells nice, it goes to your head, it takes your breath away, it makes you feel you're being tickled, and you haven't got a clue what it's made with, it's a kind of sorcery, trickery, an absolute miracle!' Then he burst out laughing: 'It shouldn't be allowed!' Then he paused, looked up with a very serious expression, and, adopting a deep bass note which he tried to bring into harmony, he added: 'and it's so *true*!'

Except at the moment when he had said the painting was better than *The Night Watch*, a blasphemy that had provoked a protest from Madame Verdurin, for whom *The Night Watch* was the greatest master-piece in the world along with the 'Ninth' and the *Winged Victory*,* and at the word 'poo', which had made Forcheville glance quickly round the table to see whether the word was acceptable and had then formed his mouth into a prudish and conciliatory smile, all the guests, except for Swann, had been gazing at the painter, transfixed with admiration.

'He's so marvellous when he gets carried away like that,' cried Madame Verdurin the moment he had finished, delighted that the table-talk should have turned out so interesting on the very evening that Monsieur de Forcheville was dining with them for the first time. 'And you, what are you doing sitting there like that, with your mouth wide open like a simpleton?' she said to her husband. 'You know how well he can talk. Anyone would think,' she went on, turning to the painter, 'that he had never heard you speak before. You should have seen him while you were talking, he was hanging on every word. And tomorrow he'll repeat everything you said, word for word.'

'But I'm not joking!' said the painter, delighted with his success. 'You look as if you think I was just spinning a yarn, that I was having you on; well, I'll take you there and you can see for yourself whether I'm exaggerating. I bet you anything you like, you'll come away even more impressed than I was!'

'But we don't think you're exaggerating. We just want you to eat your dinner, and my husband should too; give Monsieur some more sole, you can see that his has gone cold. You're serving as if the house was on fire, we're not in any hurry. Wait a little while before you bring in the salad.'

Madame Cottard, who was a modest woman and never said much, did not lack self-assurance when a moment of inspiration provided her with a witty remark. She felt it would be well received, and this increased her confidence, but what she did with it was not so much in order to shine herself as to give support to her husband in his career. And so she did not allow the word 'salad' to leave Madame Verdurin's lips without saying in an undertone, turning to Odette:

'It's not a Japanese salad, is it?'

Then, in her delight and confusion at the aptness and daring of this allusion, so discreet yet unmistakable, to the highly successful new play by Dumas, she broke into a charming, girlish laugh, not at all loud but so compulsive that for a few moments she could not control it. 'Who is that lady?' asked Forcheville. 'She's terribly witty.'

'No, it's not, but you can all have one if you come to dinner on Friday.'

'You'll think I'm terribly provincial, Monsieur,' Madame Cottard said to Swann, 'but I haven't yet seen this famous *Francillon** everybody's talking about. The Doctor has been (in fact, I remember he said he had the great pleasure of spending the evening with you) and I must confess I didn't think it would be very sensible for him to book two seats to go again with me. Of course, an evening at the Théâtre-Français is never disappointing, the acting is always so good, but we have some very nice friends' (Madame Cottard rarely uttered a proper name, finding it more 'distinguished' to refer simply to 'some friends of ours' or 'one of my friends', speaking of them in an affected tone and with the self-importance of someone who provides names only when she chooses) 'who often have a box and are kind enough to take us to all the new productions worth seeing, so I'm bound to see *Francillon* sooner or later and be able to make my own mind up about it. I must confess, though, that I feel rather stupid, because in every drawing-room I find myself in, naturally the only thing they're all talking about is that wretched Japanese salad.' Then, seeing that Swann seemed less interested in such a burning topic than she would have thought, she added: 'It's actually becoming rather tiresome. But I must admit that it can sometimes give people some amusing ideas. I've got a friend, for instance, who's quite eccentric, though she's very pretty as well as being very popular and very sought after, who claims she got her cook to make that Japanese salad in her own kitchen, using all the ingredients mentioned by Dumas *fils* in his play. Then she invited some friends to come and try it. Unfortunately, I was not one of the chosen few. But she told us all about it at her next "at home"; apparently it was revolting, she made us laugh until we cried. But of course it's all in the telling,' she said, seeing that Swann was still not amused.

And imagining that it was perhaps because he had not enjoyed *Francillon*, she went on: 'Anyway, I think I'll be disappointed. I don't suppose it's as good as *Serge Panine*, which Madame de Crécy absolutely adores. That play at least has real substance, it makes you think. But to giving a recipe for a salad on the stage of the Théâtre-Français! Really! *Serge Panine*, on the other hand . . .! But it's like everything by Georges Ohnet, it's always so well written. You may know *Le Maître de Forges*, which I like even better than *Serge Panine*.'*

'You'll have to forgive me,' Swann said ironically, 'but I must confess that my lack of admiration is divided roughly equally between those two masterpieces.'

'Really? What don't you like about them? Are you sure you're not prejudiced against them? Perhaps you think they're a little too sad? Anyway, as I always say, people should never argue about novels or plays. We've all got our own way of looking at things, and what you might hate I might absolutely love.'

She was interrupted by Forcheville, who had turned to address Swann. In fact, while Madame Cottard was discussing *Francillon*, Forcheville had been telling Madame Verdurin how much he admired what he called the painter's 'little speech'. 'The gentleman has a way with words! And what a memory!' he said to her when the painter had finished. 'I've rarely come across anything like it. By Jove, I wish I could be like that. He'd make an excellent preacher. With him and Bréchot you have two amazing characters, both virtuosos, though when it comes to the gift of the gab, I think the painter might even beat the professor. He sounds more natural, less affected. Although now and then he does use some words that are a little vulgar, but that's the thing nowadays. But I've seldom seen anyone hold the floor so cleverly—"hold the spittoon", as we used to say in the Army; in fact, I had a friend in my Army days the gentleman rather reminds me of. You could give him any subject, anything at all, this wine-glass, for example, and he could rattle on about it for hours; well no, not about this glass, that's a silly thing to say, but about the Battle of Waterloo, or something like that, he'd spin such a yarn out of it! In fact, Swann was in the same regiment; he must have known him.'

'Do you see much of Monsieur Swann?' asked Madame Verdurin.

'Oh no,' replied Monsieur de Forcheville, and then, thinking that he would be able to get closer to Odette if he were pleasant to Swann, he decided to take this opportunity to flatter him by mentioning his distinguished friends, but to do so as a man of the world himself, in a tone of friendly criticism and not as if he were congratulating Swann on some unexpected success: 'Isn't that so, Swann? I never see you. In any case, how could anyone manage to see him? The devil spends all his time with the La Trémoïlles, the Laumes, and all that lot! . . .' This imputation was especially false since, for the past year, Swann had hardly gone anywhere except to the Verdurins'. But the mere name of people the Verdurins did not know was greeted by them with a disapproving silence. Monsieur Verdurin, fearing the painful effect the names of these 'bores' must have had on his wife, especially when flung at her so tactlessly in front of all the faithful, cast a furtive glance at her, full of worry and concern. But he saw that in her resolve to take no notice, to remain unmoved by the news that had just been imparted to her, not merely to remain dumb but to have been deaf as well, as we pretend to be when a friend who has behaved badly towards us tries to slip into the conversation an excuse we would seem to accept if we listened to it without objection, or when someone utters in our presence the forbidden name of an enemy, Madame Verdurin, so that her silence should not look like approval but like the meaningless silence of inanimate objects, Madame Verdurin had suddenly emptied her face of all life, all mobility; her domed forehead had become simply a fine piece of sculpture in the round, which the name of those La Trémouïlles with whom Swann spent all his time had been unable to penetrate; her slightly wrinkled nose revealed the curve of a nostril that seemed copied from life. You would have sworn that her half-open mouth was about to speak. She was now merely a wax cast, a plaster mask, a maquette for a monument, a bust for the Palais de l'Industrie,* in front of which the public would be bound to stop in order to admire the way in which the sculptor, by evoking the inalienable dignity of the Verdurins as opposed to that of the La Trémoïlles and the Laumes,* whose equals they certainly were, just as they were the equals of all the 'bores' on the face of the earth, had managed to give an almost papal majesty to the whiteness and rigidity of the stone. Then at last the marble came to life and was heard to say that people must be very easy to please if they went to that house, because the wife was always drunk and the husband such an ignoramus that he said 'collidor' instead of 'corridor'.

'You'd have to pay me a fortune to let that lot into my house,' concluded Madame Verdurin, casting an imperious glance at Swann.

She could hardly have expected him to be so submissive as to echo the saintly simplicity of the pianist's aunt, who had exclaimed: 'Would you believe it! It amazes me that they can still find anyone willing to speak to them! I think I'd be too afraid: one can't be too careful. How can there still be people common enough to go running after them?' But he might at least have replied, like Forcheville: 'Well, dash it all, she's a Duchess! Some people are still impressed by that sort of thing.' This had at least allowed Madame Verdurin to reply: 'And much good may it do them!' But instead, Swann merely laughed in a way that suggested he could not even take such an outrageous remark seriously. Monsieur Verdurin, still casting furtive glances at his wife, was saddened to see, but understood all too well, that she was consumed with rage, like a Grand Inquisitor who has failed to stamp out heresy, and in an attempt to induce Swann to recant, since having the courage of one's convictions always seems to be calculated and cowardly in the eyes of those who do not share those convictions, asked him directly: 'Tell us frankly what you think of them. We'll keep it to ourselves, of course.'

To this, Swann replied: 'Oh, I'm not in the least intimidated by the Duchess (if it's the La Trémoïlles you're talking about). I can assure you that everyone likes going there. I wouldn't say she's in any way "profound"' (he pronounced 'profound' as if it was a ridiculous word, for his speech still bore the traces of mental habits which the recent change in his life, a rejuvenation marked by his enthusiasm for music, had temporarily made him lose, so that sometimes he would state his views quite robustly) 'but, in all honesty, she's an intelligent woman, and her husband is genuinely cultured. They're charming people.'

Whereupon Madame Verdurin, feeling that because of this one infidel she would be prevented from achieving total orthodoxy among the little clan, was unable to restrain herself, in her fury at Swann's stubborn refusal to see how much his words were making her suffer, and screamed at him from the depths of her heart: 'You can think that if you want, but at least don't say so to us.'

'It all depends on what you call intelligence,' said Forcheville, thinking it was his turn to shine. 'Come on, Swann, tell us what you mean by intelligence.'

'Exactly!' exclaimed Odette. 'That's the sort of big subject I'm always asking him to talk to me about, but he never does.'

'Yes I do,' protested Swann.

'Fibber!' said Odette.

'Fibber who?' asked the doctor.

'As you see it,' Forcheville went on, 'does intelligence mean having the gift of the gab, knowing how to ingratiate yourself?'

'Finish your dessert, so they can take your plate away,' Madame Verdurin said rather sourly to Saniette, who was lost in thought and had stopped eating. Then, perhaps a little ashamed at her ungracious tone, she added: 'It's all right, you can take your time. I only said that for the others, because it holds up the next course.'

'That gentle anarchist Fénelon,'* said Brichot, rapping out the syllables, 'has a very curious definition of intelligence . . .'

'Listen!' said Madame Verdurin to Forcheville and the doctor. 'He's going to give us Fénelon's definition of intelligence. Most interesting. It's not often you get a chance to hear that!'

But Brichot was waiting for Swann to put forward his definition. Swann, however, was not forthcoming, and by this fresh evasion spoiled the brilliant contest Madame Verdurin had been dying to offer Forcheville.

'You see! He's like that with me,' said Odette sulkily. 'I'm glad to discover I'm not the only one he thinks is not up to his standard.'

'Those de la Trémouilles,* whom Madame Verdurin has presented as being so undesirable,' said Brichot, articulating his words with special force, 'are they descended from the de la Trémouilles whom that grand old snob Madame de Sévigné said she was so pleased to know because it was good for her peasants? Of course, the Marquise had another reason, which must have been more important for her, because she was a woman of letters to the core, and always put good "copy" before everything else. And in the journal she used to send regularly to her daughter, it was Madame de la Trémouilles, always well informed through all her grand connections, who supplied the foreign politics.'

'Yes, but I don't actually think it's the same family,' hazarded Madame Verdurin.

Saniette, having hurriedly given the butler his untouched plate, had fallen back into a state of silent meditation, but now emerged at last to tell them, with a laugh, about a dinner he had attended with the Duc de la Trémoïlle where it became clear that the Duke did not know that George Sand* was the pseudonym of a woman. Swann, who was quite fond of Saniette, felt that he ought to give him some facts about the Duke's culture proving that ignorance of that sort on his part was utterly impossible; but he suddenly stopped, realizing that Saniette did not need this proof, but knew already that the story was untrue for the simple reason that he had just invented it. The worthy man suffered acutely from being regarded as so boring by the Verdurins; and, knowing full well that he had been even duller than usual at this dinner, he had not wanted to let it end without saying something amusing. He capitulated so quickly, looked so crestfallen at his failure to achieve the effect he had intended, and his reply ('My mistake, my mistake! But it's not a crime to be wrong, is it?') was such an abject appeal to Swann not to persist with a refutation that was now superfluous, that Swann wished he had been able to say that the story was both true and delightfully funny. The doctor, who had been listening to them, thought this was the right moment to say *Se non è vero,** but he was not quite sure of the words and was afraid of getting them wrong.

When dinner was over, Forcheville went up to the doctor:

'She can't have been bad-looking at one point, Madame Verdurin; and she's a woman you can talk to, which is the main thing as far as I'm concerned. Of course she's getting on a bit. But Madame de Crécy— now there's a little lady who's got her wits about her. My word, yes, you can see straight away she knows what's what! We're talking about Madame de Crécy,' he added, as Monsieur Verdurin joined them, his pipe in his mouth. 'I'd say that as a specimen of the female form . . .'

'I'd rather have her in my bed than have a slap in the face with a wet fish,' blurted Cottard, who for some moments had been waiting for Forcheville to pause for breath so that he could interject that old joke for which he feared there would be no opportunity if the conversation changed course, and which he delivered with the excessive spontaneity and confidence that mask the coldness and anxiety inseparable from a prepared recitation. Forcheville was familiar with the joke, understood it, and was amused. As for Monsieur Verdurin, he was unsparing with his mirth, having recently discovered a way of expressing it that was different from his wife's, but just as simple and obvious. Scarcely had he begun the movement of head and shoulders of a man shaking with laughter than he would immediately begin to cough, as if, in laughing too violently, he had swallowed a mouthful of pipe-smoke. And by keeping the pipe in one corner of his mouth, he was able to prolong indefinitely the pantomime of suffocation and hilarity. Thus both he and Madame Verdurin (who, on the opposite end of the room, was listening to one of the painter's stories and closing her eyes and making ready to bury her face in her hands) were like two theatre masks each representing Comedy in a different way.

Monsieur Verdurin had in fact been wise not to take his pipe out of his mouth, for Cottard, who needed to leave the room for a moment, murmured a witticism he had only recently picked up and which he repeated each time he had to go to the same place: 'I must go and see a man about a dog.' This resulted in a renewed coughing fit on the part of Monsieur Verdurin.

'Do take that pipe out of your mouth,' said Madame Verdurin, handing round liqueurs. 'You'll choke to death if you try so hard not to laugh.'

'What a charming man your husband is,' declared Forcheville to Madame Cottard. 'He's incredibly witty. Oh, thank you, Madame. An old soldier like me never says no to a drink.'

'Monsieur de Forcheville thinks Odette is charming,' said Monsieur Verdurin to his wife.

'Well, as a matter of fact she'd like to come and have lunch with you one day. We can arrange that, but on no account must Swann hear about it. He tends to put a damper on things, you know. And you can still come to dinner, of course; we hope we'll be seeing a lot of you. With summer coming, we'll often be having dinner out of doors. That won't bother you, will it—little dinner-parties in the Bois? Good, good, it'll be very nice.' Then: 'I say, aren't you going to go and do your job?' she cried to the young pianist, in order to display, before a newcomer of Forcheville's importance, both her wit and her despotic power over the 'faithful'.

'Monsieur de Forcheville was saying bad things about you,' Madame Cottard said to her husband when he returned to the drawing-room. And he, pursuing the idea of Forcheville's noble birth, which had been preoccupying him all through dinner, said to him: 'I'm treating a baroness at the moment, Baroness Putbus. The Putbuses took part in the Crusades, if I'm not mistaken. They have a lake in Pomerania that must be ten times the size of the Place de la Concorde. I'm treating her for rheumatoid arthritis. Charming woman. I believe she knows Madame Verdurin, actually.'

This enabled Forcheville, a moment later, finding himself alone again with Madame Cottard, to complete the favourable judgement he had passed on her husband: 'And he's so interesting, you can see he knows a lot of people. My word, those medical men know such a lot!'

'I'm going to play the phrase from the sonata for Monsieur Swann,' said the pianist.

'Good heavens! It's not the "Sonata-Snake", is it?' asked Monsieur de Forcheville, trying to show off.

But Dr Cottard, who had never heard this pun, did not understand, and thought that Monsieur de Forcheville was making a mistake. He hurried over to correct him. 'No, no, it's not *serpent à sonates*,* it's *serpent à sonnettes*,' he said in a tone of eager, impatient self-congratulation.

Forcheville explained the pun to him. The doctor blushed.

'You must admit it's not bad, Doctor!'

'Oh, I've heard it many times,' answered Cottard.

Then they fell silent; beneath the agitated sounds of the violin tremolos which protected it with their quivering sostenuto two octaves above it—as in a mountainous landscape, behind the seeming immobility of a vertiginous waterfall, one sees, two hundred feet below, the tiny figure of a woman walking in the valley—the little phrase had just appeared, distant, graceful, protected by the slow, continuous unfurling of its transparent curtain of sound. And Swann, in his heart, appealed to it as to a confidant of his love for Odette, as to a friend of hers who ought to tell her to pay no attention to that man Forcheville.

'Ah, you're late!' said Madame Verdurin to a regular whom she had invited to drop in for coffee. 'Brichot was in top form! He's gone now, but he was quite superb! Wasn't he, Monsieur Swann? I believe it was the first time you and he had met,' she added, in order to make the point that he had her to thank for the introduction. 'Wasn't our Brichot delightful?'

Swann bowed politely.

'What? Didn't you find him interesting?' Madame Verdurin asked him rather sharply.

'But of course, Madame, he was most interesting. I was enthralled. He's perhaps a little too arrogant, and a little too jolly, for my taste. I'd prefer it if he were rather less sure of himself, less categorical, now and then, but one can see he knows a lot and he seems a very decent sort.'

It was very late by the time everyone had left. Cottard's first words to his wife were. 'I've rarely seen Madame Verdurin in such good form as she was this evening.'

'What kind of person exactly is this Madame Verdurin of yours? Rather difficult to make out, isn't she?' said Forcheville to the painter, to whom he had offered a lift.

Odette watched with regret as he went off; she dared not decline to ride with Swann, but was in a bad mood in the carriage, and when he asked if he could come in, she gave an impatient shrug and said: 'I suppose so.'

When all the guests had gone, Madame Verdurin said to her husband: 'Did you notice the stupid way Swann laughed when we mentioned Madame La Trémoïlle?'

She had noticed, too, that several times Swann and Forcheville had omitted the 'de' in front of La Trémoïlle. Convinced that they only did this to show they were not intimidated by titles, she wanted to follow suit, but had not worked out by which grammatical form to express it. And so her debased habits of speech won out over her intransigent republicanism, so she carried on saying 'the de la Trémoïlles', or rather, using an abbreviation common in *café-concert* songs and cartoon captions, which elided the *de*, she referred to them as the d'la Trémoïlles, but compensated for it by saying: 'Madame La Trémoïlle', adding 'The *Duchess*, as Swann calls her', with an ironic smile that showed she was just quoting and would accept no responsibility for such a naïve and ridiculous appellation.

'I must say I thought him utterly stupid,' she said.

And Monsieur Verdurin replied: 'He's not sincere. He's quite sly, always sitting on the fence, always wanting to run with the hare and hunt with the hounds. How different from Forcheville! There at least is a man who tells you straight out what he thinks. You either agree with him or you don't. He's not like the other one, who's neither fish nor fowl. Odette certainly seems to prefer Forcheville, and I can't say I blame her. In any case, if Swann wants to show us what a great society man he is, the defender of duchesses, at least the other one has got a title—he is, after all, the Comte de Forcheville,' he added delicately, as if, being familiar with the history of that title, he could very accurately judge its particular value.

'Do you know,' said Madame Verdurin, 'he saw fit to make some nasty and quite ludicrous insinuations about Brichot. Naturally, once he saw that Brichot is well liked in this house, it was a way of getting back at us, and spoiling our party. He's the sort of person who pretends to be your friend and stabs you in the back as soon as he's out of the door.'

'That's exactly what I mean,' replied Monsieur Verdurin. 'He's a typical failure, one of those small-minded individuals who are envious of anything that's at all grand.'

In reality there was not one of the 'faithful' who was not more malicious than Swann; but they all took care to season their slander with familiar pleasantries, with little touches of feeling and cordiality; whereas the slightest reservation Swann allowed himself, unadorned by such conventional formulas as 'I don't mean to be unkind', to which he did not deign to stoop, seemed to them treachery. There are certain original authors in whom the slightest boldness of expression is found offensive because they have not begun by pandering to public taste by offering the usual commonplaces; it was by the same process that Swann infuriated Monsieur Verdurin. In his case as in theirs, it was the novelty of his language that was thought to betray the sinister nature of his designs.

Swann was still unaware of the disgrace that threatened him at the Verdurins' and continued to regard their absurdities in a rosy light, through the eyes of love.

Most of the time, he met Odette only in the evenings; he was afraid he would make her tired of him if he visited her during the day as well, but he wanted at least to remain in her thoughts and was always looking for opportunities to make her think of him, in a way that would be pleasant for her. If, in the window of a florist or a jeweller, the sight of a shrub or a precious stone took his fancy, he would at once think of sending them to Odette, imagining that the pleasure they had given him would be felt by her too, and would increase her affection for him, and he would have them delivered forthwith to her house in the Rue La Pérouse, so as not to delay the moment when, because she was receiving something from him, he would feel he was in some way close to her. He especially wanted her to receive them before she went out, so that her gratitude would win him a more affectionate welcome when she saw him at the Verdurins', or even— who knows?—if the shopkeeper was especially prompt, a letter she would send him before dinner, or her arrival in person at his house, in a supplementary visit of thanks. Just as he had once tested Odette's nature for reactions of resentment, so now he sought by reactions of gratitude to extract from her intimate particles of feeling that she had not yet revealed to him.

She often had money troubles and would ask him to help her pay urgent debts. He was happy to assist, as he was happy about anything that could impress Odette with his love for her, or simply with how influential he was and how useful he could be to her. No doubt if someone had said to him in the beginning: 'It's your position that attracts her', and now: 'What she loves about you is your money', he would not have believed it, but would not have minded too much if people thought that her attachment to him—if they felt they were bound to each other—was by something as powerful as snobbery or money. But even if he had believed it to be true, he might not have

been upset to discover that Odette's love for him had a more durable
buttress than his charm or the personal qualities she might see in
him: namely, self-interest, a self-interest that would prevent the day
ever coming when she might be tempted to stop seeing him. For the
moment, by heaping gifts upon her, by doing her favours, he could
rely on advantages extraneous to his person or his intellect to relieve
himself of the arduous task of making himself attractive to her. And
the pleasure of being in love, of living by love alone, the reality of
which he sometimes doubted, was greatly enhanced for him, as a dilettante of intangible sensations, by the price he was paying for it—as
we see how people who are uncertain whether the sight of the sea and
the sound of the waves are really enjoyable become convinced that
they are, and convinced also of the rare quality and disinterested
nature of their own tastes, by paying a hundred francs a day for a hotel
room from which that sight and that sound may be enjoyed.

One day, when reflections of this kind recalled once more the memory
of the time when people had spoken of Odette as a kept woman, and
he was amusing himself yet again by contrasting that strange per-
sonification, the kept woman—a shimmering amalgam of unknown
and diabolical elements, set, like some vision by Gustave Moreau,*
among poisonous flowers interwoven with precious jewels—with the
Odette on whose face he had seen the same feelings of pity for someone in distress, revolt against an injustice, gratitude for a favour, that
he had seen on his own mother's face and on the faces of his friends,
the Odette whose conversation so often turned on the things he knew
better than anyone, his collections, his bedroom, his old servant, the
banker who looked after his securities, it happened that the thought of
the banker reminded him that he must call on him soon to draw some
cash. In fact, if this month he was helping Odette less liberally with
her material difficulties than he had the previous month, when he had
given her five thousand francs, and if he did not buy her the diamond
necklace she wanted, he would not be renewing her admiration for his
generosity, the gratitude that made him so happy, and he would even
risk making her think, as she saw the tokens of his love grow smaller,
that his feelings for her had also waned. Then, suddenly, he wondered
whether this was precisely what was meant by 'keeping' her (as if, in
fact, the option of keeping could be derived from elements not at all
mysterious and perverse but from the intimate substance of his daily
life, like the familiar and domestic thousand-franc note, torn and

glued together again, which his manservant, after paying the month's accounts and the rent, had locked in the drawer of the old desk from which Swann had taken it out again to send it with four others to Odette) and whether one could not after all apply to Odette, at least since he had come to know her (because he did not suspect for a moment that she could ever have received money from anyone before him), the expression he had believed so irreconcilable with her: 'kept woman'. He was unable to pursue this idea any further, for at that moment an attack of the mental laziness which in him was congenital, intermittent, and providential extinguished all light in his brain, just as, at a later period, one could suddenly cut off the electricity in a house. His mind groped for a moment in the dark, he took off his glasses, wiped the lenses, passed his hand over his eyes, and did not see any light until he found himself faced with a completely different idea, namely that he ought to try to send six or seven thousand francs to Odette the following month instead of five, because it would give her such a pleasant surprise.

In the evening, when he did not stay at home until it was time to go and meet Odette at the Verdurins', or rather at one of the open-air restaurants in the Bois and especially at Saint-Cloud, he would dine at one of the fashionable houses where he had once been a habitual guest. He did not want to lose touch with people who might one day prove useful to Odette, and thanks to whom, in the meantime, he often succeeded in pleasing her. Also, his long acquaintance with the world of high society and luxurious living had given him both a disdain for that world and an addiction to it, so that by the time he had come to consider the most modest abodes as being exactly on a par with the most palatial, his senses were so accustomed to the latter that he would have felt quite uncomfortable to find himself in the former. He had the same regard—to a degree of identity they would not have believed—for a petit bourgeois family which invited him to a little party on the fifth floor, Staircase D, left at the landing, as for the Princess of Parma, who gave the most lavish parties in Paris; but he did not feel that he was actually at a dance as he stood with husbands and fathers in the hostess's bedroom, while the sight of the wash-stands covered with towels and the beds transformed into cloakrooms, their quilts piled high with hats and overcoats, gave him the same stifling sensation that, nowadays, people who have been used to electricity for the past twenty years may experience at the smell of a smoky oil-lamp or a guttering candle. On the days when he dined in town, he would have the horses harnessed for half-past seven; as he dressed, his thoughts would dwell on Odette, and so he would not feel alone, for the constant thought of her would give the time during which he was separated from her the same special charm as the time he spent with her. He would get into the carriage, but he felt that this thought had jumped in with him and settled on his lap like a beloved pet which he would take everywhere and keep with him at the dinner-table, unbeknown to the other guests. He would stroke it, warm himself with it, and, experiencing a kind of languor, would yield to a slight quivering sensation, quite new to him, that made his neck and his nostrils tense, as he fastened the bunch of columbines in his button-hole. Having felt unwell and depressed for some time, especially since Odette had introduced Forcheville to the Verdurins, Swann would have liked to go to the country to relax. But he would not have dared to leave Paris for a single day while Odette was there. The air was warm; spring was now at its most beautiful. And although he would traverse a city of stone to immure himself in some town house, what he constantly saw in his mind's eye was a park he owned near Combray, where, by four in the afternoon, thanks to the breeze from the meadows of the Méséglise, if you walked down to the asparagus-bed you could enjoy the cool evening air beneath an arbour in the garden as much as by the edge of the pool fringed with forget-me-nots and irises, and where, if he dined out of doors, redcurrants and roses, intertwined by his gardener, surrounded the table.

After dinner, if the meeting that evening was early, and in the Bois or at Saint-Cloud, he would leave so quickly after getting up from the table—especially if it looked like rain and that the 'faithful' would be forced to go home earlier than usual—that on one occasion the Princesse des Laumes (at whose house they had dined late and from whom Swann had taken his leave before coffee was served in order to join the Verdurins on the island in the Bois) had said: 'I must say, if Swann was thirty years older and had bladder trouble, no one would mind his running off like that. But he doesn't seem to care what people think.'

He told himself that the delights of spring which he could not go and enjoy at Combray he could at least savour on the Île des Cygnes* or at Saint-Cloud. But as he could think only of Odette, he did not even know if he had smelt the scent of the young leaves, or if the moon had been shining. He would be greeted by the little phrase from the sonata, played in the garden on the restaurant piano. If there was no piano there, the Verdurins would take great pains to have one brought down from one of the rooms or from a dining-room. Not that Swann was now back in favour; far from it. But the idea of organizing an ingenious form of entertainment for someone, even for someone they disliked, stimulated in them, during the time required for its preparation, transient feelings of warmth and cordiality. Now and then he would reflect that another spring day was slipping past, and would force himself to pay attention to the trees and the sky. But the agitation he felt in the presence of Odette, together with a slightly feverish indisposition that had persisted for some time now, robbed him of the calm and well-being which are the indispensable background to the impressions we derive from nature.

One evening, when Swann had agreed to dine with the Verdurins, and had mentioned during dinner that the following day he would be attending the annual banquet of an old comrades' association, Odette had replied across the table, in front of Forcheville, who was now one of the 'faithful', in front of the painter, in front of Cottard:

'Yes, I know you've got your banquet to go to, so I won't see you until I get home, but don't be too late.'

Although Swann had never yet taken serious offence at Odette's friendly relations with one or other of the faithful, he felt an exquisite pleasure on hearing her confess in front of everyone, with such calm immodesty, to their nightly meetings, his privileged position in her house, and the preference for him that it implied. It was true that Swann had often reflected that Odette was in no way a remarkable woman, and the supremacy he exercised over a woman so inferior to him was not something that ought to appear especially flattering when proclaimed in this way to all the 'faithful', but ever since he had noticed that many other men found Odette a beautiful and desirable woman, the attraction her body had for them had aroused in him a painful need to assert his complete mastery of even the tiniest parts of her heart. He had begun to attach immeasurable value to the times he spent at her house in the evening, when he would sit her on his knee, make her tell him what she thought about one thing or another, and list the only possessions on earth which he still valued. And so, when dinner was over, he took her aside and made a point of thanking her effusively, endeavouring to show her by the degree of his gratitude the great range of the pleasures it was in her power to bestow on him, the supreme pleasure being to safeguard him, for as long as his love should last and render him vulnerable, from attacks of jealousy.

When he came away from the banquet the next day, it was pouring with rain, and all he had was his victoria; a friend offered to drive him home in his brougham,* and since Odette, by the fact of having invited him to come, had given him to understand that she was not expecting anyone else, he could have gone home to bed, his mind at rest and his heart untroubled, rather than set off in the rain like this. But perhaps, if she saw that he did not seem to want to insist on spending the late evening with her, without exception, she might neglect to keep it free for him just at a time when he particularly wanted to see her.

It was after eleven when he reached her house, and as he apologized for not having been able to come earlier, she complained that it was indeed very late, the storm had made her feel unwell, she had a headache, and warned him he could not stay for more than half an hour, that at midnight she would send him away; soon afterwards she said she felt tired and wanted to sleep.

'So, no cattleya tonight?' he said. 'I was so looking forward to a nice little cattleya.'

Sounding slightly sulky and irritable, she replied:

'No, no, darling, no cattleya tonight. You can see I'm not well.'

'It might have done you good, but I won't insist.'

She asked him to put out the light as he went; he drew the bed-curtains and left. But when he was back home, it suddenly occurred to him that Odette might have been waiting for someone else that night, had only pretended to be tired, and had asked him to put out the light simply to make him think she was going to sleep, and that as soon as he had left she had lit the lamp again and opened the door for the man who was going to spend the night with her. He looked at the time. It was about an hour and a half since he had left her. He went back out and took a cab to a spot very close to Odette's house, in a little street perpendicular to the one her house overlooked at the back and where he would sometimes go and tap on her bedroom window so that she would let him in. He got out of the cab; the whole neighbourhood was dark and deserted. He walked the few steps to the other little street and came out almost opposite her house. Amid the darkness of the row of windows in which the lights had long since been put out, he saw just one from which there spilled out—between the slats of its shutters, closed like a wine-press over its mysterious golden pulp—the light that filled the bedroom and which, on so many other nights, as soon as he saw it from afar as he turned into the street, gave him a thrill of excitement with its message: 'She's there, waiting for you', but which now tortured him by saying: 'She's there, with the man she was expecting.' He wanted to know who it was; he crept along the wall as far as the window, but was unable to see anything between the oblique slats of the shutters; all he could hear in the silence of the night was the murmur of a conversation. It was agonizing for him to see that light and to know that in its golden glow, behind the sash, the hateful, invisible pair were moving about, to hear the murmur of voices that revealed the presence of the man who had arrived after he himself had left, the duplicity of Odette, and the pleasure she was at that moment enjoying with him.

Yet he was glad he had come back: the torment that had forced him to leave his house had become less acute now that it had become less vague, now that Odette's other life, of which he had had, before leaving, a sudden helpless suspicion, was there, within his grasp, fully exposed by the light of the lamp unknowingly imprisoned in that room, and all he had to do, when he chose, was to go in and capture it; or rather, he would knock on the shutters as he often did when he came very late; in that way, at least, Odette would learn that he knew, that he had seen the light and heard the voices, and that, although a moment ago he had pictured her laughing with the other man at his illusions, now he was the one who saw them, deceivers mistakenly confident but tricked by him, whom they believed to be far away but who was there, poised to knock on the shutters. And perhaps what he felt at that moment, a feeling that was almost pleasurable, was something more than the calming of doubt or relief from distress: it was an intellectual pleasure. If, since he had fallen in love, things had regained a little of the delightful interest they held for him in the past, but only in so far as they were illuminated by the thought of Odette, now it was another of the faculties of his studious youth that his jealousy reawakened, a passion for truth, but for a truth that was similarly interposed between himself and his mistress, receiving its light only from her, an entirely personal truth whose sole object, of infinite value and almost disinterested in its beauty, was what Odette was doing, the people she saw, her plans for the future, her past life.

At all other periods of his life, the details and everyday actions of another person had always seemed devoid of interest to Swann if reported to him as the subject of gossip; he found such talk meaningless, and, although he listened, it was only the most vulgar part of his mind that was engaged; these were moments when he felt at his most ordinary. But in this strange phase of love, when everything about another person assumes such profound importance, the curiosity he felt awakening within him concerning the most trifling activities of this woman was the same curiosity he had once had about History. And all the things of which he would previously have been ashamed, such as spying outside a window, and tomorrow perhaps, for all he knew, wheedling information out of casual witnesses, bribing servants, listening behind doors, seemed to him now to be no different from the deciphering of texts, the weighing of evidence, and the interpretation of monuments—just so many methods of scientific investigation with real intellectual value and appropriate to the search for the truth.

On the point of knocking on the shutters, he felt a pang of shame at the thought that Odette would now know he had been suspicious, that he had come back, that he had posted himself in the street. She had often told him how much she hated jealous men, lovers who spied. What he was about to do was extremely heavy-handed, and from now on she would detest him, whereas now, for the moment, so long as he had not knocked, perhaps even as she was deceiving him, she loved him still. How often we sacrifice the prospect of happiness because of our insistence on immediate gratification! But his desire to know the truth was stronger and seemed to him nobler. He knew that the reality of certain circumstances which he would have given his life to reconstruct accurately could be read behind that window, with its slats of light, as beneath the gold-illuminated cover of one of those precious manuscripts by whose artistic richness itself the scholar who consults them cannot remain unmoved. He felt a sensuous pleasure in learning the truth that so excited him in those unique, ephemeral, and precious pages, on that translucent material, so warm and so beautiful. Moreover, the advantage he felt he had—that he so needed to feel he had—over them, lay perhaps less in knowing than in being able to show them that he knew. He stood on tiptoes. He knocked. They had not heard, he knocked again more loudly, the conversation stopped. A man's voice, which he tried to identify from among the voices of the men-friends of Odette whom he knew, asked:

'Who's there?'

He was not sure he recognized it. He knocked once more. The window was opened, then the shutters. It was too late now to draw back and, since she was going to realize what he was doing there, in order not to appear too miserable, too jealous and inquisitive, he simply called out in a cheerful, casual tone:

'Sorry to disturb you. I just happened to be passing and saw the light. I wanted to know if you were feeling better.'

He looked up. Facing him, two old gentlemen were standing at the window, one of them holding a lamp, and then he saw the bedroom, a bedroom he had never seen before. Since he was in the habit, when he came to see Odette late at night, of recognizing her window by the fact that it was the only one with a light among the windows that were otherwise all alike, he had made a mistake and had knocked at the window beyond hers, which belonged to the neighbouring house. He went away apologizing and returned home, glad that the satisfaction of his curiosity had left their love intact, and that, having simulated for so long a sort of indifference towards Odette, he had not given her, by his jealousy, that proof of loving too much, which, between lovers, for ever exempts the other from loving enough. He never spoke to her about this misadventure, and he gave it no further thought himself. But now and then his wandering thoughts would come across the memory they had not noticed, and bump into it, driving it in, and Swann would feel a sudden, deep pain. As though it were an actual physical pain, his mind could do nothing to alleviate it; but at least with physical pain, because it is independent of the mind, the mind can focus on it, note that it has diminished or momentarily ceased. But with this type of pain the mind, merely by recalling it, created it afresh. To wish not to think about it was still to think about it, to continue to suffer from it. And when, talking with friends, he forgot about it, all of a sudden one of them would say something that would make him wince, like a wounded man whom some clumsy person has just carelessly touched on his bad arm or leg. When he left Odette, he was happy, he felt calm, he recalled her smiles, gently mocking when she spoke of other people but affectionate towards him; the weight of her head as she tilted it on its axis to let it fall, almost in spite of herself, on his lips, as she had done the first time in the carriage; the languishing looks she had given him as she lay in his arms, nestling her head against her shoulder as if shrinking from the cold.

But at once his jealousy, as if it were the shadow of his love, provided him with a complementary version of the new smile with which
she had greeted him that very evening—and which, conversely now,
mocked Swann, filled as it was with her love for another—with the
same inclination of the head, but leaning towards different lips, with
all the marks of affection she had given him, but given to another.
And all the sensuous memories he carried away from her house
were like so many sketches, rough plans like those a decorator might
submit, enabling Swann to form an idea of the passionate or swooning attitudes she might adopt with other men. The result was that
he came to regret every pleasure he enjoyed with her, every new
caress whose sweetness he had been so imprudent as to point out to
her, every fresh charm he found in her, for he knew that a moment
later they would be added to the collection of instruments in his
torture-chamber.

This torture became even more cruel when Swann remembered
a fleeting expression he had noticed a few days earlier, and for the first
time, in Odette's eyes. It was after dinner at the Verdurins'. Whether
it was because Forcheville, sensing that Saniette, his brother-in-law,
was no longer in favour, wanted to use him as a whipping-boy in order
to shine at his expense, or because he had been irritated by a clumsy
remark Saniette had made to him, though in fact it had gone unnoticed
by the others present, who were unaware of any unpleasant allusion
it might unintentionally have contained, or because, for some time
now, he had been waiting for an opportunity to have banished from
the house someone who knew too much about him, and whom he
knew to be so sensitive that at times he felt embarrassed merely by his
presence, Forcheville responded to Saniette's clumsy remark in such
a crudely aggressive manner, hurling abuse at him, emboldened, the
more he shouted, by Saniette's distress, alarm, and entreaties, that
the poor man, after asking Madame Verdurin whether he should stay
or leave, and receiving no answer, had left the house stammering in
confusion, with tears in his eyes. Odette had looked on impassively,
but when the door had closed on Saniette, she had lowered by several
notches, as it were, her face's normal expression, so as to put herself
on the same level of baseness as Forcheville, and her eyes had gleamed
with a sly smile of congratulations for his boldness, and mockery
for the man who had been its victim, she had cast him a glance of
complicity in the crime which so clearly implied: 'That was a real

execution, if ever there was one! Did you see how pathetic he looked? He was crying', that Forcheville, when his eyes met hers, suddenly lost all the anger or the pretence of anger with which he was still flushed, and smiled as he answered: 'Well, if he had been a bit nicer, he would still be here. A good dressing-down never does a man any harm, at any age.'

One day when Swann had gone out in the middle of the afternoon to pay a call, and had found that the person he wanted to see was not at home, he had the idea of going round to Odette's house instead, at an hour when he never called on her, but when he knew she was always at home having her nap or writing letters before tea-time, and when he would enjoy seeing her for a little while without disturbing her. The concierge told him he thought she was in; he rang the bell, thought he heard a noise, and then footsteps, but no one came to the door. Anxious and irritated, he went round to the little street at the back and stood under Odette's bedroom window; the curtains prevented him from seeing anything, he knocked hard on the window-panes, and called out; no one opened. He saw that some neighbours were watching him. He went away, thinking that after all he might have been mistaken in believing he had heard footsteps, but he remained so preoccupied that he could not think of anything else. An hour later, he went back. He found her there; she told him she had been in the house when he rang, but was sleeping; the bell had woken her, she had guessed it was Swann, she had run out to look for him, but he had already gone. She had, of course, heard him knock at the window. Swann immediately recognized in her story one of those fragments of true fact which liars, when caught off guard, console themselves by introducing into the composition of the falsehood they are inventing, thinking they can incorporate it there and give their story a semblance of Truth. Of course, when Odette had done something she did not want to reveal, she would hide it deep inside herself. But as soon as she found herself face to face with the man to whom she intended to lie, she became uneasy, all her ideas evaporated, her faculties of invention and reasoning were paralysed, her brain became empty; yet she had to say something, and all she would find within reach was the very thing she had wanted to conceal and which, being true, was all that had remained. She would detach a little piece from it, insignificant in itself, telling herself that, after all, it was the best thing to do, since the detail was authentic and less dangerous, therefore, than a fictitious

one. 'At least that bit is true,' she would say to herself, 'and that's all
to the good. He can make enquiries, he'll find it's true, so at least it
won't be that that gives me away.' She was wrong, it was precisely
what gave her away; she did not realize that her little fragment of
truth had corners that could fit only into the contiguous fragments
of the truth from which she had arbitrarily detached it, corners that,
no matter into what invented details she placed them, would always
reveal, by the bits that stuck out and the gaps they did not fill, that
that was not where they belonged. 'She admits that she heard me ring
the bell and then knock, that she thought it was me, and that she
wanted to see me,' Swann said to himself. 'But that hardly accords
with the fact that nobody came to the door.'

But he did not point out this contradiction, because he thought
that, left to herself, Odette might produce some falsehood that would
give him a faint indication of the truth. She went on talking, and
he did not interrupt, but listened, with an avid, painful piety, to her
every word, feeling (rightly so, because she was hiding the truth behind
them as she spoke) that, like the sacred veil, they retained a vague
imprint, a blurred outline, of that reality so infinitely precious and,
alas, undiscoverable—what she had been doing that afternoon at three
o'clock, when he had called—of which he would never possess anything other than her lies, illegible and divine traces, and which now
existed only in the secretive memory of this woman who could contemplate it without appreciating its value but would never reveal it to
him. Of course, it had occurred to him more than once that in themselves Odette's daily activities were not passionately interesting, and
that the relationships she might have with other men did not exhale
naturally, universally, or for every intelligent soul, a morbid sadness
capable of infecting one with a feverish desire to commit suicide.
He would then realize that this interest, this sadness, existed in him
alone, like a disease, and that, once he was cured of this disease,
Odette's actions, the kisses she might have bestowed, would become
once again as innocuous as those of so many other women. But his
realization that the painful curiosity he now brought to them had its
origin only in himself was not enough to make him think it was unreasonable to consider this curiosity as important and to take every possible step to satisfy it. For Swann was reaching an age at which one's
philosophy—encouraged by the prevailing philosophy of the day, and
also by that of the circle in which he had spent much of his life, the

Princesse des Laumes and her set, where the accepted view was that intelligence is in direct ratio to scepticism and that nothing is real and incontestable except the particular tastes of the individual—is no longer that of youth, but a positivistic, almost medical philosophy, the philosophy of men who, instead of exteriorizing the objects of their aspirations, try to extract from the accumulation of the years a stable residue of habits and passions which they can regard as characteristic and permanent, and which they will deliberately make it their primary concern to satisfy by the kind of life they choose to adopt. Swann thought it wise to make allowance in his life for the pain he felt at not knowing what Odette had been doing, just as he made allowance for the fact that his eczema would become worse in inclement weather; to provide in his budget for sizeable sums to be expended on the procurement of information about how Odette spent her days, without which he would feel unhappy, just as he reserved certain amounts for the gratification of other tastes from which he knew he could expect to derive pleasure, at least before he had fallen in love, such as his taste for collecting art and for good food.

When he began to say goodbye to Odette to return home, she asked him to stay a while longer and even held him back by the arm as he was opening the door to go. But he paid no special attention to this, because among the multiplicity of gestures, remarks, and little incidents that go to make up a conversation, it is inevitable that we should pass close by, without noticing anything to attract our attention, those that hide a truth our suspicions are blindly seeking, and stop, on the other hand, to examine others behind which there is nothing. She kept saying: 'What a shame—you never come in the afternoon, and the one time you do come, I miss you.' He knew very well that she was not so in love with him that she had been very distressed at having missed his visit, but, because she was good-natured, anxious to please him, and often sad when she had offended him, he found it quite natural that she should be sorry for having deprived him of the pleasure of spending an hour in her company, which was a very great pleasure, if not for her, then certainly for him. Yet it was a matter of such relative unimportance that the doleful expression she continued to wear finally began to surprise him. She reminded him, even more than usual, of the faces of some of the women portrayed by the painter of the 'Primavera'.* She had at this moment their dejected, sorrowful expression, which seems to betoken the unbearable weight of some terrible burden of grief, whereas they are merely letting the Infant Jesus play with a pomegranate or watch Moses pour water into a trough.* He had seen her wear this expression of profound sorrow once before, but had forgotten when. Then, suddenly, he remembered: it was when she had lied to Madame Verdurin the day after the dinner to which she had not come on the pretext of illness, but in reality so that she could spend time alone with him. Surely, even if she had been the most scrupulously honest of women, she would hardly have felt remorse for such an innocent little lie. But the lies Odette normally told were less innocent, and served to prevent discoveries that might involve her in terrible difficulties with one or another of the people she knew. So when she lied, she felt assailed by fear, poorly prepared for her defence, plagued by doubts, and would be close to tears, from sheer exhaustion, like a child who has not slept. She knew, moreover, that through her lie she was usually seriously hurting the man to whom she was telling it, and at whose mercy she would perhaps find herself if she lied badly. And so she felt at once humble and guilty in his presence. And when she had to tell a little white lie, the association of sensations and memories would make her feel faint, as if by overexertion, and penitent, as when one does someone a bad turn.

What depressing lie was she now telling Swann that gave her this pained look, this plaintive voice, which seemed to falter under the effort she was forcing herself to make, to beg for forgiveness? It suddenly crossed his mind that it was not merely the truth about what had occurred that afternoon that she was trying to hide from him, but something more immediate, that had perhaps not yet happened and was quite imminent, something that might enlighten him about the earlier event. At that moment, he heard the bell ring. Odette did not stop talking, but her words had become a single, long lament: her regret at not having seen Swann that afternoon, at not having opened the door to him, had turned into an endless cry of despair.

The front door could be heard closing, then the sound of a carriage, as if someone was going away—presumably the person Swann was not meant to meet—after being told that Odette was not at home. Then, after reflecting that merely by coming at an unusual time of day he had managed to disturb so many arrangements she did not want him to know about, he was overcome with a feeling of despondency, almost of anguish. But since he loved Odette, since he was in the habit of turning all his thoughts towards her, instead of feeling sorry for himself, he felt sorry for her, and he murmured: 'Poor darling!' When he finally left, she picked up several letters that were lying on her table and asked him if he could post them for her. He took them with him and, once he was home, realized that they were still in his pocket. He walked back to the post office, took the letters out of his pocket, and, before dropping them in the box, glanced at the addresses. They were all for tradesmen, except one which was for Forcheville. He stood holding the envelope in his hand. 'If I knew what was inside,' he thought, 'I would know what she calls him, the way she talks to him, if there's anything between them. In fact, if I don't look inside, I'd be doing Odette a disservice, because it's the only way to rid myself of a suspicion that may be slanderous, in any case bound to cause her suffering, and that nothing thereafter can remove, once the letter has been posted.'

He returned home after leaving the post office, but he had kept this last letter in his pocket. He lit a candle and held up close to its flame the envelope he had not dared to open. At first he could not read anything, but the envelope was thin, and by pressing it against the stiff card it contained he managed to make out, through the semi-transparent paper, the concluding words. It was a very stiff, formal ending. If Forcheville had been looking at a letter addressed to him, rather than himself reading a letter addressed to Forcheville, then Forcheville would have seen words far more redolent of affection! He took a firm hold of the card which kept moving about in the envelope, which was too large for it, and then, sliding it with his thumb, brought one line after another under the part of the envelope which was not of double thickness, the only part through which it was possible to read.

But he still had great difficulty in deciphering the words. Not that it mattered, because he had seen enough to realize that the letter was about some trivial event that had no connection with a love affair; it was something to do with an uncle of Odette's. Swann had been able to read at the beginning of the line: 'I was right', but could not understand what Odette had done that was right, when a word he had not at first been able to decipher suddenly became clear and explained the meaning of the whole sentence: 'I was right to open the door, it was my uncle.' Open the door! So Forcheville had been there when Swann rang the bell, and she had made him leave, which was the reason for the noise he had heard.

Then he read the whole letter; at the end she apologized for having treated him so unceremoniously, and told him he had forgotten his cigarette-case, the same sentence she had written to Swann after one of his first visits to her house. But to Swann she had added: 'If you had left your heart here too, I would not have let you have it back.' To Forcheville, nothing of the sort, nor any allusion that might suggest they were having an affair. In fact, if anyone was being deceived in all this it was Forcheville, for the purpose of Odette's letter was to make him believe that the visitor had been her uncle. So that he, Swann, was the one she really cared about, the one for whom she had sent the other man away. And yet, if there was nothing between Odette and Forcheville, why had she not opened the door right away, why had she said: 'I did the right thing to open the door, it was my uncle'? If she was not doing anything wrong, what on earth could Forcheville have made of the fact that she had not opened the door? Swann sat there, bewildered, forlorn, yet happy, gazing at this envelope which Odette had entrusted to him without the slightest hesitation, so absolute was her confidence in his integrity, but through the transparent screen of which had been revealed to him, together with the secret of an incident which he would never have believed it possible to discover, a fragment of Odette's life, like a narrow illuminated section cut directly out of the unknown. Then his jealousy rejoiced at this discovery, as though that jealousy had an independent, selfish existence, voracious for anything that would feed it, even at Swann's own expense. Now it had something to feed on, and Swann could begin to worry every day about the visitors Odette had received at about five o'clock, and begin trying to learn where Forcheville had been at that time. For Swann's affection for Odette still retained the form imprinted on it from the beginning by his ignorance of how she spent her days and by the mental laziness that prevented him from supplementing his ignorance by his imagination. He had not been jealous, at first, of the whole life Odette led without him, but only of the moments when some incident, which he had perhaps misinterpreted, had led him to suppose that Odette might have deceived him. His jealousy, like an octopus which throws out a first, then a second, and finally a third tentacle, battened on that particular moment, five o'clock in the afternoon, then on another, then on yet another. But Swann was not capable of inventing his sufferings. They were merely the memory, the perpetuation, of a suffering that had come to him from elsewhere.

But here, everything brought him more suffering. He decided to remove Odette from Forcheville's company altogether by taking her to the Midi for a few days. But he imagined that all the men in the hotel desired her and that she desired them. And so, although in his travels in the past he had looked out for new people and new groups, he now seemed unsociable, avoiding company as if it gave him deep offence. And how could he not be misanthropic, when in every man he saw a potential lover of Odette? And thus his jealousy, even more than the happy, sensual feelings he had initially had for Odette, altered Swann's character, completely changing, in the eyes of other people, even the outward signs by which that character manifested itself.

A month after the day on which he had read Odette's letter to Forcheville, Swann went to a dinner the Verdurins were giving in the Bois. Just as people were getting ready to leave, he noticed a number of confabulations between Madame Verdurin and several of the guests, and thought he heard the pianist being reminded to come to a party at Chatou the next day—to which he, Swann, had not been invited.

The Verdurins had spoken only in whispers, and in vague terms, but the painter, probably without thinking, exclaimed: 'We must make sure there's no light, and have him play the Moonlight Sonata* in the dark so that things can become clear!'

Madame Verdurin, seeing that Swann was within earshot, assumed that expression in which the desire to silence the speaker and the desire to maintain an air of innocence in the eyes of the listener cancel each other out in a gaze of intense vacuity, in which the motionless sign of complicity is concealed beneath an innocent smile, which, as everyone who has ever noticed a social gaffe is aware, reveals it instantly, if not to its author, at least to its victim. Odette seemed suddenly to have the desperate look of someone who has given up the struggle against the crushing difficulties of life, and Swann anxiously counted the minutes he would have to endure before he could leave the restaurant and, during the drive home, ask her for an explanation, persuade her not to go to Chatou the next day or make sure he was invited, and find solace in her arms for the anguish he was feeling. At last the carriages were brought round. Madame Verdurin said to Swann: 'So, goodbye. See you soon, I hope?', attempting by her friendly manner and fixed smile to prevent him from realizing that she was not saying, as she had always said until now: 'We'll see you tomorrow, then, at Chatou, and at my house the day after.'

Monsieur and Madame Verdurin invited Forcheville to get in with them. Swann's carriage had pulled up behind theirs, and he was waiting for them to move on so that he could help Odette into his.

'Odette, you can come with us,' said Madame Verdurin, 'we've kept a little place for you here, next to Monsieur de Forcheville.'

'Yes, Madame,' replied Odette.

'But I thought you were coming with me!' exclaimed Swann, not mincing his words, because the carriage door was open, there were just a few seconds left, and, in the state he was in, he could not possibly leave without her.

'But Madame Verdurin has asked me . . .'

'For heaven's sake!' said Madame Verdurin. 'You can surely go home without her for once; we've let you have her to yourself often enough!'

'But there's something important I need to say to Madame de Crécy!'

'Well, you can write her a letter . . .'

'Goodbye,' said Odette, holding out her hand.

He tried to smile but looked utterly dejected.

'Did you see the way Swann thinks he can treat us now?' said Madame Verdurin to her husband when they were back home. 'I thought he was going to bite my head off, just because we offered Odette a lift! It's quite indecent! He might as well say straight out that he thinks we're running a brothel! It's a mystery to me how Odette can put up with such manners! His whole way of behaving seems to say: "You belong to me." I'll tell Odette exactly what I think, I hope she'll understand.'

A moment later she burst out once more: 'No, but really! The filthy creature!', using, without realizing it, perhaps responding to the same obscure need to justify herself—like Françoise at Combray, when the chicken refused to die—the same words which the final convulsions of a harmless animal wring from the peasant who is engaged in slaughtering it.*

When Madame Verdurin's carriage had left and Swann's took its place, his coachman looked at him and asked if he was feeling unwell or whether there had been some accident.

Swann sent him away; he wanted to walk, and he returned home on foot through the Bois. He talked to himself out loud, and in the same artificial tone he had always adopted when enumerating the charms of the little clan and extolling the magnanimity of the Verdurins. But just as the conversation, the smiles, the kisses of Odette seemed as hateful to him as he had once found them delightful, if they were addressed to other men, so the Verdurins' salon, which that very evening had still seemed an agreeable place, inspired with a genuine enthusiasm for art and even with a sort of moral nobility, appeared to him with all its absurdities, its foolishness, its ignominy, now that it was a man other than himself whom Odette was going there to meet, and love quite freely.

He pictured to himself, with disgust, the soirée at Chatou. 'The very idea of going to Chatou anyway! Like a gang of grocers taking a day off! How unspeakably bourgeois they are! They can't actually be real, they must all have stepped out of a play by Labiche!'*

The Cottards would be there, and perhaps Brichot too. 'Could anything be more grotesque than the lives of these nonentities, living constantly in each other's pockets. They would feel completely lost, I'm sure they would, if they didn't all meet up again tomorrow *at Chatou!*' Oh God! The painter would be there too, the painter who was so fond of 'matchmaking', who would invite Forcheville to visit his studio with Odette. He could see Odette, terribly overdressed for a country outing, 'because she's so vulgar, and especially, the poor thing, so stupid!'

He could hear the jokes Madame Verdurin would make after dinner, jokes which, whoever the 'bore' might be at whom they were aimed, had always amused him because he saw Odette laughing, laughing with him, her laughter mingling with his. Now he felt that perhaps they would make Odette laugh at him. 'What a fetid sense of humour they have!' he said, twisting his mouth into an expression of disgust so violent that he could feel the muscles in his neck press against his shirt collar. 'How on earth can a creature whose face is made in God's image find anything to laugh at in those nauseating jokes? Anyone with the slightest sense of smell has to turn away in horror to avoid the offensive stench. It's quite incredible to think that a human being can fail to understand that, by smiling at the expense of a fellow human being who has held out a trusting hand, she is allowing herself to sink into a slimy pit from which it will be impossible, with the best will in the world, ever to rescue her. I exist on a level so many miles above the swamp where those filthy vermin squat gabbing and blabbing, that I can't possibly be spattered by the jokes of a Verdurin!'

he cried, tossing his head and proudly throwing back his shoulders. 'God knows I've honestly tried to pull Odette up out of there, and lift her into a nobler and purer atmosphere. But any human being has just so much patience, and mine is exhausted,' he said to himself, as though this mission to tear Odette away from an atmosphere of sarcasms dated from longer ago than the last few minutes, and as though he had not embarked upon it only when it had occurred to him that their sarcasms might be aimed at him and were intended to separate Odette from him.

He could see the pianist sitting down to play the Moonlight Sonata, and the faces Madame Verdurin would pull as she grew increasingly alarmed at the disastrous effect Beethoven's music would have on her nerves: 'Idiot! Liar!' he exclaimed. 'And the woman makes out that she loves *Art*!' She would say to Odette, after cleverly slipping in a few words of praise for Forcheville, as she had so often done for him: 'Make some room next to you for Monsieur de Forcheville.' 'In the dark, too! She's a pimp! A procuress!' 'Procuress' was the name he applied also to the music that would invite them to sit quietly, to dream together, to gaze into each other's eyes, to take each other by the hand. He felt that there was something to be said for the austere view of the arts held by Plato and Bossuet, and the old system of education in France.*

In fact, the life one led at the Verdurins', which he had so often described as 'the kind of life one should lead', seemed to him now the worst type of all, and their little clan the lowest of social circles. 'They really are', he said, 'at the bottom of the social ladder, the last circle of Dante.* It's obvious that that venerable text refers to the Verdurins! When you think about it, real society people, whatever you may say about them, are quite other than that uncouth lot, and demonstrate their profound wisdom in refusing to know them, or so much as sully the tips of their fingers with them! What sound intuition there is in that *Noli me tangere** of the Faubourg Saint-Germain!' He had now left far behind the avenues of the Bois and had almost arrived home, but still, having not yet got over his pain and the feats of insincerity which the false tones and artificial sonority of his own voice were raising to ever greater heights, he went on perorating aloud in the silence of the night: 'Society people have their faults, as no one knows better than I do, but all the same they are people for whom certain things are simply impossible. I used to know a certain society lady who was far from perfect, but all the same had a basic delicacy and a sense of honour in her dealings with people that would have made her incapable, under any circumstances, of any sort of treachery, and that is enough to show the vast gulf between her and a harridan like that Verdurin woman. Verdurin! What a name! Oh, we can certainly say they're the perfect, the ultimate specimens of their kind! Thank God—it was high time I stopped demeaning myself by mixing with those vile, dreadful people!'

But just as the virtues he was still attributing to the Verdurins that very afternoon would not have been enough, even if they had actually possessed them but had not favoured and encouraged his love, to arouse in Swann the state of intoxication in which he felt moved by their magnanimity and which, even though it was propagated through other people, could only reach him through Odette—similarly, the immorality he now saw in the Verdurins, had it been real, would have been powerless, if they had not invited Odette with Forcheville and without him, to unleash his wrath and induce him to denounce 'their infamy'. And no doubt Swann's voice was more perceptive than he was himself, when it refused to pronounce these words of revulsion towards the Verdurin circle and his joy at being free of it, except in an affected tone, and as if they had been chosen to relieve his anger rather than to express his thoughts. Indeed, his thoughts, while he was giving vent to his invectives, were probably, without his noticing it, occupied with a wholly different matter, for when he arrived home, scarcely had he closed the main door behind him than he suddenly clapped his hand to his forehead and, reopening the door, went out again exclaiming in a natural voice this time: 'I think I've found a way of getting myself invited to the dinner at Chatou tomorrow!' But it must not have been a good way, for he was not invited: Dr Cottard, who had been called away to attend to a patient in the country and had therefore not seen the Verdurins for several days and had been unable to go to Chatou, said, the day after the dinner, as he sat down at their table: 'So, aren't we going to see Monsieur Swann this evening? He's surely what one calls a personal friend of the . . .'

'I should certainly hope not!' exclaimed Madame Verdurin. 'God forbid! He's terribly dull, stupid, and ill-mannered.'

At these words Cottard showed his surprise and, simultaneously, his submission, as though confronted with a truth contrary to everything he had believed until then, but which was incontrovertibly obvious; and looking rather nervous and fearful, buried his nose in his plate and simply replied: 'Ah! Ah! Ah! Ah! Ah!', traversing, on a descending scale, the entire register of his voice in his forced but orderly retreat into the depths of his being. Swann was never mentioned again at the Verdurins'.

So the drawing-room that had brought Swann and Odette together became an obstacle to their meetings. She no longer said, as in the early days of their love: 'We'll see each other tomorrow night anyway, there's a supper at the Verdurins'', but: 'We won't be able to see each other tomorrow night, there's a supper at the Verdurins'.' Or else the Verdurins would have arranged to take her to the Opéra-Comique to see *Une nuit de Cléopâtre** and Swann would read in Odette's eyes her fear of his asking her not to go, to which, quite recently, he would not have been able to stop himself responding with a kiss as it flitted across his mistress's face, but which now exasperated him. 'Yet it's not anger I feel,' he said to himself, 'when I see that she wants to go and dip into that excremental music. It's sadness, not for myself of course, but for her; sadness at seeing that after more than six months of living in daily contact with me, she hasn't managed to change enough to reject Victor Massé spontaneously! Especially that she hasn't managed to understand that there are evenings when a person of any sensitivity at all must be able to give up a pleasure when asked to do so. She ought to be able to say "I won't go", if only because it's the intelligent thing to do, because it's by her answer that her innermost qualities will be judged once and for all.' And having persuaded himself that it really was only in order to have a higher opinion of Odette's spiritual worth that he wanted her to stay with him that evening instead of going to the Opéra-Comique, he followed the same line of reasoning with her, with the same degree of insincerity that he had used with himself, and even with one degree more, for now he was also in the grip of his desire to catch her through her vanity.

'I swear', he said to her a few moments before she left for the theatre, 'that in asking you not to go, I would really be wishing, if I were thinking only of myself, that you would refuse, because I have a thousand things to do this evening and I will feel caught out and quite annoyed if you tell me now all of a sudden that you aren't going. But my own occupations, my own pleasures, aren't everything, I must think of you. There may come a day when, seeing me separated from you

for ever, you will be entitled to reproach me for not having given you
warning in those crucial moments when I felt I was about to make
one of those judgements of you of a severity that love cannot long
endure. You see, *Une nuit de Cléopâtre* (what a title!) has nothing to
do with what I'm saying. What is important is whether you are really
a creature of lowly intellect and even limited charm, the sort of
despicable creature who is incapable of giving up a pleasure. If that
is what you are, how could anyone love you, because you're not even
a person, a clearly defined entity, imperfect but at least perfectible.
You're just a formless stream of water running down any slope it
finds, a fish devoid of memory, incapable of thought, which no matter
how long it spends in its aquarium, will always mistake the glass for
water and bump against it a hundred times a day. Do you realize that
your answer will have the effect—I won't say of making me stop loving you immediately, of course, but of making you less attractive in
my eyes when I realize that you're not a person, that you're a slave
to everything and don't know how to rise above anything? Obviously
I would have preferred to ask you as a thing of no importance to give
up your *Nuit de Cléopâtre* (since you oblige me to soil my lips with
that despicable name) in the hope that you would go anyway. But
since I've decided to take such account of your answer and draw these
inferences from it, I thought it would only be fair to let you know.'

For a few moments Odette had been showing signs of being upset and
confused. Although she was unable to grasp the meaning of this speech,
she did understand that it might belong to the general category of
'scoldings' and scenes of reproach and supplication, and her familiarity
with the ways of men enabled her, without paying attention to the details
of what they said, to conclude that they would not make such pro
nouncements unless they were in love, and that since they were in love it
was not necessary to obey them, as they would only be more in love
afterwards. And so she would have listened to Swann with the utmost
calm if she had not noticed that the time was getting on and that if he
went on talking much longer, she would, as she told him with a smile
that was loving, obstinate and abashed, 'end up missing the Overture!'

On other occasions he told her that the one thing that was more
likely than anything else to make him stop loving her was her refusal
to stop lying. 'Even from the point of view of your attractiveness as
a woman,' he said, 'can't you see how unattractive you make yourself
when you stoop to lying? Think how many faults you could redeem

with a single confession! You're really far less intelligent than I thought!' But it was in vain that Swann thus expounded for her all the good reasons she had for not lying; they might have undermined some general and systematic approach to lying, but Odette had no such system; whenever she did not want Swann to know about something she had done, she simply did not tell him. In other words, lying was for her an expedient of a particular order; and the only thing that could determine whether she should make use of it or tell the truth was a reason also of a particular order, the greater or lesser likelihood of Swann's discovering that she had not told him the truth.

Physically, she was going through a bad phase: she was putting on weight; and the expressive, doleful charm, the wide, dreamy eyes she used to have seemed to have disappeared with her first youth, with the result that she had become most dear to Swann at the very moment, as it were, when he found her distinctly less pretty. He would gaze at her for minutes at a time, trying to rediscover the charm he had once seen in her, and could not find it. But knowing that within the new chrysalis, what lived on was still Odette, still the same will, evanescent, elusive and sly, was enough to make Swann pursue her with as much passion as before. He would also look at photographs of her taken two years before, and remember how exquisite she had been. And that would console him a little for all the trouble he took over her.

When the Verdurins carried her off to Saint-Germain, or to Chatou, or to Meulan, as often as not, if the weather was fine, they would suggest on the spot that they should stay the night and not go back until the next day. Madame Verdurin would try to allay the scruples of the pianist, whose aunt had stayed behind in Paris: 'She'll be very pleased to be rid of you for a day. And why should she be worried, she knows you're with us; in any case, I can take the blame.'

But if she did not succeed, Monsieur Verdurin would be detailed to find a telegraph office or a messenger and enquire as to which of the 'faithful' had someone they needed to notify. But Odette would thank him and say she did not need to send anyone a telegram, because she had told Swann once and for all that if she were to send him one in front of everybody, she would be compromising herself. There were times when she would be gone for several days, when the Verdurins took her to see the tombs at Dreux, or, on the recommendation of the painter, to Compiègne to admire the sunsets in the forest, from where they would go as far as the chateau at Pierrefonds.

'To think she could visit real historic buildings with me, who studied architecture for ten years and am forever being implored to take people of very high standing to Beauvais or Saint-Loup-de-Naud, but would do it only for her, and instead she goes off with those absolute dullards to swoon over the dejecta of Louis-Philippe and Viollet-le-Duc! If you ask me, you don't need to be very artistic to do that, and you don't need to have a particularly sensitive nose to decide not to spend your holidays in the latrines in order to be closer to the smell of excrement.'

But when she had left for Dreux or Pierrefonds—without, alas, allowing him to go too, and turn up there as if by chance, because 'that would make a terrible impression', she said—he would plunge into that most intoxicating of romances, the railway timetable, which showed him the various means by which he could join her, in the afternoon, in the evening, or that very morning! Not just the means, but more than that, almost the authorization. Because, after all, the timetable and the trains themselves were not meant for dogs. If the public was informed, by means of the printed word, that at eight o'clock in the morning a train left for Pierrefonds and arrived there at ten, it could only be because going to Pierrefonds was a lawful act, for which permission from Odette was superfluous; an act, moreover, that could have a motive completely different from the desire to see Odette, since people who had never heard of her performed it every day, and in large enough numbers for it to be worth the trouble of stoking the locomotives.

So, all things considered, she could hardly stop him from going to Pierrefonds if he felt like it! In fact, he felt that he did want to, and that, if he had not known Odette, he certainly would have gone. For ages he had wanted to become more familiar with Viollet-le-Duc's restoration work. And since the weather was so good, he felt an overwhelming desire to go for a walk in the forest at Compiègne.

It really was bad luck that she had forbidden him the only spot that tempted him today. Today! If he ignored her prohibition and went there, he might see her *today*! But whereas, if at Pierrefonds she had met someone who did not matter, she would have said joyfully: 'I say! What are you doing here!', and would have invited him to come and see her at the hotel where she was staying with the Verdurins; if on the other hand it was himself, Swann, that she ran into, she would be offended, she would think she was being followed, she would love him less, perhaps she would turn away in anger when she saw him. 'So, I'm not allowed to travel any more!' she would say to him on their return, whereas he was the one who was not allowed to travel!

At one point, he had had the idea, in order to be able to go to Compiègne and Pierrefonds without making it appear that he was doing so to meet Odette, of arranging to be taken there by one of his friends, the Marquis de Forestelle, who had a chateau in that part of the country. The Marquis, to whom he had mentioned his plan without revealing the reason for it, was beside himself with joy and marvelled at the fact that Swann, for the first time in fifteen years, was finally consenting to come and see his estate, and since he did not want to stay there, as he had told him, at least promised to spend a few days going on walks and excursions with him. Swann could already picture himself with Monsieur de Forestelle. Even before seeing Odette there, even if he did not succeed in seeing her there, how happy he would be to set foot on that earth where, not knowing the exact location, at any given moment, of her person, he would feel all around him the thrilling possibility of her suddenly appearing: in the courtyard of the chateau, which now seemed so beautiful because it was on her account that he had gone to see it; in every street of the town, which to his eyes took on a fantastical air; on every path of the forest, rosy in the deep, soft sunset—in an infinity of alternative nooks where, in the uncertain ubiquity of his hopes, his happy, errant and multiple heart would simultaneously take refuge. 'On no account,' he would warn Monsieur de Forestelle, 'must we run into Odette and the Verdurins. I've just heard, as it happens, that they're at Pierrefonds today. We have plenty of time to see each other in Paris, it would hardly be worth the trouble of leaving Paris if neither of us could take a step without the other.' And his friend would not understand why, once he was there, he would change his plans twenty times a day, inspect the dining-rooms of all the hotels in Compiègne without making up his mind to sit down in any of them even though they bore no trace of the Verdurins, seeming to be searching for the very thing he had said he wanted to avoid (and would indeed avoid) as soon as he found it, for if he had come upon the little group, he would have made a show of avoiding them, happy to have seen Odette and that she had seen him, especially that she had seen him apparently not thinking of her at all. But no, she would certainly guess that it was on her account that he was there. And when Monsieur de Forestelle came to pick him up, and it was time to set off, he said: 'Alas, no, I can't go to Pierrefonds today, Odette is there, you see.' And Swann was happy despite everything to feel that if he, alone among mortals, was not allowed to go to Pierrefonds that day, it was because for Odette he was in fact someone different from other people, her lover, and that the restriction that was applied in his case alone to the universal right to freedom was merely one of the forms of that servitude, that love which was so dear to him. It was certainly better not to risk quarrelling with her, to be patient, to wait for her to come back to Paris. He spent his days poring over a map of the forest of Compiègne as though it was the *Carte du Tendre*,* and surrounded himself with photographs of the chateau at Pierrefonds. On the first day when it was just possible that she might be on her way back, he opened the timetable again, calculated which train she must have taken and, in the event of her being delayed, those she could still take. He did not leave the house for fear of missing a telegram, did not go to bed in case she had returned on the last train and wanted to surprise him by coming to see him in the middle of the night. In fact he heard the bell at the street door, and it seemed to him that they were slow to open it, he wanted to wake up the concierge, went to the window to call out to Odette if it was she, for in spite of the instructions he had more than a dozen times gone down to give the servants himself, they were quite capable of telling her he was not at home. It was a servant coming in. He noticed the incessant stream of carriages passing by, to which he had never paid attention in the past. He listened to each one coming from far off, drawing near, and passing his door without stopping, and bearing far away a message that was not for him. He waited all night, quite pointlessly, for the Verdurins had decided to come back early, and Odette had been in Paris since noon; it had not occurred to her to tell him, and not knowing what to do with herself she had spent the evening alone at a theatre, had long since gone to bed, and was now asleep.

In fact, she had not even given him a thought. And occasions such as this, when she forgot Swann's very existence, were more useful to Odette, did more to attach Swann to her, than all her coquetry. Because in this way he was kept in that state of painful agitation which had already been powerful enough to make his love blossom on the night when he failed to find her at the Verdurins' and had looked for her all evening. And he did not have, as I had at Combray in my

childhood, happy days in which to forget the sufferings that return at
night. Swann spent his days without Odette; and there were times
when he said to himself that to allow such a pretty woman to go out
alone in Paris was like leaving a case full of jewels in the middle of the
street. Then he would glare at all the men passing by as if they were
so many thieves. But their faces, formless and collective, escaped the
grasp of his imagination and did not feed his jealousy. Swann's mind
would become exhausted until, putting his hand over his eyes, he would
cry out: 'Heaven help me!', like people who, having worn themselves
out grappling with the problem of the reality of the external world or
the immortality of the soul,* relieve their weary minds with an act of
faith. But the thought of his absent mistress was always indissolubly
mingled with the simplest actions of his life—having lunch, receiving his mail, leaving the house, going to bed—by the very sadness he
felt at having to perform them without her, like the initials of Philippe
le Beau, which, in the church at Brou, because of the longing she felt
for him, Margaret of Austria* intertwined everywhere with her own.
On certain days, instead of staying at home, he would go and have his
lunch in a nearby restaurant to which he had once been attracted
by its good cooking and to which he now went only for one of those
reasons, at once mystical and absurd, that we call romantic; because
the restaurant (which still exists) bore the same name as the street in
which Odette lived: *Lapérouse*. Sometimes, when she had gone away
for a short period, it was only after several days that she thought of
letting him know she had returned to Paris. And then she would say
quite simply, no longer taking the precaution as she once had of
covering herself, just in case, with a little fragment borrowed from the
truth, that she had at that very moment returned by the morning
train. These words were false; at least for Odette they were false, lacking substance, not having what they would have had if true—a basis
in her memory of her arrival at the station; indeed, she was prevented
from picturing them to herself at the moment she uttered them, by
the contradictory image of whatever quite different thing she had
been doing at the moment when she claimed she was getting off the
train. In Swann's mind, however, there was no such obstacle to her
words and they encrusted themselves, assuming the indelibility of
a truth so absolute that if a friend told him he had come by the same
train and had not seen Odette, Swann would be convinced that it was
the friend who was mistaken about the day or the hour, since his

account did not agree with what Odette had said. Her words would
have seemed to him false only if he had suspected beforehand that
they were. For him to believe she was lying, a previous suspicion was
a necessary condition. In fact it was also a sufficient condition. Then
everything Odette said to him would seem suspect. If he heard her
mention a name, it was certainly the name of one of her lovers; once
the supposition was forged, he would spend weeks in a state of torment; on one occasion he even contacted a private investigator to
ascertain the address and occupation of his unknown rival, who would
give him no peace until he went away, and who, he eventually learned,
was an uncle of Odette's who had died twenty years ago.

   Although as a rule she did not allow him to meet her in public
places, saying that people would talk, it happened now and again that
he would attend a soirée to which she had also been invited—at
Forcheville's, at the painter's, or at a charity ball in one of the minis-
tries—and would find himself there at the same time as she. He saw
her but did not dare to stay for fear of irritating her by seeming to be
spying on the pleasures she was enjoying with other people, pleasures
which—as he drove home alone, and went to bed as troubled, as I was
to be some years later, on the evenings when he came to dine with us
at Combray—appeared boundless to him because he had not seen
their end. And once or twice on such evenings he experienced the
sort of happiness which, had it not been so violently affected by the
shocking return of an anxiety that had so suddenly ceased, it might be
tempting to call a tranquil happiness, because it consisted of a return
to a state of calm: he had dropped in on a party at the painter's and
was about to depart, leaving behind him Odette transformed into
a brilliant stranger, surrounded by men to whom her glances and her
gaiety, which were not for him, seemed to speak of some sensual
pleasure to be enjoyed there or elsewhere (perhaps at the 'Bal des
Incohérents',* where he dreaded she might go afterwards) and which
caused Swann more jealousy even than physical intimacy because he
found it more difficult to imagine; he was on the point of going
through the studio door when he heard himself being called back with
these words (which, by removing from the party the possible ending
that had filled him with such dread, made the party seem innocent in
retrospect, made Odette's return home something no longer incon-
ceivable and terrible, but sweet and familiar, something that would
stay beside him, like a part of his everyday life, in his carriage, and

divested Odette herself of her too brilliant and too gay appearance, showing that it was only a disguise she had assumed for a moment, for its own sake, not with a view to mysterious pleasures, and of which she was already tired), with these words that Odette tossed to him as he was crossing the threshold: 'Would you mind staying another five minutes? I'm about to leave, we could go together and you could take me home.'

It was true that on one occasion Forcheville had asked to be taken back at the same time, but when they arrived at Odette's door and he asked to be allowed to come in too, Odette had responded by pointing to Swann and saying: 'Ah! That depends on this gentleman here. Ask him. Well, you can come in for a little while if you want, but you mustn't stay too long, because, I warn you, he likes to have a quiet chat with me, and he doesn't much like me to have visitors when he's here. Ah, if you knew that creature as well as I do! Isn't that so, *my love*, I'm the only one who really knows you?'

And Swann was perhaps even more touched to see her addressing him in this way, in front of Forcheville, not only with these words of affection and special favour, but also with certain criticisms like: 'I'm sure you haven't answered your friends yet about that dinner on Sunday. Don't go if you don't want to, but at least be polite', or: 'Now, have you left your essay on Vermeer here so you can do a little more of it tomorrow? You're so lazy! I'll make you work—you'll see!', which proved that Odette kept abreast of his social engagements and his writings on art, and that the two of them really did have a life together. And as she said this she gave him a smile which made him feel she was entirely his.

At moments like this, while she was making orangeade for them, suddenly, as when a faulty reflector starts to cast on the wall, around a certain object, big fantastic shadows, which then shrink and disappear into it, all the terrible shifting ideas he had formed about Odette would vanish, would dissolve into the charming body that Swann saw before him. He had the sudden suspicion that this hour spent at Odette's house, in the lamplight, was perhaps not an artificial hour, invented just for him (intended to disguise that alarming and delightful thing that was constantly in his thoughts without his ever being able to form a clear picture of it, an hour in Odette's real life, in Odette's life when he was not there), with stage-props and imitation fruit, but was perhaps a real hour of Odette's life, and that if he had not been there she would have offered the same armchair to Forcheville and poured for him not some unknown drink, but that same orange-ade, that the world inhabited by Odette was not that other frightful and supernatural world in which he regularly placed her, and which perhaps existed only in his imagination, but the real world, with no special aura of sadness, and including that table at which he was going to be able to write and that drink which he would be allowed to taste, all those objects which he contemplated with as much admiration and curiosity as gratitude, for if by absorbing his dreams they had delivered him from them, they in return had been enriched by them, they showed him the palpable realization of those dreams, and they intrigued his mind, taking shape before his eyes at the same time that they soothed his heart. Ah, if fate had but allowed him to share a single dwelling with Odette, so that in her house he would be at home, if he asked the servant what there was for lunch, it would have been Odette's menu he was given in reply, and if when Odette wanted to take a morning walk in the Avenue du Bois de Boulogne, his duty as a good husband would have obliged him to accompany her, even if he had no desire to go out, and to carry her coat when she was too warm, and if after dinner she wanted to spend a relaxed evening at home, if he had been forced to stay there with her, doing whatever she wanted; then how completely all those trivial details of Swann's life which seemed to him so sad, would, on the contrary, have taken on, because they would also be part of Odette's life, even the most familiar of them—like that lamp, that orangeade, that armchair, things that con-tained so much of his dreams, materialized so much desire—a sort of superabundant sweetness and a mysterious density.

And yet he suspected that what he yearned for was a state of tran-quillity, of peace, which would not have provided a propitious atmos-phere for his love. When Odette ceased to be for him a creature always absent, longed for, imagined, when the feeling he had for her was no longer the same mysterious disturbance provoked in him by the phrase from the sonata, but affection and gratitude, when normal relations were established between them, putting an end to his madness and his melancholy, then no doubt the actions of Odette's daily life would seem of little interest in themselves—as he had several times already suspected they were, for instance on the day when he had read through the envelope the letter addressed to Forcheville. Contemplating his malady with as much analytical detachment as if he had inoculated himself with it in order to study it, he told himself that when he had recovered, whatever Odette might do would be a matter of indifference to him. Even so, the truth was that, in his morbid state, he feared such a recovery as much as death itself, for it would in fact have meant the death of everything that he then was.

After these quiet evenings, Swann's suspicions would subside; he would think kindly of Odette, and the next day, early in the morning, he would order the finest jewellery to be sent round to her house, because her kind attentions of the night before had excited either his gratitude, or a desire to see them repeated, or a paroxysm of love which needed to find expression.

But at other times his torment would return, he would imagine that Odette was Forcheville's mistress, and that when, the day before the outing to Chatou to which he had not been invited, the two of them had sat watching him from the depths of the Verdurins' landau* in the Bois, as he begged her in vain, with that look of despair which even his coachman had noticed, to go back with him, and then turned away, alone and defeated, she must have had, as she pointed him out to Forcheville, saying: 'Look how furious he is!', the same gleam in her eyes, the same malicious, base, sly expression as on the day when Forcheville had driven Saniette from the Verdurins' house.

At moments like this, Swann hated her. 'Just look at me, I'm such a fool', he would tell himself. 'I'm actually paying for other people's pleasures. All the same, she'd better be careful and not push her luck, because I might well decide to stop forking out for her altogether. At any rate, let's put an end, for the time being, to all the extra favours! To think that only yesterday, when she said she wanted to go to Bayreuth* for the season, I was stupid enough to offer to rent, for the two of us, one of those pretty little castles the King of Bavaria has in the neighbourhood! But she didn't seem awfully keen. She hasn't said yes or no yet; let's hope she'll decide against it. My God! The idea of spending two weeks listening to Wagner with a woman like that, who couldn't care less about music—what fun that would be!' And since his hatred, like his love, needed to find an outlet and be acted upon, he took pleasure in pursuing his evil fantasies further and further, since, because of the perfidies he attributed to Odette, he hated her even more, and, if they turned out to be true (something he tried very hard to picture), he would have an opportunity to punish her and to vent on her his mounting rage. Thus he went so far as to imagine that he would soon receive a letter from her in which she would ask him for money to rent the castle near Bayreuth, but with the warning that he should not go there himself, because she had promised to invite Forcheville and the Verdurins. How he would have liked her to be so bold! How he would have enjoyed refusing, as he wrote the vengeful answer, the terms of which he took satisfaction in choosing, in declaiming out loud, as if he had actually received the letter!

Yet, this was what happened the very next day. She wrote that the Verdurins and their friends had expressed a desire to attend these performances of Wagner, and that, if he would be so good as to send her the money, she would at last have the pleasure, after having been invited so often to their house, of inviting them in her turn. As for him, she said not a word, the implication being that their presence excluded his.

And so, the terrible answer, every word of which he had carefully chosen the day before without daring to hope that they could ever be used, could now, to his delight, be sent round to her. But sadly, he felt certain that, whether with her own money or with money she could easily find elsewhere, she would still be able to rent something at Bayreuth, since she wanted to do so, she who was incapable of telling the difference between Bach and Clapisson.* However, she would have to live more modestly. There was no way, as there would have been had he simply sent her a few thousand-franc bills, of organizing every evening, in some castle, one of those exquisite supper-parties after which she might indulge the whim—which it was possible she had never yet had—of falling into Forcheville's arms. At least he, Swann, would not be the one who would foot the bill for this loathsome trip! If only he could do something to prevent it! If she could sprain an ankle before setting out, or if the coachman who was to take her to the station would agree, at no matter what price, to drive her to some place where she could be kept for a while in seclusion—that perfidious woman, her eyes glittering with a smile of complicity with Forcheville, that Odette had become for Swann in the last forty-eight hours!

But she was never that for very long; after a few days, the sly gleam in her eyes would fade, and the picture of a hateful Odette saying to Forcheville: 'Look how furious he is!' would fade and dissolve. Then, gradually, the face of the other Odette would reappear and rise up, gently radiant, the Odette who also offered a smile to Forcheville, but a smile in which there was nothing but affection for Swann, when she said: 'You mustn't stay too long, because this gentleman doesn't much like me to receive visitors when he wants to be with me. Ah, if you only knew that creature as well as I do!'—the same smile she wore when thanking Swann for an instance of his courtesy, which she prized so highly, or for some advice for which she had asked during one of those times of difficulty when he was the only person she felt she could turn to.

Then, thinking of this other Odette, he would ask himself how he could have written that outrageous letter, of which until now she had probably thought him incapable, and which must have brought him down from the high, the very special place which by his kindness and devotion he had won in her esteem. He would now become less dear to her, because it was for those qualities, which she did not find in Forcheville or in any other man, that she loved him. It was because of them that Odette so often showed a warmth towards him that counted for nothing when he was jealous, because it was not a sign of desire, and even gave proof of affection rather than love, but whose importance he began once more to feel in proportion as the spontaneous relaxation of his suspicions, a relaxation often accelerated by the distraction he found in reading about art or in conversation with a friend, caused his passion to become less demanding of reciprocities.

Now that, after this oscillation, Odette had naturally returned to the place from which Swann's jealousy had momentarily removed her, to the angle from which he found her charming, he pictured her to himself as full of tenderness, with a look of consent in her eyes, and so pretty thus that he could not help offering her his lips as if she had been there and he had been able to kiss her; and he felt as strong a sense of gratitude towards her for that enchanting, kindly glance as if it had been real, as if he had not simply conjured it up in his imagination to satisfy his desire.

How he must have hurt her! Of course, he could find valid reasons for his resentment, but they would not have been enough to make him feel that resentment if he had not loved her so much. Had he not had equally serious grievances against other women, for whom he would nevertheless have been happy to do favours now, feeling no anger towards them because he no longer loved them? If the day ever came when he found himself in the same state of indifference towards Odette, he would understand that it was his jealousy alone that had made him find something repugnant, unforgivable, in her desire (so understandable, after all, springing as it did from an element of childishness in her nature and also from a certain delicacy of spirit), to be able in her turn, since the opportunity had arisen, to return some of the Verdurins' hospitality, and to play the lady of the house herself.

He returned to this other point of view—which was the opposite of the one based on his love and jealousy, and which he adopted sometimes through a sort of intellectual equity and in order to allow for the various probabilities—and tried to judge Odette as if he had never been in love with her, as if she were like any other woman, as if her life, as soon as he was no longer present, had not been different, like a plot being hatched against him behind his back.

Why should he think that there she would enjoy, with Forcheville or with other men, intoxicating pleasures which she had never experienced with him and which his jealousy alone had fabricated out of nothing? In Bayreuth as in Paris, if Forcheville happened to think of him at all, it would only be as of someone who occupied an important place in Odette's life, to whom he was obliged to defer when they met at her house. If Forcheville and she gloated at the idea of being there together in spite of him, it was he who was to blame for it by trying in vain to prevent her from going, whereas if he had approved of her plan, which was in fact defensible, she would have appeared to be there on his recommendation, she would have felt that she had been sent there, housed there by him, and she would have had him to thank for the pleasure of entertaining those people who had so often entertained her.

And if—instead of letting her go off on bad terms with him, without having seen him again—he sent her the money, if he encouraged her to make the trip and did all he could to make it pleasant for her, she would come running to him, happy and grateful, and he would have the joy of seeing her, a joy he had not experienced for nearly a week and which nothing could replace. Because as soon as Swann could picture her without a feeling of revulsion, as soon as he saw once again the warmth of her smile, and as soon as the desire to take her away from any other man was not mixed in with his love by jealousy, that love became once again mainly a taste for the sensations that Odette's person gave him, for the pleasure he took in admiring as a spectacle, or exploring as a phenomenon, the dawn of one of her glances, the formation of one of her smiles, the sound of a certain tone of voice. And this pleasure, different from all others, had in the end created in him a need for her that she alone, by her presence or her letters, could satisfy, almost as disinterested, almost as artistic, as perverse, as another need that characterized this new period in Swann's life, in which the aridity, the depression of earlier years had been succeeded by a sort of spiritual over-abundance, without his knowing to what he owed this unexpected enrichment of his inner life, any more than a person of poor health knows why, at a certain moment, he begins to grow stronger, put on weight, and seems for a time to be on the road to a complete recovery: that other need, which was also developing independently of the material world, was the need to hear and learn about music.

And so, through the very chemistry of his disease, after he had created jealousy with his love, he began again to manufacture affection and pity for Odette. She had become once more his sweet, enchanting Odette. He was full of remorse at having treated her badly. He wanted her to come to him, and, before she came, wanted to have prepared for her some pleasure, so as to see her gratitude take shape in her face and mould her smile.

And Odette, certain that she would see him come back to her after a few days, as loving and submissive as before, to ask her for a reconciliation, lost all fear of displeasing him or even of making him angry, and refused him, whenever it suited her, the favours he valued most.

Perhaps she did not realize how sincere he had been with her during their quarrel, when he had told her that he would not send her any money and would try to hurt her. Perhaps she did not realize, either, how sincere he was, if not with her, at least with himself, on other occasions when, for the sake of the future of their relationship, so as to show Odette that he was capable of living without her, that a break between them was always possible, he decided to let some time pass without going to see her again.

Sometimes it would be after several days during which she had given him no fresh cause for anxiety; and since he knew that his next few visits to her house would not give him any great joy, but more probably some annoyance that would put an end to his present state of calm, he would send her a note to say that he was very busy and would not be able to see her on any of the days he had suggested. Then a letter from her, crossing with his, asked him to change one of those very meetings. He wondered why; his suspicions, his anguish, took hold of him again. He could no longer abide, in the new state of agitation in which he found himself, by the commitment he had made to himself in his earlier state of relative calm, and he would hurry round to her house and demand to see her on every one of the following days. And even if she had not written first, if she simply acknowledged his letter, agreeing to his request that they stop seeing each other for a while, this was enough to make him unable to go on without seeing her. For, contrary to Swann's expectations, Odette's agreement to his suggestion had brought about a complete change in his attitude. Like all those who possess some particular thing, in order to know what would happen if he ceased for a moment to possess it, he had removed it from his mind, leaving everything else in the same state as when it was there. But the absence of a thing is not merely that, it is not simply a partial lack, it is a disruption of everything else, it is a new state which cannot be foreseen in the old.

But there were other occasions—Odette's imminent departure on a trip, for instance—when, using some trivial dispute as his excuse, he would resolve not to write to her and not to see her again until her return, thus giving the appearance, and expecting the benefit, of a serious rupture, which she would perhaps imagine to be final, to a separation the greater part of which was the unavoidable consequence of her trip, which he was simply allowing to begin a little earlier than planned. Already he could picture Odette worried and distressed at having received neither a visit nor a letter from him, and this image of her, by soothing his jealousy, made it easier for him to break the habit of seeing her. At times, no doubt, in a remote part of his mind where his resolution had thrust it because of the long intervening period of the three weeks of accepted separation, it was with pleasure that he contemplated the idea that he would see Odette again on her return; but it was also with so little impatience that he began to wonder whether he would not happily double the duration of an abstinence so easy to bear. It had lasted so far only three days, a much shorter time than he had often spent without seeing Odette and without having, as now, planned it in advance. And yet at this point a slight irritation or physical discomfort—by inciting him to regard the present moment as an exceptional moment, outside the rules, one in which common sense would allow him to accept the relief afforded by a pleasure and, until there might be some point in resuming the effort, to give his will a rest—suspended the action of his will, which relaxed its grip; or, less than that, the recollection of something he had forgotten to ask Odette, such as whether she had decided on the colour in which she would have her carriage repainted, or, with regard to an investment, whether it was ordinary or preference shares that she wanted him to buy (it was all very well to show her that he could live without seeing her, but if it meant that the carriage had to be painted all over again, or the shares yielded no dividends, a lot of good it would have done him), and, like a stretched elastic band that is released or the air in a pneumatic machine when a slight opening is made, the thought of seeing her again sprang back from the far distance where it had been kept into the field of the present and of immediate possibilities.

It sprang back without meeting any further resistance, and was so irresistible, in fact, that Swann had found it far less difficult to face the approach, one after another, of the fifteen days he was to be separated from Odette than to wait the ten minutes his coachman needed to harness the carriage that was going to take him to her, minutes he spent in transports of impatience and joy, his mind returning constantly, in order to lavish upon it all his affection, to the idea of seeing her again, an idea which, by returning so suddenly, just when he thought it so remote, had leapt back to the forefront of his consciousness. For this idea no longer encountered the obstacle of his desire to attempt immediately to resist it, a desire which had ceased to have any place in Swann's mind since, having proved to himself—or so he believed—that he was so easily capable of resisting it, he no longer saw any risk in postponing a plan of separation that he was now certain he could easily put into operation whenever he wished. Furthermore, this idea of seeing her again came back to him adorned with a novelty, a seductiveness, endowed with a virulence, which habit had dulled but which had been retempered in that privation, not of three days but of two weeks (for a period of abstinence must be calculated, by anticipation, as having lasted already until the final date assigned to it), and had converted what had been until then an expected pleasure which could easily be sacrificed into an unhoped-for happiness which he was powerless to resist. Finally, the idea came back to him embellished by his ignorance of what Odette might have thought, might perhaps have done, on seeing that he had given no sign of life, so that what he was now going to find was the thrilling revelation of an almost unknown Odette.

She, however, just as she had assumed that his refusal of the money was only a sham, took as a mere pretext to see her his coming to ask about the repainting of the carriage and the purchase of shares. For she was unable to reconstruct the various phases of the crises through which he was passing, and in the notion she had formed of them there was no attempt to understand the way they worked; she considered them only in the light of what she knew beforehand—their necessary, unfailing, and always identical termination. A notion that was incomplete—and therefore all the more profound, perhaps—if it were to be judged from the point of view of Swann, who would no doubt have thought he was misunderstood by Odette, just as a drug-addict or a consumptive, persuaded that they have been prevented, one by some outside event just when he was about to free himself from his inveterate habit, the other by a chance indisposition just when he was about to be finally cured, feel misunderstood by the doctor who does not attach the same importance to these alleged contingencies, which he sees as mere disguises, assumed, so as to make themselves felt again by his patients, by the vice and the morbid condition which, in reality, have not ceased to weigh heavily and incurably upon them while they were indulging their dreams of reformation or recovery. Indeed, Swann's love had reached the stage where the boldest of doctors and, in certain affections, of surgeons ask themselves whether depriving a patient of his vice or ridding him of his disease is still reasonable or even possible.

Certainly, of the extent of this love Swann had no direct awareness. When he tried to measure it, it sometimes seemed to him diminished, reduced to almost nothing; for example, on certain days he would recall the lack of pleasure, amounting almost to displeasure, which, before he fell in love with Odette, he had felt for her expressive features and dull complexion. 'I'm definitely making progress,' he would say to himself the next day. 'When I really think about it, I hardly enjoyed myself at all yesterday when I was in bed with her: it's odd, I actually found her ugly.' And, of course, he was quite sincere, but his love extended well beyond the domain of physical desire. Odette's person, in fact, now had very little to do with it. When his eyes fell upon the photograph of Odette on his study table, or when she dropped in to see him, he found it difficult to identify her face, in the flesh or on pasteboard, with the constant, painful anxiety in his mind. He would say to himself, almost with surprise: 'It is she!', as though suddenly we were to be shown in a particular, external form one of our illnesses, and found that it bore no resemblance to our suffering. 'She'—he tried to ask himself what that actually meant; for what love and death have in common, much more than the vague things people are always saying, is that they make us probe deeper, for fear that its reality will elude us, into the mystery of personality. And this malady which Swann's love had become had spread to such an extent, was so intermingled with all his habits, with his every act and thought, with his health, his sleep, his whole existence, even with what he wished for after his death, was now so much part of him, that it could not have been torn out of him without destroying him almost entirely: as they say in surgery, his love was no longer operable.

This love of Swann's had so detached him from all other interests that when by chance he reappeared in society, telling himself that his connections in that world, like a beautiful setting (though Odette would probably not have been able to form any clear estimate of its worth) might restore a little of his own value in her eyes (as indeed they might have done had these connections not been devalued by his love, which for Odette depreciated everything it touched by seeming to proclaim them less precious), what he felt there, along with his distress at being in places and among people she did not know, was the same disinterested pleasure as he would have derived from a novel or a painting depicting the amusements of a leisured class, just as, in his own house, he enjoyed contemplating the smooth functioning of his domestic life, the elegance of his wardrobe and of his servants' liveries, the soundness of his investments, in the same way as, when reading Saint-Simon, who was one of his favourite authors, he enjoyed descriptions of the mechanics of daily life, the menus at Madame de Maintenon's dinners, or Lulli's* shrewd avarice and lavish lifestyle. And to the small extent that this detachment was not absolute, the reason for the new pleasure Swann was savouring was that he could migrate for a while into the few and distant parts of himself that had remained almost untouched by his love and his pain. In this respect the personality which my great-aunt attributed to him as 'young Swann', as distinct from the more individual personality of Charles Swann, was the one in which he was now happiest. One day, wishing to send the Princesse of Parma some fruit for her birthday (and because she could often be useful to Odette indirectly, by enabling her to have seats at galas and jubilees), but not being sure how to order it, he had entrusted the task to a cousin of his mother's, a lady who, delighted to run an errand for him, had written to him, when sending the account, that she had not ordered all the fruit at the same place, but the grapes from Crapote, whose speciality they were, the strawberries from Jauret, the pears from Chevet, who always had the best, and so on, 'each piece of fruit hand-picked and inspected by me'. And indeed, from the way the Princesse had thanked him, he had been able to judge the flavour of the strawberries and the ripeness of the pears. But, above all, the words 'each piece of fruit hand-picked and inspected by me' had soothed his suffering by transporting his mind to a region he rarely visited, even though it was his by right as the heir to a rich, upper-bourgeois family which had handed down from generation to generation, at his disposal whenever he wanted, a knowledge of the 'right addresses' and the art of placing an order.*

Indeed, he had forgotten he was 'young Swann' for too long not to feel, when he became that person again for a moment, a keener pleasure than any he might have felt at other times but which had palled; and if the kindness shown towards him by the bourgeois, for whom he had never been anything else than 'young Swann', was less marked than that of the aristocracy (but in fact was more flattering, for with them at least it is always inseparable from respect), no letter from a royal personage, whatever princely entertainment it offered, could ever give him as much pleasure as a letter asking him to be a witness, or merely to be present, at a wedding in the family of some old friends of his parents, some of whom had continued to see him from time to time—like my grandfather, who, the year before, had invited him to my mother's wedding—while others barely knew him personally, but felt certain obligations of courtesy towards the son, the worthy successor, of the late Monsieur Swann.

But, because of his close ties, already so well established, with members of high society, they too, in a sense, were part of his house, his household, his family. He felt, when contemplating his distinguished connections, the same external support, the same reassurance, as when he gazed upon the fine properties, the fine silverware, the fine table linen, that had come down to him from his family. And the thought that if he were struck down at home by a sudden illness, his manservant would naturally run for help to the Duc de Chartres, the Prince de Reuss, the Duc de Luxembourg, and the Baron de Charlus, brought him the same consolation as our old Françoise derived from the knowledge that she would one day be wrapped in a shroud of her own fine sheets, marked with her name, and not darned (or with such care that it gave an even clearer idea of her skill as a seamstress), a shroud which, since she saw it so often in her mind's eye, gave her a certain satisfactory sense, if not of well-being, at least of self-esteem. But above all, since every action or thought of Swann's that concerned Odette was shaped and controlled by his unavowed feeling that he was, if not less dear to her, at any rate less pleasant to be with than anyone, even the most boring of the Verdurins' faithful—when he returned to a social world in which he was regarded as the very incarnation of elegance, was constantly sought after, whom people were always sorry not to see, he began once again to believe in the existence of a happier life, almost to feel an appetite for it, like an invalid who, bedridden for months, and on a strict diet, suddenly sees in a newspaper the menu for an official luncheon or an advertisement for a cruise around Sicily.

If he was obliged to make his excuses to people in society for not visiting them, those he made to Odette were for not staying away from her. He even paid for his visits to her (asking himself at the end of each month, imagining he had tried her patience somewhat by going to see her too often, whether it would be enough if he sent her four thousand francs) and for each one found a pretext, a present to bring her, a piece of information he needed, Monsieur de Charlus whom he had bumped into going to her house and who had insisted that he accompany him. And, in the absence of an excuse, he would ask Monsieur de Charlus if he would run over to her house and mention in the course of conversation, as if spontaneously, that he had just remembered something he had to tell Swann, and would she be so kind as to ask him to come round right away; but more often than not Swann would wait in vain, and Monsieur de Charlus would tell him in the evening that his ruse had not succeeded. The result was that, if she was now frequently away from Paris, even when she was there she saw very little of him, and she who, when she was in love with him, used to say: 'I'm always free' and 'What do I care what others think?', now, each time he wanted to see her, would invoke social conventions or plead some prior engagement. When he mentioned that he might be going to a charity event, or a private viewing, or a first-night which she, too, would attend, she would tell him that he was trying to flaunt their affair, that he was treating her like a prostitute.

It reached the point that, in order to avoid being debarred from meeting her anywhere, Swann, knowing that she was acquainted with and was very fond of my great-uncle Adolphe, and having once been a friend of his himself, went to see him one day in his little apartment in the Rue de Bellechasse to ask him to use his influence with Odette. Since she always adopted a lyrical tone when she spoke to Swann about my uncle, saying: 'Ah, yes, he's not like you, his friendship with me is such a splendid thing, a great and beautiful thing! He would never have so little regard for me that he would want to be seen with me everywhere in public!', Swann was perplexed, and did not know quite how lofty his own tone should be in talking about Odette to my uncle. He began by invoking her a priori excellence, her axiomatic and seraphic super-humanity, the revealed truth of her virtues, which could neither be demonstrated nor deduced from experience. 'I must talk to you. You know what an adorable creature Odette is, an absolute angel. And you also know what people are like in Paris. Not everyone sees Odette in the same way you and I see her. There are some people who think I'm cutting a rather ridiculous figure; she won't even let me be seen out with her, at the theatre, for example. She has enormous respect for your opinion, so couldn't you have a word with her for me, to assure her that she's exaggerating the harm I might be doing to her reputation by greeting her in public?'

My uncle advised Swann not to see Odette for a little while, saying that this would make her love him all the more; and he advised Odette to let Swann meet her wherever he liked. A few days later, Odette told Swann she had just had the disappointing experience of discovering that my uncle was no different from other men: he had tried to take her by force. She calmed Swann down, for his first impulse was to go and challenge my uncle to a duel, but he refused to shake his hand the next time they met. He regretted this falling out all the more because he had hoped, had he seen my uncle again a few times and had managed to chat with him in complete confidence, to get him to shed some light on certain rumours regarding the life Odette had led when she lived in Nice. For my uncle was in the habit of spending his winters there, and Swann thought that it might even have been there that he had first known Odette. The few words that someone had let slip in Swann's presence about a man who had purportedly been Odette's lover had greatly disturbed him. But the things which, before knowing them, he would have regarded as the most terrible to learn and the

most impossible to believe, when he did learn of them, were incorporated for ever into his general sadness; he accepted them, he would
no longer have been able to understand their not existing. But each
one of them left an indelible mark on the picture he was forming
of his mistress. He was even given to understand, at one point, that
Odette's easy virtue, which he would never have suspected, was more
or less common knowledge, and that in Baden and in Nice, when she
used to go and spend a few months there, she had had a sort of
amorous notoriety. He sought out certain womanizers, in order to
question them; but they were aware that he knew Odette; and besides,
he was afraid of reminding them of her, of putting them on her track.
But he, to whom nothing hitherto could have seemed as tedious as
everything relating to the cosmopolitan life of Baden or Nice, having
learned that Odette had perhaps led a rather wild life in those two
pleasure-spots, though he could never find out whether it had been
solely to satisfy financial needs which, thanks to him, she no longer
had, or from some form of capricious desire which might easily return,
now leaned in impotent, blind, dizzy anguish over the bottomless
abyss that had swallowed up the early years of the Septennate,* when
one spent the winter on the Promenade des Anglais and the summer
beneath the linden-trees at Baden, and saw in them a painful but
magnificent profundity, such as a poet might have lent them; and he
would have devoted to the reconstruction of the petty details of life
on the Côte d'Azur in those days, if it could have helped him to
understand something of Odette's smile or the look in her eyes—
candid and straightforward though they were—more passion than an
aesthete studying the extant documents of fifteenth-century Florence
in order to gain greater insight into the soul of Botticelli's Primavera,
his fair Vanna, or his Venus.* Often he would sit gazing at her pen-
sively, not saying a word, and she would say: 'You look so sad!' It was
not very long since he had switched from the idea that she was a good
person, the equal of the finest women he had ever known, to the idea
that she was a kept woman; conversely, he had more recently reverted
from the Odette de Crécy who was perhaps too well known among
a merry crowd of rakes and philanderers, to this face whose expression was at times so gentle, to this nature so human. He would ask
himself: 'What does it matter that in Nice everyone has heard of
Odette de Crécy? Reputations like that, even if true, are based on
gossip and rumour.' He would reflect that the legend surrounding

Odette, even if it was authentic, was something extraneous to her, was not innate, an irreducible and pernicious aspect of her personality; that the creature who might have been led into bad ways was a woman with kind eyes, a heart full of pity for the suffering of others, a docile body which he had held, clasped in his arms and felt with his hands, a woman whom he might one day come to possess entirely, if he succeeded in making himself indispensable to her. She would sit there, often tired, her face drained for a moment of that febrile, excited preoccupation with the unknown things that made Swann suffer; she would push back her hair with her hands; her forehead, her whole face, would seem larger; then, suddenly, some ordinary human thought, some generous feeling such as may be found in all individuals when, in a moment of relaxation or reclusion, they are able to be themselves, would spring from her eyes like a beam of golden sunlight. And immediately her whole face would light up like a grey landscape covered in clouds that suddenly part, leaving it transfigured by the setting sun. The life he glimpsed within Odette at such moments, even the future of which she seemed to be dreaming, Swann could have shared with her; no troubling disturbance seemed to have left its residue there. Rare though they became, these moments were not without value. In memory, Swann joined the fragments together, abolished the intervals between them, cast, as if in gold, an Odette of kindness and calm, for whom in later years (as we shall see in the second part of this story)* he made sacrifices which the other Odette would never have won from him. But how rare these moments were, and how seldom he now saw her! Even in the case of their evening rendezvous, she told him only at the last minute if she would be able to see him, for she counted on his always being free and she wanted first to make sure that no one else would invite her out. She would claim that she had to wait for a message of the greatest importance, and if, after she had already told Swann that he could come, some friends asked her, halfway through the evening, to join them at the theatre or at supper, she would jump for joy and run off to dress. As she progressed in her preparations, every movement she made brought Swann closer to the moment when he would have to leave her, when she would dash off on an irresistible impulse; and when at last she was ready, shooting a final glance at the mirror, her eyes sharp and bright with concentration, she applied a little more lipstick, fixed a stray lock of hair over her forehead, and called for her sky-blue evening cape with gold tassels,

Swann looked so downcast that she could not repress a gesture of impatience as she snapped: 'So that's the thanks I get for letting you stay here until the last minute. And I thought I was being nice. I'll know better next time!' Sometimes, at the risk of annoying her, he resolved to try to find out where she had gone, and he even imagined an alliance with Forcheville, who might perhaps have been able to enlighten him. In any case, when he had ascertained with whom she was spending the evening, it was not difficult for him to discover, among his acquaintances, someone who knew, if only indirectly, the man in question, and could easily obtain this or that piece of information about him. And while he was writing to one of his friends, to ask him for help in clearing up some point or other, he would feel a sense of relief on ceasing to ask himself his unanswerable questions and on transferring to someone else the tiring task of interrogation. It is true that Swann was hardly better off for the information he did obtain. Knowing something does not always enable us to prevent it, but the things we know, we can at least hold on to, if not with our hands, at least in our minds, where we can do with them what we like, which gives us the illusion of having some sort of control over them. He was happy whenever Monsieur de Charlus was with Odette. He knew that nothing would happen between Charlus and her, that when Monsieur de Charlus went out with her, it was out of friendship for him and he would have no qualms about telling him what she had done. Sometimes her refusal to see Swann on a particular evening would be so categorical, she would seem so keen to go out somewhere, that Swann would feel it most important that Charlus should make himself available to go with her. The next day, not daring to question Charlus too closely, he would pretend to misunderstand his answers, thus obliging him to give further details; and after each further answer he would feel more relieved, because it soon became clear that Odette had occupied her evening with the most innocent of pleasures: 'What are you saying, Mémé old chap?* I don't quite follow . . . You didn't go straight to the Musée Grévin from her house? You went somewhere else first? No? How funny! You don't know how entertaining you are, Mémé old boy. What a strange idea of hers to go on to the Chat Noir afterwards. But quite typical . . . No? Oh, so it was your idea? How odd. But not such a bad idea, really; she must have seen a lot of people she knew there? No? She didn't speak to anyone? That's extraordinary. So you sat there, the two of you, all by yourselves? I can just picture it. What a good chap you are, my dear Mémé. I'm very fond of you.' Swann felt relieved. It had occasionally happened to him, when chatting casually with people to whom he was barely listening, to hear certain stray remarks (such as: 'I saw Madame de Crécy yesterday with a gentleman I don't know'), remarks which, as soon as they entered his heart, turned into a solid state, grew hard like an encrustation, and cut into him, irremovable; so that he was greatly soothed, in contrast, by the words: 'She knew no one, she spoke to no one', which flowed freely through him, fluid, easy, breathable! And yet, a moment later, he was telling himself that Odette must find him very dull if those were the pleasures she preferred to his company. And their triviality, though reassuring, pained him as if they had been an act of betrayal.

Even when he was unable to find out where she had gone, it would have been enough, to alleviate the anguish he felt at such times, and for which Odette's presence, the sweet pleasure of being with her, was the sole remedy (which in the long run aggravated the disease, like many remedies, but at least brought temporary relief), it would have been enough for him, if only Odette had allowed it, to remain in her house while she was out, to wait for her there until the hour of her return, into whose stillness and appeasement would have flowed the hours which some special quality or magic spell had made him believe to be different from all others. But she did not want this; he had to return home; he forced himself, on the way, to form various plans, he stopped thinking about Odette; he even succeeded, as he undressed, in turning over in his mind some quite cheering thoughts; and it was with a heart full of hope of going to see some great painting the next day that he got into bed and put out the light; but no sooner, as he prepared to go to sleep, did he cease to exert the self-control of which he was not even aware, because it had become so habitual, than at that very instant an icy shiver would run through him and he would begin to sob. He did not even want to know why, he wiped his eyes, and said to himself with a little laugh: 'That's nice! I'm turning into a real neurotic!' After which he could not think without a feeling of great weariness that the next day he would have to resume his quest to find out what Odette had been doing, and consider what influences he could bring to bear in order to see her. This compulsion to engage in activity that was relentless, unchanging, and fruitless, was so painful to him that one day, noticing a swelling in his abdomen, he felt genuinely delighted at the thought that he might have a fatal tumour, that he would no longer need to bother about anything, that illness would take him over, make him its plaything, until his imminent demise. And indeed if, during this period, he often longed for death without admitting it to himself, it was in order to escape not so much from the intensity of his suffering as from the monotony of his struggle.

And yet he would have liked to live until such time as he no longer loved her, when she would have no reason to lie to him, and he could at last learn from her whether, that afternoon when he had dropped in to see her, she was or was not in bed with Forcheville. Often, for several days, the suspicion that she was in love with someone else would draw his mind away from that question about Forcheville, would make it almost a matter of indifference to him, in the way that a new stage in an illness can seem to provide momentary relief from the preceding stages. There were even days when he was not tormented by any suspicions. He thought he was cured. But the next morning, when he woke up, he felt the same, persistent pain which, the day before, he had diluted with a stream of different sensations. But the seat of the pain was unchanged. In fact, it was the sharpness of the pain that had woken him.

Since Odette never gave him any information about those very important things which occupied so much of her time every day (although he had lived long enough to know that these things are never anything other than pleasures), he could not try to imagine them for very long at a time; his brain would become quite empty; then he would pass a finger over his weary eyelids, as if wiping his pince-nez, and would stop thinking altogether. But floating up from that great unknown were certain occupations that reappeared from time to time, vaguely connected by Odette to some obligation towards distant relatives or old friends who, since they were the only ones she regularly mentioned as preventing her from seeing him, seemed to Swann to form the necessary, fixed framework of her life. Because of the tone in which she referred from time to time to 'the day I go to the Hippodrome with my girlfriend', if, having felt unwell and thought: 'Perhaps Odette will be prepared to come and see me', he suddenly remembered that it was one of those days, he would say to himself: 'Oh, no! There's no point in asking her to come. I should have thought of it before, today's her day for going to the Hippodrome with her woman-friend. Let's confine ourselves to what's possible; there's no point wearing ourselves out suggesting things that are unacceptable and have already been ruled out in advance.' The duty incumbent upon Odette of going to the Hippodrome, to which Swann thus gave way, seemed to him not only inescapable, but the mark of necessity with which it was stamped seemed to make plausible and legitimate everything that was in any way related to it. If a man passing in the street greeted Odette and thus aroused Swann's jealousy, she answered his questions by linking the man to one of the two or three great duties to which she regularly referred; if, for example, she said: 'He was in my friend's box at the Hippodrome', this explanation would allay Swann's suspicions, since it struck him as inevitable that the friend would have other guests besides Odette in her box, but he had never tried or managed to form any clear picture of them. How he would have loved to make the acquaintance of the friend who went to the Hippodrome, and to be invited along with Odette! How gladly he would have given up all his elegant society friends in exchange for a single person Odette was in the habit of seeing, even a manicurist or a shop assistant! He would have gone to more trouble for them than for a queen. Wouldn't they have given him, with the knowledge of Odette's life they bore within them, the only effective sedative for his pain? With what joy he would have hastened to spend his days at the home of one or other of those humble people with whom Odette kept up friendly relations, whether out of self-interest or genuine simplicity! How gladly he would have elected to live the rest of his days in the garret of some sordid but enviable apartment house where Odette went but never took him and where, if he had lived with the little retired dressmaker, whose lover he would willingly have pretended to be, he would have had a visit from Odette nearly every day! In these almost working-class neighbourhoods, what a modest existence, abject but sweet, and filled with calm and happiness, he would gladly have led for ever.

It still happened occasionally that when, after meeting Swann somewhere, Odette saw some man approaching whom he did not know, he could discern on her face the same look of dismay she had worn on the day he had come to see her while Forcheville was there. But this was rare; for on the days when, despite everything she had to do, and her fear of what people might think, she managed to see Swann, the main impression she gave now was self-assurance: in striking contrast, whether unconscious compensation or a natural reaction, to the timidity she had shown in the early days of their relationship, even when she was not with him, when she began a letter with the words: 'My dear Charles, my hand is shaking so much that I can hardly write' (at least so she claimed, and a little of that emotion must have been sincere for her to want to feign more). She had felt attracted to Swann then. We only ever tremble for ourselves, or for those we love. When our happiness is no longer in their hands, what calm, what ease, what boldness we enjoy in their presence! When she spoke to him, she no longer used any of those words by which she had sought to give herself the illusion that he belonged to her, creating opportunities for saying 'my' or 'mine' when she referred to him—'You are my possession, it's the sweet scent of our friendship, and I shall keep it'—and for talking to him about the future, about death itself, as if it were something they would share together. In those days, to everything he said she would answer admiringly: 'You're so unlike other people!'; she would gaze at his long face and his balding head (which made those who knew of his success with women think: 'He's not conventionally good-looking, it's true, but he has style: that quiff, that monocle, that smile!'), and, perhaps more out of curiosity to know what he was really like than a desire to become his mistress, she would say: 'If only I knew what goes on in that head of yours!'

Now, however, whatever Swann said, she would respond in a tone that was sometimes irritable, at other times indulgent: 'Can't you ever be like other people!' She would look at his face, which was only a little aged by worry (but about which everyone now thought, with the same aptitude that enables one to discover the meaning of a piece of symphonic music after reading the programme, or to see family resemblances in a child once one knows its parentage: 'He's not exactly ugly, it's true, but he's really quite ridiculous: that monocle, that quiff, that smile!'—creating in their suggestible imaginations the invisible boundary that separates, by a few months, the head of an adored lover from the head of a cuckold), she would say: 'Oh, if only I could change what goes on in that head of yours and put some sense into it!' Always ready to believe in the truth of what he hoped, if Odette's behaviour towards him left the slightest room for doubt, he would seize upon her words, and say: 'You can if you want.'

And then he would try to convince her that to comfort him, guide him, make him work, would be a noble task, to which many women would ask nothing better than to devote themselves, though it is only fair to add that in their hands the noble task would have seemed to him a tactless and intolerable usurpation of his freedom: 'If she didn't love me a little,' he would tell himself, 'she wouldn't want to change me. And to change me, she will have to see me more often.' Thus he saw her reproaches as proof of her interest, of her love perhaps; and indeed she now gave him so few of those that he was obliged to regard as such the various prohibitions she imposed on him. One day she declared that she did not like his coachman, who, she felt, was perhaps turning him against her, and in any case did not show the punctiliousness and deference towards him that she would have liked to see. She felt that Swann wanted her to say: 'Don't use him any more when you come to see me', just as he might have wanted her to kiss him. Since she was in a good mood, she said it; he was touched. That evening, talking to Monsieur de Charlus, with whom he could at least enjoy the relief of being able to talk about her openly (since every word he uttered now, even to people who did not know her, always related in some way to her), he said: 'I do believe, though, that she loves me; she's so nice to me, and she certainly seems interested in what I do.' And if, when he was setting off to her house, getting into his carriage with a friend to whom he was giving a lift, the friend said: 'I say, that's not Lorédan on the box', with what melancholy joy Swann would reply:

'Indeed not! I can't use Lorédan, you know, when I go to the Rue La Pérouse. Odette doesn't like me to use Lorédan, she doesn't think he behaves properly towards me. Well, what can one do? You know what women are like! You know that would greatly upset her. Oh, yes, if I used Rémi, I'd never hear the end of it!'

This new manner, indifferent, offhand, irritable, which Odette had adopted towards him, certainly made him suffer; but he was not aware of the extent of his suffering; since it was only gradually, day by day, that Odette had cooled towards him, it was only by comparing what she was now with what she had been in the beginning that he could have measured the depth of the change that had taken place. Yet that change was his deep, secret wound, which hurt him day and night, and every time he felt that his thoughts were straying a little too close to it, he would quickly lead them in another direction for fear of suffering too much. He would say to himself in an abstract way: 'There was a time when Odette loved me more', but he never looked back at that time. Just as there was a desk in his study that he managed not to look at, which he made a detour to avoid as he came and went, because in one of its drawers he had locked away the chrysanthemum she had given him that first evening when he had driven her home, and the letters in which she had said: 'If you had left your heart here too, I would not have let you have it back', and: 'At whatever time of the day or night that might be convenient for you to see me, send for me and I'll be only too happy to come', so there was a place inside him which he never allowed his thoughts to approach, forcing them, if necessary, to make the detour of a lengthy argument so that they would not have to pass in front of it: this was the place in which dwelled his memory of happier times.

But his extreme caution was foiled one evening when he had gone out to a party.

It was at the home of the Marquise de Saint-Euverte, the last, for that year, of the evenings on which she invited people to hear the musicians she would use, later on, for her charity concerts. Swann, who had intended to go to each of the previous evenings in turn but had not been able to make up his mind, was dressing for this one when he received a visit from the Baron de Charlus, who had come to offer to accompany him to the party, if this would help him to be a little less bored there, a little less miserable. But Swann responded:

'You know, of course, how much I'd like to go with you. But the greatest pleasure you can give me is to go and see Odette instead. You know what an excellent influence you have on her. I don't think she'll be going anywhere this evening before she goes to see her old dressmaker, and I'm sure she'd be delighted if you went with her. In any case, you'll find her at home before that. Try to entertain her, and see if you can talk some sense into her. Perhaps you can arrange something she would like for tomorrow, something the three of us could do together . . . And try to make a few suggestions for the summer, see if there's anything she might want to do, a cruise we could all three go on, something like that. As for tonight, I don't expect to see her; but if she did want to see me, or you thought of something, you'd need only to send me a word at Madame de Saint-Euverte's up until midnight, and afterwards here at home. Thank you for everything you do for me. You know how fond I am of you.'

The Baron promised to pay the visit Swann wanted after depositing him at the door of the Saint-Euverte house, where Swann arrived calmed by the thought that Monsieur de Charlus would be spending the evening in the Rue La Pérouse, but in a state of melancholy indifference to everything that did not concern Odette, and especially to all that concerned fashionable life—a state which gave them the charm to be found in anything which, when it is no longer an object of our desire, appears to us as it is. As soon as he stepped down from the carriage, in the foreground of that fictitious summary of their domestic life which hostesses like to offer their guests on ceremonial occasions, and in which they strive to observe accuracy of costume and setting, Swann was very pleased to see the descendants of Balzac's 'tigers',* the grooms, who normally followed their mistress on her daily outing, but who were now hatted and booted and posted outside in front of the house on the soil of the avenue, or in front of the stables, like gardeners lined up next to their flower-beds. The tendency he had always had, to look for analogies between living people and portraits in art galleries, was still active, but in a more constant and general way; it was fashionable society as a whole, now that he was detached from it, that presented itself to him as a series of pictures. In the entrance-hall (which, in the old days, when he still attended such functions, he would have entered wrapped in his overcoat and left in his tails, without knowing what had happened during the few moments he had spent there, his mind having been either still at the party he had just left or already at the party into which he was about to be introduced) he noticed for the first time, roused by the unexpected arrival of such a tardy guest, the scattered pack of tall, magnificent, idle footmen who were dozing here and there on benches and chests, and who, raising their noble, sharp, greyhound profiles, now rose to their feet and gathered around him in a circle.

One of them, particularly ferocious-looking, and rather like the executioner in certain Renaissance paintings depicting scenes of torture, advanced towards him with an implacable air to take his things. But the hardness of his steely gaze was compensated for by the softness of his cotton gloves, so that, as he approached Swann, he seemed to exhibit both contempt for his person and regard for his hat. He took it with a care to which his posture imparted something meticulous and a delicacy that was rendered almost touching by his evident strength. Then he passed it to one of his inexperienced and timid assistants, who expressed the terror he was feeling by casting wild glances in all directions, and showing the agitation of a captive animal in the first hours of its domestication.

A few feet away, a burly fellow in livery stood musing, motionless, statuesque, useless, like the purely decorative warrior one sees in the most tumultuous paintings by Mantegna,* lost in thought, leaning on his shield, while those around him are rushing about slaughtering each other; standing apart from the group of his colleagues as they bustled round Swann, he seemed similarly resolved to take no part in this scene, which he followed vaguely with his cruel sea-green eyes, as if it had been the Massacre of the Innocents or the Martyrdom of St James. He seemed indeed to belong to that vanished race—if, in fact, it ever existed, except in the altarpiece of San Zeno and the frescoes of the Eremitani, where Swann had come in contact with it, and where it dreams on still—which issued from the impregnation of an ancient statue by one of the Master's Paduan models or one of Albrecht Dürer's Saxons.* And the locks of his red hair, crinkled by nature but glued by brilliantine, were treated as they are in the Greek sculptures which the painter from Mantua never stopped studying and which, if out of all creation it represents only man, is at least able to derive from his simple forms such rich variations, as though borrowed from the whole of animate nature, that a head of hair, in the smooth rolls and sharp beaks of its curls, or in the superimposition of the triple diadem of its tresses, can look at once like a bunch of seaweed, a brood of doves, a bed of hyacinths, and a coil of snakes.

Still others, also colossal, stood on the steps of a monumental staircase for which their decorative presence and marmoreal immobility might have inspired the same name as the one in the Doges' Palace— 'The Giants' Staircase'*—and which Swann began to climb with the sad thought that Odette had never climbed it. Oh, with what joy, by contrast, he would have gone up the dark, evil-smelling, rickety flights to the little dressmaker's, in whose garret he would gladly have paid more than the price of a weekly stage-box at the Opera for the right to spend the evening there when Odette came to visit, and even on other days, so that he could talk about her, be among the people she was in the habit of seeing when he was not there, and who for that reason seemed to possess a part of his mistress's life that was more real, more inaccessible, and more mysterious than anything he knew. In the old dressmaker's foul-smelling but longed-for staircase, since the building had no service stair, one saw in the evening outside every door an empty, unwashed milk-can put out in readiness on the mat; whereas on the magnificent but despised staircase that Swann was now climbing, on either side, at different levels, in front of each recess made in the wall by the window of the concierge's lodge or the door to an apartment, representing the domestic service which they controlled and paying homage to the guests, a concierge, a majordomo, a steward (worthy men who for the rest of the week lived semi-independently in their own quarters, dined there by themselves like small shopkeepers, and might before long take up more prosaic service in the household of a doctor or an industrialist), all of them careful to carry out to the letter the instructions they had been given before being allowed to put on the dazzling livery they wore only at rare intervals and in which they did not feel entirely at ease, stood beneath the arch of their doorways, their stately splendour tempered by their plebeian friendliness, like saints in their niches, while an enormous usher, dressed like a verger in church, struck the flagstones with his staff as each new guest passed by. Having reached the top of the staircase, up which he had been followed by a pale-faced servant with his hair tied with a ribbon in a short pigtail, like one of Goya's sextons* or a notary in an old play, Swann passed in front of a desk at which valets seated like scriveners before huge registers stood up and inscribed his name. He then crossed a little hall which—like certain rooms arranged by their owners to serve as the setting for a single work of art, from which they take their name, and, kept deliberately bare, contain nothing else—displayed at its entrance, like some priceless effigy by Benvenuto Cellini* of a watchman, a young footman, his body bent slightly forward, showing above his red gorget a face even redder from which gushed torrents of fire, timidity, and zeal, who, piercing with his intense, impetuous, watchful gaze the Aubusson tapestries* hung before the room where the music was being performed, seemed, with his appearance of soldierly impassiveness or supernatural faith—an allegory of alarm, an incarnation of alertness, or commemoration of the call to arms—to be watching, angel or sentinel, from the tower of a castle or cathedral, for the approach of the enemy or for the Day of Judgement. Now Swann had only to enter the concert-room, the doors of which were opened for him by an usher loaded with chains, who bowed low before him as though handing him the keys of a conquered city. But he thought of the house in which he might have been at that very moment, if Odette had allowed it, and the memory of an empty milk-can he had glimpsed on a doormat wrung his heart.

Swann quickly recovered his sense of how ugly the male of the species can be when, beyond the tapestry hanging, the spectacle of the servants was followed by that of the guests. But even the ugliness of these faces, though so familiar, seemed new to him now that their features—instead of being signs of practical utility in the identification of this or that person who until then had represented a set of pleasures to pursue, annoyances to avoid, or courtesies to repay—now rested on purely aesthetic connections, on the autonomy of their lines. And in the midst of this press of men, everything, down to the monocles that many of them wore (and which previously would at most have enabled Swann to say that they were wearing monocles), released from indicating a habit, the same one for all of them, now appeared to him to be endowed with a sort of individuality. Perhaps because he now saw General de Froberville and the Marquis de Bréauté, who were chatting just inside the door, as no more than two figures in a painting, whereas they were the old, useful friends who had introduced him to the Jockey Club* and supported him in duels, the General's monocle, stuck between his eyelids like a piece of shrapnel in his vulgar, scarred, triumphant face, standing out in the middle of his forehead like the single eye of the Cyclops, looked to Swann like a monstrous wound that might have been glorious to receive but was indecent to display; whereas the monocle that the Marquis had added, as a sign of festivity, to his pearl-grey gloves, opera hat, and white tie, substituting it for the familiar pince-nez (as Swann himself did) when going out in society, bore, glued to its other side, like a natural history specimen under a microscope, an infinitesimal gaze swarming with affability, that never ceased to gleam with delight at the loftiness of the ceilings, the excellence of the entertainments, the interesting programmes, and the quality of the refreshments.

'I say, fancy seeing you! We haven't seen you for ages,' said the General to Swann. Then, noticing how drawn he looked and thinking that a serious illness might have kept him away, he added: 'You're looking very well, old chap!' while Monsieur de Bréauté exclaimed 'My dear fellow, what on earth are you doing here?' to a society novelist who had just slotted into the corner of his eye a monocle that was his sole instrument of psychological investigation and merciless analysis, and who replied with an air of mystery and self-importance, rolling the 'r's: 'I'm here as an observer!'

The Marquis de Forestelle's monocle was minute and rimless, and, as it required a constant, painful clenching of the eye in which it was encrusted like a superfluous piece of cartilage whose presence was inexplicable and its composition very rare, gave his face an expression of melancholy refinement, and made women imagine that he was capable of suffering greatly in love. But that of Monsieur de Saint-Candé, encircled by a huge ring, like Saturn, was the centre of gravity of a face that continually adjusted itself in relation to it, a face whose quivering red nose and sarcastic thick-lipped mouth attempted by their grimaces to keep up with the endless sparks of wit gleaming in the glass disc, and saw itself preferred to the most handsome eyes in the world by snobbish and depraved young women in whom it inspired dreams of artificial charms and exquisite sensual pleasures; meanwhile, behind him, Monsieur de Palancy, who with his big carp's head and bulging eyes moved slowly through the festivities clenching and unclenching his mandibles as if to orient himself, seemed to be carrying about on his person only an accidental and perhaps purely symbolic fragment of the glass of his aquarium, a part intended to represent the whole, reminding Swann, a great admirer of Giotto's *Vices* and *Virtues* at Padua,* of the figure of *Injustice*, by whose side a leafy bough evokes the forests where his lair lies hidden.

Swann had moved further into the room at Madame de Saint-Euverte's insistence, and in order to listen to an aria from *Orfeo** that was being performed on the flute, had positioned himself in a corner where, unfortunately, his view was blocked by two ladies of mature years seated next to each other, the Marquise de Cambremer and the Vicomtesse de Franquetot, who, because they were cousins, spent all their time at parties wandering about clutching their handbags and followed by their daughters, looking for each other as though at a railway station, and could never relax until they had reserved two adjacent chairs with a fan or a handkerchief: Madame de Cambremer, since she knew hardly anyone, being all the more glad to have a companion, Madame de Franquetot, who, in contrast, was extremely well-connected, thinking there was something elegant and original about showing all her fine friends that she preferred to their company an insignificant lady with whom she shared youthful memories. Full of melancholy irony, Swann watched them as they listened to the piano intermezzo (Liszt's 'Saint Francis Preaching to the Birds')* which had come after the flute, and followed the dizzy feats of the virtuoso; Madame de Franquetot appearing anxious, her eyes almost popping out of her head as if the keys over which he ran his fingers so nimbly were a series of trapezes from which he might fall from a height of two hundred feet, and at the same time casting at her companion looks of astonishment and disbelief, as if to say: 'This is amazing! I would never have thought that a man could do that!'; Madame de Cambremer, as a woman who had received a sound musical education, beating time with her head, like a metronome pendulum which swung so far and so fast from side to side (and with the sort of wild abandonment in her eyes that suggested a level of pain that had gone beyond what was bearable, can no longer be controlled, and cries out: 'I can't help it!') that her diamond earrings kept getting caught in the straps of her bodice and she was obliged to straighten the black grapes she had in her hair, while continuing to accelerate her wild oscillations. On the other side of Madame de Franquetot, but a little further forward, was the Marquise de Gallardon, absorbed in her favourite subject for reflection, namely her relationship to the Guermantes, which in her eyes and, she believed, the eyes of the world was a source of great glory as well as some shame, for the most brilliant of the Guermantes kept her at a certain distance, perhaps because she was a bore, or because she was unkind, or because she came from an inferior branch of the family, or possibly for no reason at all. When she found herself next to someone she did not know, as at this moment with Madame de Franquetot, she suffered terribly from the fact that her awareness of her kinship with the Guermantes could not be made outwardly manifest in visible characters like those which, in the mosaics in Byzantine churches, placed one beneath another, inscribe in a vertical column next to some holy personage the words he is supposed to be uttering. At this moment she was pondering the fact that, in the six years that her young cousin the Princesse des Laumes had been married, not once had she received an invitation or a visit from her. This thought filled her with anger, but also with pride; for, by dint of saying to people who expressed surprise at not seeing her at Madame des Laumes's house that it was because she risked meeting the Princesse Mathilde there—for which her ultra-Legitimist family would never have forgiven her*—she had come to believe this actually was the reason why she never visited her young cousin. Yet she remembered having asked Madame des Laumes several times whether there was some way she could meet her, but remembered this only vaguely and, in any case, more than neutralized this slightly humiliating recollection by muttering to herself: 'After all, it's not up to me to make the first move, I'm twenty years older than she is.' Fortified by these muttered words, she threw her shoulders proudly back so that they seemed detached from her torso, while her head was positioned almost horizontally upon them in a manner reminiscent of the 'restored' head of a roast pheasant that is brought to the table with all its feathers. She had been endowed by nature with a squat, plump, mannish figure; but the snubs she had received had straightened her up like those trees which, having taken root in an unfortunate position on the edge of a precipice, are forced to grow backwards to keep their balance. Obliged, in order to console herself for not being altogether the equal of the other Guermantes, to tell herself incessantly that it was because of her uncompromising principles and her pride that she saw so little of them, this thought had ended up moulding the very shape of her body and giving her a kind of bearing that passed among bourgeois ladies as a sign of breeding, and at times even generated a flicker of desire in the jaded eyes of old clubmen. If Madame de Gallardon's conversation had been subjected to those analyses which, by establishing the frequency of given words and phrases, enables one to discover the key to a coded text, it would have become clear that no expression, even the most common, recurred in it as often as 'at my cousins the Guermantes's', 'at my aunt Guermantes's', 'Ezéar de Guermantes's health', 'my cousin de Guermantes's box'. When anyone spoke to her about a celebrated personage, she would reply that, although she did not know him personally, she had seen him hundreds of times at the home of her aunt de Guermantes, but she would deliver this reply in such a glacial tone and in a voice so low that it was clear that if she did not know him personally it was because of all the stubborn and ineradicable principles which her shoulders leaned against, like the ladders on which gymnastic instructors make you stretch in order to develop your chest.

As it happened, the Princesse des Laumes, whom no one would have expected to see at Madame de Saint-Euverte's, had just arrived. To show that she was not trying to flaunt her superior rank in a salon to which she had come only out of condescension, she had entered with shoulders hunched, her arms pressed close to her sides, even though there was no crowd to squeeze through and no one attempting to get past her, and she stayed deliberately at the back of the room, with the air of being in her proper place, like a king queueing at the door of a theatre for as long as the management are unaware he is there; and, confining her gaze—so as not to seem to be indicating her presence and demanding attention—to the study of a pattern in the carpet or in her own skirt, she stood in the spot that had seemed to her the most unassuming (and from which, as she was well aware, she would be drawn by a cry of delight from Madame de Saint-Euverte as soon as the latter noticed her), next to Madame de Cambremer, whom she did not know. She stood watching her neighbour's pantomime of musical appreciation, but refrained from imitating it. This did not mean that, having for once agreed to spend a few minutes at the Marquise de Saint-Euverte's, she did not wish (so that the courtesy she was doing her hostess might count double) to show herself as agreeable as possible. But she had a natural horror of what she called 'overdoing things', and would make it very clear that she 'did not intend to' indulge in displays of emotion that were not in keeping with the 'tone' of her usual circle, but on the other hand could not help but make an impression on her by virtue of that spirit of imitation akin to timidity which is developed even in the most self-confident people by the atmosphere of a new environment, even if it is inferior to their own. She began to wonder whether Madame de Cambremer's gesticulations were not, perhaps, a necessary response to the piece being played, which bore little resemblance to the type of music she was used to hearing, and whether to refrain from such behaviour might not be taken as evidence of incomprehension with respect to the work and rudeness towards the lady of the house: so that, in order to express by a compromise both of her contradictory inclinations, at one moment she merely straightened her shoulder-straps or raised a hand to her blonde hair to secure the little balls of coral or pink enamel, flecked with diamonds, which formed her simple and charming coiffure, and the next moment she studied her impassioned neighbour with cold curiosity, while keeping time to the music for a few moments with her fan, but, so as not to forfeit her independence, against the rhythm. When the pianist had finished the Liszt intermezzo and begun a prelude by Chopin, Madame de Cambremer gave Madame de Franquetot a fond smile of knowing satisfaction and allusion to the past. As a girl she had learned how to caress those long sinuous phrases of Chopin, so free, so flexible, so tactile, which begin by seeking out and exploring a place for themselves far outside and away from the direction in which they started, far beyond the point which one might have expected them to reach, and which disport themselves in these byways of fantasy only to return more deliberately—with a more premeditated reprise, with more precision, as upon a crystal bowl that resonates until it makes you want to cry out—to strike you in the heart.

Having been brought up in a provincial household that had little contact with anyone, hardly ever going to a ball, she had become intoxicated, in the solitude of her old manor house, with the idea of all those dancing couples, imagining their movements, slowing them down, speeding them up, scattering them like flowers, even leaving the ballroom for a moment to listen to the wind blowing in the pine trees at the edge of the lake, and seeing all of a sudden, as he came towards her, more unlike anything one had ever dreamed of than an earthly lover could be, a slender young man in white gloves whose voice had a strange and false lilt to it. But nowadays the old-fashioned beauty of this music seemed stale. Having fallen, during the last few years, in the esteem of the discriminating public, it had lost its place of honour and its charm, and even those with poor taste no longer took more than moderate and unavowed pleasure in it. Madame de Cambremer cast a furtive glance behind her. She knew that her young daughter-in-law (full of respect for her new family, except regarding the things of the mind, about which, with her knowledge of Harmony and even Greek, she was especially enlightened) despised Chopin, and felt almost ill when she heard him played. But Madame de Cambremer, freed from the vigilant eye of the Valkyrie, who was sitting at a distance with a group of people of her own age, was now able to abandon herself to a few moments of sheer delight. And the Princesse des Laumes shared this delight. Though without a natural gift for music, she had had lessons fifteen years earlier from a piano teacher in the Faubourg Saint-Germain, a woman of genius who at the end of her life had been reduced to poverty and had returned, at the age of seventy, to giving lessons to the daughters and granddaughters of her old pupils. She was now dead. But her method, her lovely style of playing, came back to life sometimes under the fingers of her pupils, even those who had become in other respects very ordinary people, had given up music, and hardly ever opened a piano. And so Madame des Laumes could nod approvingly, very knowledgeably, with a true appreciation of the way the pianist was playing this prelude, which she knew by heart. The final notes of the phrase he had just begun came spontaneously to her lips. And she murmured: 'It's always so *ch*arming', with a double *ch* at the beginning of the word which was a mark of refinement and with which she felt her lips crinkling so romantically, like a beautiful flower, that she instinctively brought her eyes into harmony with them by giving them at the very same time an expression of dreamy sentimentality. Meanwhile, Madame de Gallardon was thinking how annoying it was that she had so few opportunities to meet the Princesse des Laumes, for she wanted to teach her a lesson by snubbing her. She did not know her cousin was actually there. But as Madame de Franquetot moved her head, the Princesse came into view. Immediately Madame de Gallardon rushed over to her, disturbing everybody; but although she was keen to maintain a distant and glacial manner that would remind everyone that she had no desire to be on friendly terms with a person in whose house one might find oneself coming face to face with the Princesse Mathilde, and to whom it was not for her to make advances since she belonged to 'a different generation', she decided to make up for this air of haughtiness and reserve by some simple remark that would justify her overture and force the Princesse to engage in conversation; and so, when she reached her cousin, Madame de Gallardon, with a stern expression and a hand thrust out as if trying to 'force' a card, said 'How is your husband?' in the concerned tone she would have used if the Prince had been seriously ill. The Princesse, bursting into a laugh which was peculiar to her and was intended at once to show that she was making fun of someone and also to make herself look prettier by concentrating her features around her animated lips and sparkling eyes, replied: 'Oh, he's never been better!' And she went on laughing.

Whereupon Madame de Gallardon, drawing herself up and putting on an even chillier expression, and still concerned about the Prince's health, said to her cousin:

'Oriane' (and at this point Madame des Laumes looked with an air of surprise and amusement in the direction of an invisible third party, before whom she seemed anxious to testify that she had never authorized Madame de Gallardon to call her by her first name), 'I'd be so pleased if you would stop by for a moment tomorrow evening to hear a clarinet quintet by Mozart. I'd love to know what you think of it.'

She seemed not so much to be making an invitation as asking a favour, and to want the Princesse's appraisal of the Mozart quintet as if it were a dish prepared by a new cook, whose culinary skills she was keen to have assessed by a gourmet.

'But I know that quintet, and I can tell you now . . . that I like it!'

'You know, my husband isn't well; it's his liver . . . He'd be so very pleased to see you,' resumed Madame de Gallardon, thus making it a charitable obligation for the Princesse to appear at her soirée.

The Princesse never liked to tell people she did not wish to visit them. Every day she would write notes expressing her regret at having been prevented—by an unexpected visit from her mother-in-law, by an invitation from her brother-in-law, by the Opera, by an outing to the country—from attending a soirée to which she would never have dreamed of going. In this way she gave many people the joy of believing that she was one of their friends, that she would have been glad to visit them, and that she had been unable to do so because of some aristocratic contretemps which they were flattered to see competing with their own soirée. Also, since she belonged to that witty Guermantes set in which there survived something of the quick wit, unburdened by platitudes and conventional sentiments, which goes back to Mérimée and has found its latest expression in the plays of Meilhac and Halévy,* she adapted it to her social relations, transposing it even into her style of politeness, which endeavoured to be positive and precise, to approximate to the plain truth. She would never develop at any length to a hostess the expression of her desire to attend her soirée; she thought it kinder simply to put to her a few little facts on which would depend whether or not it was possible for her to come.

'Well, the fact is,' she said to Madame de Gallardon, 'tomorrow evening I must go and see a friend who has been asking me for ages to fix a day. If she takes us to the theatre, with the best will in the world there'll be no chance that I could come to you; but if we stay in the house, since I know there won't be anyone else there, I'll be able to slip away.'

'By the way, did you see your friend Monsieur Swann?'

'What? My darling Charles is here? I had no idea. I must try to catch his eye.'

'It's funny he should come to old Saint-Euverte's,' remarked Madame de Gallardon. 'Of course, I know he's very clever' (by which she meant he was very crafty), 'but all the same—a Jew in the house of the sister and sister-in-law of two archbishops!'

'Well, I'm ashamed to say I'm not at all shocked,' said the Princesse des Laumes.

'I know he's a convert, and even his parents and grandparents before him. But they say it's the converted ones that stay more attached to their religion than the rest, that it's all for show. Is that true, do you think?'

'I have no idea about those things.'

The pianist had by now finished the prelude, the first of the two Chopin pieces he was to play, and went straight into a polonaise. But from the moment Madame de Gallardon told her cousin that Swann was in the room, Chopin himself could have risen from the grave and played his entire repertoire without Madame des Laumes paying the slightest attention. She belonged to that half of the human race in whom the curiosity the other half feels about the people it does not know is replaced by an interest in those it does. As with many women of the Faubourg Saint-Germain, the presence, in a place where she was, of another member of her set, even though she had nothing in particular to say to him, monopolized her attention to the exclusion of everything else. From that moment, in the hope that Swann would notice her, the Princesse, like a tame white mouse when a lump of sugar is offered to it and then taken away, kept on turning her face, filled with a thousand signs of complicity, with no relation to the feelings expressed in Chopin's polonaise, in the direction where Swann was standing and, if he moved, she would make a corresponding adjustment to the direction of her magnetic smile.

'Oriane, please don't be angry,' resumed Madame de Gallardon, who could never prevent herself from sacrificing her highest social ambitions, and her hope of one day dazzling the world, to the immediate, obscure, and private pleasure of saying something disagreeable, 'but there are people who claim that your Monsieur Swann is the sort of man one can't have in one's house. Is that true?'

'But surely you of all people know it's true,' replied the Princesse des Laumes, 'since you've invited him scores of times and he hasn't been to your house once.'

Then, leaving her cousin to her mortification, she burst out laughing again, scandalizing the people who were listening to the music, but attracting the attention of Madame de Saint-Euverte, who had stayed near the piano out of politeness and only now caught sight of the Princesse. Madame de Saint-Euverte was especially delighted to see Madame des Laumes because she had thought she was still at Guermantes looking after her sick father-in-law.

'Good heavens, Princesse! I didn't know you were here!'

'Yes, I've been here in my little corner, and I've been hearing such lovely things.'

'What! You've been here for quite a while?'

'Oh, yes, quite a long while, but it has seemed quite short to me; if it was long, it was only because I couldn't see you.'

Madame de Saint-Euverte offered the Princesse her armchair, but she declined, saying:

'Oh, please, no! There's no need. I don't mind where I sit.' And deliberately choosing a low seat without a back, the better to show off her lordly simplicity, she said: 'There, this pouffe is good enough for me! It will make me sit up straight. Oh dear, I'm making too much noise again; if I'm not careful, I'll get myself thrown out!'

The pianist was now forcing the pace, the musical excitement was reaching a climax, a servant was passing round refreshments on a tray and making the spoons rattle, and, as happened every week, Madame de Saint-Euverte signalled to him, without his seeing her, to go away. A newly-wed, who had been told that a young woman should never appear bored, was smiling with pleasure, and was trying to catch the hostess's eye in order to send her a look of gratitude for having 'thought of her' for such a delightful occasion. However, although she remained calmer than Madame de Franquetot, it was not without some uneasiness that she followed the music; the object of her concern, however, was not the pianist, but the piano, on which a candle, jumping at each fortissimo, seemed in danger, if not of setting its shade on fire, at least of dripping wax on to the rosewood. In the end she could bear it no longer and, mounting the two steps of the dais on which the piano was placed, rushed to remove the candle-holder. Her hands were just about to touch it when a final chord rang out, the polonaise came to an end, and the pianist stood up. Nevertheless, the young woman's bold initiative, and the brief promiscuity between her and the instrumentalist which resulted from it, produced a generally favourable impression.

'Did you see what that young woman did, Princesse?' said General de Froberville to the Princesse des Laumes, having come over to greet her as Madame de Saint-Euverte moved away for a moment. 'Quite odd, wasn't it? Is she one of the performers?'

'No, she's just some young thing by the name of Cambremer,' replied the Princesse without thinking, and then hastened to add: 'I'm only repeating what I've heard—I have no idea who she is, someone behind me was saying they're neighbours of Madame de Saint-Euverte in the country, but I don't think anyone knows them. They must be "country cousins"! By the way, I don't know whether you're on familiar terms with all the brilliant people here tonight, but I can't put a name to any of them. What do you think they do when they're not attending one of Madame de Saint-Euverte's soirées? She must have hired them along with the musicians, the chairs, and the refreshments. You must admit these guests from the Belloir agency* are most impressive. How can she have the nerve to hire all these "extras" week after week? I've never seen anything like it!'

'Ah! But Cambremer is a good name, and old too,' said the General.

'It may well be,' snapped the Princesse, 'but that doesn't mean it's *euphonious.*' She gave a special emphasis to the word, as though putting it in quotation marks, a little affectation of speech that was peculiar to the Guermantes set.

'Really? She's quite gorgeous, though,' said the General, keeping his eyes fixed on Madame de Cambremer. 'Don't you think so, Princesse?'

'She's too forward; I don't think that's very nice in such a young woman. Of course, she's not my generation,' replied Madame des Laumes, using an expression that was common to the Gallardons and the Guermantes. Then, seeing that the General could not take his eyes off Madame de Cambremer, she added, half out of spite towards the young woman, half out of indulgence towards the General: 'Not very nice . . . for her husband! I'm sorry I don't know her, seeing that you're so taken with her; I could have introduced you' (which, if she had known her, she would have made a point of not doing). 'I'll have to say goodnight soon; it's the birthday of a friend of mine today, and I must go and give her my best wishes.' Her tone of matter-of-fact modesty reduced the fashionable gathering to which she was going to the level of a tiresome ceremony which she was obliged, yet touched, to attend. 'And I have to meet Basin there, too. While I've been here, he's been seeing some friends of his; I believe you know them, they're called after a bridge—the Iénas.'

'It was the name of a victory before it was a bridge,* Princesse,' said the General. 'You know,' he went on, removing his monocle and wiping it, as he would have changed the dressing on a wound, while the Princesse instinctively looked away, 'for an old trooper like me, that Empire nobility, it wasn't the same, of course, but, for what it was, it was very fine in its own way. Those people really fought like heroes.'

'Oh, I have the greatest respect for heroes,' said the Princesse in a slightly ironic tone. 'If I don't go with Basin to see this Princesse d'Iéna, it's not because of that, not at all, it's simply because I don't know them. Basin knows them, he's very fond of them. And it's not what you might think—there's no flirting involved, there's no reason for me to object. Besides, what good does it do when I object!' she added in a melancholy voice, for everyone knew that the day after the Prince des Laumes married his ravishing cousin, he had been unfaithful to her, and had not stopped being unfaithful ever since. 'It isn't that at all, they're old friends of his, he gets on swimmingly with them and I'm very pleased for him. In any case, what he's told me about their house is enough. Can you imagine, all their furniture is "Empire"!'

'Naturally, Princesse; it was their grandparents' furniture.'

'I'm not saying it wasn't, but that doesn't make it less ugly. I understand very well that people can't always have nice things, but at least the things they have shouldn't be ridiculous. I really can't think of anything more pretentious, more bourgeois, than that horrible style—cabinets with swans' heads, like bathtubs '

'Nevertheless, I believe they do have some beautiful things; they must have that famous mosaic table that was used for the Treaty of . . .'*

'Oh, I'm not saying they haven't got a few things that are interesting from a historical point of view. But they can't be very nice . . . because they're simply horrible! I've got things like that myself, which Basin inherited from the Montesquious. Only they're in the attics at Guermantes, where nobody can see them. But, in any case, that's not the point, I'd rush round to see them with Basin, I'd even see them among all their sphinxes and brasses if I knew them, but . . . I don't know them! I was always told when I was little that it isn't polite to call on people one doesn't know,' she said, putting on a childish voice. 'So I'm just doing what I was taught. Just imagine how those good people would react if someone they don't know came bursting into their house. They might give me a very hostile reception!'

And she coquettishly enhanced the charm of the smile which this supposition had brought to her lips, by giving her blue eyes, which were fixed on the General, a dreamy, gentle expression.

'Oh, Princesse, you know full well they would be utterly delighted . . .'

'Not at all. Why would they?' she asked him very sharply, either because she did not wish to give the impression that she knew it would be because she was one of the foremost ladies in France, or in order to have the pleasure of hearing the General tell her so. 'Why? What makes you say that? It might be most disagreeable for them. I don't know, but speaking for myself, I find it tiresome enough to see the people I know, and I'm quite sure that if I had to see people I don't know, even if they had "fought like heroes", I would go mad. In any case, except when it's an old friend like you, whom one knows quite apart from that, I'm not sure that heroism gets people very far in society. I often find it boring enough to give a dinner-party, but if I had to take the arm of Spartacus . . . No, really, if I had to make up the numbers, I'd never dream of asking Vercingetorix.* I think I'd keep him for big occasions. And since I don't have any of those . . .'

'Ah, Princesse, you're not a Guermantes for nothing. You've got all the family wit!'

'People always say "the Guermantes' family wit". I've never understood why. Do you know any *others* who have it?' she added, with a burst of joyful, bubbly laughter, her features concentrated, combined in a network of animation, her eyes sparkling, blazing with a radiant sunshine of gaiety that could be kindled only by remarks, even if made by the Princesse herself, in praise of her wit or her beauty. Then she said: 'Look, there's Swann. He seems to be talking to your young Cambremer; over there, next to old Madame Saint-Euverte, can't you see him? Go and ask him to introduce you. But you'd better hurry, he's getting ready to leave!'

'Did you notice how terribly ill he's looking?' said the General.

'My dear Charles! Ah! He's coming over at last. I was beginning to think he didn't want to see me!'

Swann was very fond of the Princesse des Laumes, and the sight of her reminded him of Guermantes, the estate next to Combray, and the whole of the surrounding countryside which he loved so much and had ceased to visit so as not to be away from Odette. Using the half-artistic, half-courtly expressions which he knew the Princesse found pleasing, and which came back to him quite naturally as soon as he immersed himself in his old social milieu, and wanting anyway, for his own satisfaction, to express the longing he felt for the country:

'Ah!' he said to the company at large, in order to be heard both by Madame de Saint-Euverte, to whom he was speaking, and by Madame

des Laumes, for whom he was speaking. 'Behold the charming Princesse!
See, she has come up from Guermantes for the express purpose of
listening to Liszt's *Saint Francis of Assisi*, and has only just had time,
like a pretty little titmouse, to steal a little fruit from the plum-trees
and hawthorns to put in her hair; there are even a few dew-drops on
them still, a little of the hoar-frost that must be making the Duchess
shiver. It's very pretty indeed, my dear Princesse.'

'What! The Princesse has come up specially from Guermantes?
But that's really too much! I didn't know; I feel quite embarrassed,'
exclaimed Madame de Saint-Euverte naively, unaccustomed as she
was to Swann's wit. Then, examining the Princesse's headdress, she
said: 'Yes, you're right, it's meant to look like . . . I'm not quite sure,
not chestnuts, no—oh, it's a lovely idea! But how could the Princesse
have known what was going to be on my programme! The musicians
didn't even tell me.'

Swann, who, when he was with a woman with whom he had kept up
the habit of speaking in gallant language, usually said things in such
a delicately nuanced way that many society people found him incom-
prehensible, did not condescend to explain to Madame de Saint-Euverte
that he had been speaking metaphorically. As for the Princesse, she
exploded with laughter, because Swann's wit was highly appreciated
in her set, and also because she could never hear a compliment addressed
to her without finding it exquisitely subtle and irresistibly amusing.

'Oh, I'm so pleased, Charles, that you like my little hips and haws.
But what were you doing talking to that Cambremer woman? Is she
a neighbour of yours in the country, too?'

Madame de Saint-Euverte, seeing that the Princesse appeared
happy to chat with Swann, had moved away.

'But so are you, Princesse!'

'I am? Then they must have country houses everywhere, those
people! I'd love to be in their shoes!'

'No, not the Cambremers; her own family. She's the Legrandin girl
who used to come to Combray. I don't know whether you realize that
you are the Comtesse de Combray, and that the Chapter owes you dues.'

'I don't know what the Chapter might owe me, but I do know that
the curé touches me for a hundred francs every year, and I'd be very
pleased if he stopped! But I must say, those Cambremers have an
extraordinary name! It ends just in time, but it ends badly!' she said
with a laugh.

'And it doesn't begin any better,' Swann replied.

'Yes! The double abbreviation . . .'*

'Someone very angry and very proper didn't dare finish the first word.'

'But since he couldn't stop himself from beginning the second, he should have finished the first—then he'd have had done with it. I must say, we're making some very tasteful jokes today, my dear Charles.' Then she added, in a caressing tone: 'You know, it's such a shame I don't see you any more, I do so like talking to you. That old fool Froberville, for example, would never have understood what I meant about the Cambremers having an extraordinary name. You must admit life can be dreadful. It's only when I see you that I stop feeling bored.'

This was probably not true. But Swann and the Princesse had the same way of looking at the little things of life, the effect of which—unless it was the cause—was a great similarity in their ways of expressing themselves and even in their pronunciation. This resemblance was not easily noticeable because their voices were so utterly different. But if in one's imagination one managed to divest Swann's remarks of the sonority in which they were wrapped, of the moustache from beneath which they emerged, one realized that these were the same phrases, the same inflections, the whole general style of the Guermantes set. When it came to important matters, Swann and the Princesse could never agree about anything. But ever since Swann had become so melancholy, always in the tremulous state that precedes tears, he felt the same need to talk about his suffering as a murderer has to talk about his crime. When he heard the Princesse say that life can be dreadful, he felt as comforted as if she had been talking about Odette.

'Oh, yes! Life can be dreadful. We must see each other soon, my dear friend. What's so nice about you is that you're never cheerful. We could spend an evening together.'

'What a good idea! Why don't you come down to Guermantes? My mother-in-law would be ecstatic. People say it's very unattractive down there, but I must say I don't dislike that part of the world at all; I have a horror of "picturesque" places.'

'Yes indeed! It's delightful,' replied Swann. 'It's almost too beautiful, too alive for me just now; it's a place to be happy in. Perhaps it's because I've lived there, but there are so many things there that speak

to me! As soon as a little breeze gets up, and the cornfields begin to
stir, I feel that someone is about to appear, that I'm going to receive
some news; and those little houses by the water . . . I would be quite
miserable there!'

'Oh, look out! There's that awful Rampillon woman. She's seen
me; you must hide me. Remind me what it was that happened to her;
I get it all mixed up; she's just married off her daughter, or her lover,
I can't remember which; perhaps both . . . to each other! . . . Oh,
no, I remember now, she's been dropped by her prince . . . Pretend
you're talking to me, so that that old Bérénice* won't come over and
invite me to dinner. In any case, I must be off. Listen, my dear Charles,
now that I've seen you for once, won't you let me carry you off and
take you to the Princesse de Parme's? She'd be so pleased to see you,
and so would Basin—he's meeting me there. You know, if we didn't
get news of you from Mémé . . . Do you realize I never see you at
all now!'

Swann declined; having told Monsieur de Charlus that he would
go straight home from Madame de Saint-Euverte's, he did not want
to run the risk, by going to the Princesse de Parme's, of missing
a message that he had been hoping all evening would be brought in to
him by a servant, and that perhaps he would now get from his concierge. 'Poor Swann,' said Madame des Laumes that night to her husband, 'he's always so pleasant, but he does seem terribly miserable.
You'll see him yourself, because he has promised to come to dinner
one of these days. I do find it absurd that a man of his intelligence
should suffer over a woman like that. She isn't even interesting; I'm
told she's quite stupid,' she added, with the wisdom of people, not in
love themselves, who think that a clever man should be unhappy only
over a person who is worthwhile; which is rather like being surprised
that anyone should condescend to suffer from cholera because of so
insignificant a creature as the comma bacillus.

Swann was looking for an opportunity to leave, but just as he was
about to make his escape, General de Froberville asked him for an
introduction to Madame de Cambremer, and he was obliged to go
back into the drawing-room with him to look for her.

'I say, Swann, I'd rather be married to that little lady than slaughtered by savages! What do you say?'

The words 'slaughtered by savages' affected Swann profoundly;
and at once he felt the need to continue the conversation:

'Well, you know,' he said, 'some very fine men have died that way . . . For example, there was that navigator whose ashes were brought back by Dumont d'Urville—La Pérouse . . .'* (and Swann was at once happy again, as if he had talked of Odette). 'He was a fine character, that La Pérouse, and very interesting,' he added with a melancholy air.

'Oh yes, of course, La Pérouse,' said the General. 'He's very well-known. There's a street named after him.'

'Do you know someone in the Rue La Pérouse?' asked Swann in some agitation.

'Only Madame de Chanlivault, the sister of that fine fellow Chaussepierre. She gave a very good theatre-party the other evening. Now there's a salon that will be very chic one of these days, mark my words!'

'Ah, so she lives in the Rue La Pérouse. It's pleasant—a pretty street, and so sad-looking.'

'Not at all. You can't have been there for quite a while; there's nothing sad about it these days, there's a lot of building going on throughout that whole neighbourhood.'

When Swann finally introduced Monsieur de Froberville to the young Madame de Cambremer, since it was the first time she had heard the General's name she gave him the smile of delight and surprise with which she would have greeted him if no other name but his had ever been uttered in her presence, for as she did not know any of the friends of her new family, whenever someone was introduced to her she assumed that he must be one of them, and thinking it would be tactful to look as though she had heard such a lot about him since her marriage, she would hold out her hand with a hesitant air that was meant as proof both of the inculcated reserve she had to overcome and the spontaneous warmth of personality that enabled her to do so. And so her parents-in-law, whom she still regarded as the most eminent people in France, declared that she was an angel; all the more so because they preferred to appear, in marrying their son to her, to have yielded to the attraction of her fine qualities rather than of her great wealth.

'You clearly have the soul of a musician, Madame,' said the General, unconsciously alluding to the incident of the candle.

Meanwhile the concert had resumed, and Swann realized he would not be able to leave before the end of the new item. He was unhappy at having to remain locked among all these people whose stupidity and absurd ways struck him all the more painfully because, being unaware of his love and incapable, had they known about it, of taking any interest or of doing more than smile at it as at some childish nonsense or deplore it as sheer madness, they made it appear to him as a purely subjective state which existed for him alone, whose reality could not be confirmed by any external thing; he suffered above all, to the point where even the sound of the instruments made him want to cry out, from having to prolong his exile in this place to which Odette would never come, where no one, nothing was aware of her existence, from which she was entirely absent.

But suddenly it was as though she had entered the room, and this caused him such intense pain that he could not help clutching at his heart. What had happened was that the violin had risen to a series of high notes on which it lingered as though waiting for something, holding them in a prolonged state of expectancy, in the exaltation of already seeing the object of its expectation approaching, and with a desperate effort to try to last until its arrival, to welcome it before expiring, to keep the way open for it a moment longer, with its last remaining strength, so that it could come through, as one holds open a door that would otherwise close. And before Swann had time to understand, and say to himself: 'It's the little phrase from Vinteuil's sonata don't listen!', all his memories of the time when Odette was in love with him, which he had succeeded until now in keeping hidden in the deepest part of his being, deceived by this sudden beam of light from the time of love which they believed had returned, had taken wing, and risen to sing madly in his ears, with no pity for his present misfortune, the forgotten refrains of happiness.

In place of the abstract expressions 'the time when I was happy', 'the time when I was loved', which he had often used before now without suffering too much, for his mind had invested them only with spurious extracts of the past that preserved nothing of its reality, he now recovered everything that had fixed for ever the specific, volatile essence of that lost happiness; he saw it all again: the curled, snow-white petals of the chrysanthemums she had tossed to him in his carriage, and which he had kept pressed to his lips—the embossed address of the 'Maison Dorée' on the note-paper on which he had read: 'my hand is shaking so much that I can hardly write'—the way her eyebrows had drawn together when she said pleadingly: 'You won't leave it too long before getting in touch?'; he could smell the curling-tongs of the barber, who would crimp his hair while Lorédan went to fetch the young girl; he could feel the torrential rain that fell so often that spring, the drive home in his victoria on those icy moonlit nights; the whole network of thought-patterns, seasonal impressions, and physical reactions which had woven over a number of weeks a uniform mesh in which his body was once again held. At that time he had been satisfying a sensual curiosity by experiencing the pleasures of people who live for love alone. He had believed he could stop there, that he would not be obliged to know their sorrows too; but how small a thing Odette's charm was for him now compared with the dreadful terror thrown out from it, like a murky halo, by the immense anguish of not knowing at every moment what she had been doing, of not possessing her everywhere and always! Alas, he recalled the tone of her voice when she had exclaimed: 'But I never have anything to do! I'm always free!'—she who was never free now!—and the interest, the curiosity she had shown in his life, the passionate desire that he should do her the favour—which in fact he had then dreaded as a tedious and inconvenient waste of his time—of allowing her to be part of it; how she had had to beg him to let her introduce him to the Verdurins'; and, when he had allowed her to come and see him once a month, how she had had to tell him over and over again, before he allowed himself to give in, how delightful it would be to make a practice of seeing each other every day, a habit she longed for whereas to him it seemed only a tiresome imposition, of which she had then grown tired and finally broken off, while for him it had become such an irresistible and painful need. He had no idea how truly he spoke when, the third time he saw her, as she said to him yet again: 'But why don't you let me come more often?', he had said to her with a laugh, gallantly: 'for fear of being hurt'. Now, alas, she still wrote to him occasionally from a restaurant or hotel on note-paper that bore the establishment's printed name, but printed as if in letters of fire that burned him. 'She wrote this from the Hôtel Vouillemont. What can she have gone there for? With whom? What happened there?' He remembered the gas-lamps being extinguished along the Boulevard des Italiens, when he had met her against all hope among the wandering shades on that night which had seemed to him almost supernatural and which indeed—since it belonged to a period when he did not even have to ask himself if he would annoy her by looking for her and finding her, so sure was he that her greatest pleasure was to see him and let him take her home—was part of a mysterious world to which one may never return once its doors have closed. And Swann saw, standing motionless before that scene of remembered happiness, a wretched figure who filled him with pity because he did not recognize him at first, and he had to lower his eyes so that no one would notice they were full of tears. It was himself.

When he realized this, his pity vanished, but he was jealous of that other self she had loved, he was jealous of those men of whom he had often thought, without too much suffering, 'perhaps she loves them', for now he had exchanged the vague idea of loving, in which there is no love, for the petals of the chrysanthemum and the letterhead of the Maison d'Or, which were full of it. Then, his distress becoming too intense, he drew his hand across his forehead, let his monocle drop, and wiped its glass. If he had seen himself at that moment, he might have added, to the collection of those he had already observed, the monocle he was now removing like an importunate thought and from whose misted surface he was trying, with a handkerchief, to wipe away his cares.

There are tones in the violin—if we do not see the instrument and therefore cannot relate what we hear to its shape, which modifies its sound—so similar to those of certain contralto voices that we have the illusion that a singer has been added to the concert. When we look up we see only the wooden cases of the instruments, as delicate as Chinese boxes, but at times we are still tricked by the deceptive call of the siren; at times, too, we think we can hear a captive genie struggling deep inside the erudite, enchanted, quivering box, like a devil in a baptismal font; and at other times it is like a pure and supernatural being that goes by, unrolling its invisible message.

As though the musicians were not so much playing the little phrase as performing the rituals it required in order to make its appearance, and proceeding to the incantations necessary to obtain, and prolong for a few moments, the wonder of its evocation, Swann, who was no more able to see it than if it had belonged to an ultra-violet world, and who was experiencing something like the refreshing sense of a metamorphosis in the momentary blindness with which he was struck as he approached it, felt it to be present, like a protective goddess, a confidante of his love, who, in order to be able to come to him through the crowd and take him aside to speak to him, had assumed the disguise of this sonorous apparition. And as she passed, light and soothing as

a perfume, telling him what she had to say, every word of which he
studied closely, sorry to see them fly away so quickly, he involuntarily
made with his lips the motion of kissing the harmonious, fleeting
form as it went by. He no longer felt exiled and alone, since the little
phrase was speaking to him, talking to him quietly about Odette. For
he no longer had the impression, as he once had, that he and Odette
were unknown to the little phrase. It had so often witnessed their
moments of happiness! True, it had just as often warned him how
fragile these moments were. And in fact, whereas in those days he had
read suffering in its smile, in its limpid, disenchanted tones, he now
found in it the grace of a resignation that was almost gay. Of those
sorrows of which the little phrase used to speak to him and which,
without being affected by them, he had seen it carry along, smiling,
on its rapid and sinuous course, of those sorrows which had now
become his own, without his having any hope of ever being free of
them, it seemed to say to him, as it had once said of his happiness:
'What does it all matter? None of it means anything.' And for the first
time Swann's thoughts turned with a surge of pity and tenderness
to Vinteuil, to that unknown, sublime brother who must also have
suffered greatly. What must his life have been like? From the depths
of what sorrows had he drawn that godlike strength, that unlimited
power to create? When it was the little phrase that spoke to him about
the vanity of his sufferings, Swann found solace in that very wisdom
which, just moments before, had seemed to him unbearable when he
thought he could read it on the faces of indifferent strangers who
regarded his love as a minor aberration. For the little phrase, unlike
them, whatever its opinion of the brevity of such conditions of the
soul, saw in them something not less serious than everyday life, as
these people did, but on the contrary, something so superior that it
alone was worth expressing. The charms of an inner sadness—they
were what it sought to imitate, to recreate, and their very essence,
even though it consists in being incommunicable and appearing trivial to everyone but the one who experiences them, had been captured
and made visible by the little phrase. So much so that it caused their
value to be acknowledged, their divine sweetness savoured, by all
those same people in the audience—if they were at all musical—who
would afterwards fail to recognize these charms in real life, in every
individual love that came into being before their eyes. Doubtless
the form in which it had codified them could not be resolved into

arguments or reasonings. But ever since, more than a year before, the love of music had, for a time at least, been born in him, revealing to him many of the riches of his own soul, Swann had regarded musical motifs as actual ideas, belonging to another world, another order, ideas veiled in shadow, unknown, impenetrable to the human mind, but nonetheless perfectly distinct from one another, unequal among themselves in value and significance. When, after the Verdurin evening, he had had the little phrase played over for him again, and had sought to solve the puzzle of how it was that, like a perfume, like a caress, it took hold of him, enveloped him, he had realized that it was to the narrow intervals between the five notes that composed it, and to the constant repetition of two of them, that the impression of a sweetness, tremulously offered and withdrawn was due; but in reality he knew that he was drawing this conclusion not from the phrase itself, but from equivalents substituted, for his mind's convenience, for the mysterious entity he had perceived, before knowing the Verdurins, at that party where he had heard the sonata for the first time. He knew that the very memory of the piano falsified still further the perspective in which he saw the elements of the music, that the field open to the musician is not a miserable keyboard of seven notes, but an immeasurable keyboard as yet almost entirely unknown on which, just here and there, separated by shadows thick and unexplored, a few of the millions of keys of tenderness, of passion, of courage, of serenity, which compose it, each one as different from the others as one universe differs from another, have been discovered by a few great artists who do us the service, by awakening in us feelings that correspond to the theme they have discovered, of showing us what richness, what variety lies hidden, unbeknownst to us, within that great unfathomed and alarming night of our soul which we take to be vacuity and nothingness. Vinteuil had been one of those musicians. In his little phrase, although it might present to the intelligence an obscure surface, one sensed a content so solid, so precise, to which it gave a force so new, so original, that those who had heard it preserved it within themselves on the same footing as the ideas of the intellect. Swann referred back to it as to a conception of love and happiness whose distinctive character he recognized at once, as he would that of *La Princesse de Clèves* or of *René*,* if the titles of either of those works occurred to him. Even when he was not thinking of the little phrase, it existed latent in his mind on the same level as certain other notions without material equivalents, like the notion of light, of sound, of perspective, of physical pleasure, which are the rich possessions that diversify and adorn our inner life. Perhaps we shall lose them, perhaps they will fade away, if we return to nothingness. But for as long as we are alive, we can no more divest ourselves of our experience of them than we can do so in relation to some material thing, than we can, for example, doubt the light of the lamp we have lit and which transforms all the objects in our room, from which even the memory of darkness vanishes. In this way Vinteuil's phrase, like some theme in *Tristan*,* for example, which may also represent to us a certain emotional accretion, had espoused our mortal condition, had taken on something human that was quite affecting. Its destiny was linked to the future, to the reality of our soul, of which it was one of the most special, the most distinctive ornaments. Perhaps it is the nothingness that is real and our entire inner life is non-existent, but in that case we feel that these phrases of music, and these notions that exist in relation to that life must be nothing also. We shall perish, but we hold as hostages these divine captives who will follow us and share our fate. And death in their company is somehow less bitter, less inglorious, perhaps less probable.

Swann was, therefore, not wrong to believe that the phrase of the sonata really existed. However, though human in that respect, it belonged nevertheless to a species of supernatural creatures we have never seen, but whom, in spite of that, we recognize with delight when some explorer of the unseen succeeds in capturing one, and brings it back, from the divine realm to which he has access, to shine down for a few moments upon ours. This was what Vinteuil had done with the little phrase. Swann sensed that the composer had merely unveiled it, made it visible, with his musical instruments, following and respecting its outlines with a hand so loving, so prudent, so delicate, and so sure that the sound altered at every moment, fading to indicate a shadow, enlivened when it had to follow the track of a bolder contour. And one proof that Swann was not mistaken in believing in the real existence of this phrase, was that any lover of music with the least discernment would at once have noticed the imposture if Vinteuil, lacking the power to see its outlines clearly and to render them accurately, had added a few touches of his own here and there in order to conceal the deficiencies of his vision or the lapses of his hand.

It had disappeared. Swann knew it would reappear at the end of the last movement, after a long passage that Madame Verdurin's pianist always skipped. There were in that passage some marvellous ideas which Swann had not distinguished on first hearing the sonata but which he noticed now, as if, in the cloakroom of his memory, they had divested themselves of the uniform disguise of novelty. Swann listened to all the diverse themes that would enter into the composition of the phrase, like the premises on which an inevitable conclusion is built; he was witnessing its genesis. 'What daring!' he said to himself. 'This Vinteuil is as inspired, perhaps, as Lavoisier or Ampère,* conducting his experiments, discovering the secret laws that govern an unknown force, driving on, across a region unexplored, towards the only possible goal, the invisible team in which he has placed his trust and which he will never see!' How beautiful was the dialogue Swann heard between the piano and the violin at the beginning of the last section! The suppression of human speech, far from letting fantasy reign there, as one might have thought, had eliminated it; never had spoken language been subject to such rigid necessity, never had it known such pertinent questions, such irrefutable answers. At first the piano alone lamented, like a bird abandoned by its mate; the violin heard it and responded, as from a nearby tree. It was as at the beginning of the world, as if there were as yet only the two of them on the earth, or rather in this world removed from everything else, constructed by the logic of its creator so that there would never be more than the two of them: the world of this sonata. Was it a bird, was it the soul of the little phrase, not yet fully formed, was it a fairy—this creature invisibly lamenting, whose plaint the piano tenderly repeated? Its cries were so sudden that the violinist had to snatch at his bow to gather them up. Marvellous bird! The violinist seemed to want to charm it, tame it, capture it. Already it had passed into his soul, already the violinist's body, truly possessed, was shaking like a medium's with the presence of the little phrase. Swann knew it was going to speak one more time. And he had so completely divided himself in two that the wait for the imminent moment when he would find himself confronting it again made him shudder with one of those sobs which a beautiful line of poetry or a sad piece of news wrings from us, not when we are alone, but when we repeat them to friends in whom we can see ourselves as another person whose probable emotion affects them too. It reappeared, but this time to remain suspended in the air and play there for a moment only, as though motionless, before dying. And so Swann concentrated intently on this brief extension of its life. It was still there, like an iridescent bubble floating by itself. Like a rainbow, whose brilliance weakens, fades, then returns, and before dying away altogether, glows for a moment more gloriously than ever: to the two colours it had so far allowed to appear, it added others, chords of every hue in the prism, and made them sing. Swann did not dare to move, and would have liked to make all the other people in the room remain still too, as if the slightest movement might compromise the fragile, exquisite, supernatural magic that was so near to vanishing. No one, in fact, dreamed of speaking. The ineffable word of one man, who was absent, perhaps dead (Swann did not know if Vinteuil was still alive), breathing out above the rites of these celebrants, was enough to hold the attention of three hundred people, and made of the dais, where a soul had thus been conjured into being, one of the noblest altars on which a supernatural ceremony could be performed. So that, when the phrase had unravelled itself at last, floating in fragments in the motifs that followed and had already taken its place, if at first Swann was irritated to see the Comtesse de Monteriender, famous for her naivety, lean towards him to confide her impressions even before the sonata had ended, he could not help smiling, and perhaps also found a deeper meaning, which she could not see, in her words. Marvelling at the virtuosity of the musicians, the Comtesse exclaimed to Swann: 'It's amazing! I've never seen anything like it . . .' But then, with a scrupulous regard for accuracy, she corrected her first assertion, and qualified her remark by adding: 'anything like it . . . since the table-turning!'

From that evening on, Swann knew that the feeling Odette had once had for him would never return, that his hopes of happiness would never be fulfilled. And on the days when she again happened to show some kindness and affection towards him, if she showed him some thoughtful attention, he would note these ostensible and deceptive signs of a slight renewal of feeling with the kind of loving, sceptical concern, the desperate joy of people who, caring for a friend in the last days of an incurable illness, report as facts of great significance such things as: 'Yesterday he did his accounts himself, and he managed to spot a mistake we had made in adding up; today he ate an egg and enjoyed it—if he manages to digest it we'll try a cutlet tomorrow', although they know these things are meaningless on the eve of an inevitable death. No doubt Swann was sure that if he had now been living far away from Odette, he would eventually have lost interest in her, so that he would have been glad if she had left Paris for ever; he would have had the courage to remain; but he could not bring himself to leave.

He had often thought of it. Now that he was once again at work on his study of Vermeer, he needed to return, for a few days at least, to The Hague, Dresden, and Brunswick. He was convinced that a 'Diana with Her Companions' which had been bought by the Mauritshuis at the Goldschmidt sale as a Nicolas Maes was in fact a Vermeer.* And he would have liked to be able to examine the painting on the spot, in order to support his conviction. But to leave Paris while Odette was there, or even when she was not there—for in new places where our sensations have not been dulled by habit, we refresh and reanimate an old pain—was for him so cruel a notion that he was able to think about it constantly only because he knew he was resolved never to put it into effect. But sometimes, while he was asleep, the intention of taking the trip would come back to him—without his remembering that it was out of the question—and in his sleep he would take the trip. One night he dreamed that he was going away for a year; he was leaning out of the train window towards a young man on the platform who was weeping as he bade him farewell, and was trying to convince him to come away with him. The train began to move, he awoke in alarm, and remembered that he was not going away, that he would see Odette that evening, the next day, and almost every day thereafter. Then, still shaken by his dream, he blessed the special circumstances that had made him independent, so that he could remain near Odette, and also succeed in getting her to allow him to see her occasionally; and, as he recapitulated all these advantages—his social position; his wealth, from which she was too often in need of assistance not to shrink from contemplating a serious break with him (having even, some said, a secret hope of getting him to marry her); his friendship with Monsieur de Charlus, which in truth had never been of any great advantage to him in his dealings with Odette, but gave him the consolation of feeling that she heard flattering things about him from this mutual friend for whom she had such great esteem; and even his intelligence, which he employed entirely in devising every day a new scheme that would make his presence, if not agreeable, at least necessary to Odette—he thought about what would have become of him if he had not had all this; he thought that if, like so many men, he had been poor, humble, wretched, forced to accept any kind of work, or

tied down by his family or a wife, he might have been obliged to leave
Odette, and that dream, the terror of which was still so fresh in his
mind, might even have come true; and he said to himself: 'You don't
know when you're happy. You're never as unhappy as you think.'* But
he reflected that this existence had already lasted for several years,
that all he could now hope for was that it would last for ever, that he
would sacrifice his work, his pleasures, his friends, in fact his whole
life to the daily expectation of a meeting that could bring him no happiness, and he wondered whether he was not deceiving himself,
whether the circumstances that had favoured his love affair and kept
it from ending had not been detrimental to the whole course of his
life, whether the most desirable outcome would not in fact have been
the one which, to his great delight, had only happened in a dream: his
own departure; and he told himself that you don't know when you're
unhappy, that you are never as happy as you think.

Sometimes he hoped she would die, painlessly, in an accident, for
she was out of doors, in the streets, on the roads, from morning to
night. As she always returned safe and sound, he would marvel that
the human body was so supple and so strong, that it continued to keep
at bay, to outwit all the perils that beset it (and which to Swann seemed
innumerable now that his secret desire had assessed them), and so
allowed people to abandon themselves daily and almost with impunity to their work of mendacity, their pursuit of pleasure. And Swann
felt a bond of sympathy with Mohammed II, whose portrait by Bellini
he liked so much,* who, realizing that he had fallen madly in love with
one of his wives, stabbed her to death in order, as his Venetian biog-
rapher ingenuously says, to recover his independence of mind. Then
he would feel shocked that he should be thinking thus only of himself,
and the sufferings he had endured would seem to him to deserve no
pity since he himself had set so low a price on Odette's life.

Unable to stop seeing her altogether, if at least he had been able to
see her without any separations, his suffering would in the end have
subsided and perhaps his love would have died. And since she did not
want to leave Paris for ever, he wished she would never leave. As he
knew that her only extended absence was the annual one in August
and September, at least he had ample opportunity, several months in
advance, to dissolve the bitter thought of it in all the Time to come
which he carried within him in anticipation, and which, composed of
days identical with those of the present, flowed through his mind,

transparent and cold, nourishing his sadness but without causing him too great a pain. But that inner future, that limpid free-flowing river, was suddenly disturbed by a single remark of Odette's which, piercing Swann's heart, immobilized it like a block of ice, hardened its fluidity, froze it completely; and Swann suddenly felt he was filled with an enormous and infrangible mass that pressed on the inner walls of his being until it nearly burst; Odette had simply said, observing him with a sly smile: 'Forcheville is going on a lovely trip at Whitsun.* He's going to Egypt', and Swann had immediately taken this to mean: 'I'm going to Egypt at Whitsun with Forcheville.' And in fact, if, several days later, Swann said to her: 'About that trip you said you were going to take with Forcheville', she would answer without thinking: 'Yes, my dear boy, we're leaving on the 19th. We'll send you a post-card of the Pyramids.' Then he longed to know if she was Forcheville's mistress, to ask her point-blank. He knew that, superstitious as she was, there were some perjuries she would not commit, and besides, the fear, which had held him back up to now, of annoying Odette by questioning her, of making her hate him, had vanished now that he had lost all hope of ever being loved by her.

One day he received an anonymous letter telling him that Odette had been the mistress of countless men (several of whom it named, among them Forcheville, Monsieur de Bréauté, and the painter), and of women too, and that she frequented houses of ill repute. He was tormented by the thought that among his friends there was a person capable of sending him this letter (because certain details revealed that its author was someone who had an intimate knowledge of Swann's life). He wondered who it could be. But he had never had any suspicion with regard to the unknown actions of other people, those which had no visible connection with what they said. And when he began to wonder whether it was beneath the apparent character of Monsieur de Charlus, or Monsieur des Laumes, or Monsieur d'Orsan, that he would have to locate the uncharted region in which this ignoble act had been conceived, since he had never heard any of these men speak in favour of anonymous letters, and since everything they had ever said to him implied that they condemned them, he saw no reason to connect this infamy with the character of any one of them rather than the others. Monsieur de Charlus was somewhat eccentric, but basically good and kind; Monsieur des Laumes was a little hard, but sound and straightforward. As for Monsieur d'Orsan, Swann had never met anyone who, in even the most depressing circumstances, would approach him with more heartfelt words, in a more tactful and fitting manner. So much so that he could not understand the rather indelicate role people ascribed to Monsieur d'Orsan in the love affair he was having with a rich woman, and whenever Swann thought of him he was obliged to disregard the bad reputation which was so irreconcilable with the many clear proofs of his considerateness. For a moment Swann felt his mind clouding over, and he thought about something else in order to see things more clearly. Only then did he have the strength to return to his reflections. But now, having been unable to suspect anyone, he was forced to suspect everyone. After all, Monsieur de Charlus was fond of him, and he had a good heart. But he was a neurotic—one day he might cry on hearing that Swann was ill, and another day, out of jealousy, or anger, or acting on a sudden impulse, he might want to hurt him. Really, that kind of man was the worst of all. Of course, the Prince des Laumes was not nearly as fond of Swann as Monsieur de Charlus. But for that very reason he did not have the same susceptibilities with regard to him; and also, his was a nature which, though undoubtedly cold, was as incapable of base actions as of great ones. Swann regretted that in his life he had not formed attachments exclusively to such people. Then he mused that what prevents men from doing harm to their fellow men is goodness of heart, that really he could answer only for men whose natures were similar to his own, as was, so far as the heart was concerned, that of Monsieur de Charlus. The mere thought of causing Swann so much distress would have revolted him. But with an insensitive man, of another order of humanity, as was the Prince des Laumes, how could one begin to imagine the actions to which he might be led by motives that sprang from a totally different nature? To have a kind heart is everything, and Monsieur de Charlus had one. Monsieur d'Orsan was not lacking in heart either, and his relationship with Swann—cordial but not close, arising from the pleasure which, since they thought the same way about everything, they found in talking together—was more stable than the high-strung affection of Monsieur de Charlus, who was capable of committing acts of passion, for good or ill. If there was anyone by whom Swann had always felt himself understood and liked in a discriminating way, it was by Monsieur d'Orsan. Yes, but what of the dishonourable life he was leading? Swann regretted that he had not been more mindful of it in the past, having often confessed jokingly that he had never felt such keen feelings of sympathy and respect as in the company of a scoundrel. 'It's not for nothing,' he said to himself now, 'that when men pass judgement on their fellows, it's in terms of their actions. They are the only things that mean something, as opposed to what we say or what we think. Charlus and des Laumes may have their faults, but they are still honourable men. Orsan may not have any such faults, but he is not an honourable man. He may have acted dishonourably once again.' Then Swann suspected Rémi, who, it was true, could only have provided inspiration for the letter, but for a moment he felt he was on the right track. In the first place, Lorédan had reasons for bearing a grudge against Odette. And then, how can we not imagine that our servants, living in a situation inferior to ours, adding to our wealth and our weaknesses imaginary riches and vices for which they envy and despise us, will inevitably be led to act quite differently from the people of our own class? He also suspected my grandfather. Every time Swann had asked a favour of him, had he not always refused? Besides, with his bourgeois ideas, he might have thought he was acting for Swann's own good. Swann also suspected Bergotte, the painter, the Verdurins, and in passing admired once more the wisdom of society people in keeping their distance from those artistic circles in which such things are possible, perhaps even openly accepted as good pranks; but then he recalled some of the honest traits displayed by those Bohemians, and contrasted them with the life of expediency, almost of fraudulence, to which a lack of money, a craving for luxury, and the corrupting influence of their pleasures often drive members of the aristocracy. In short, the anonymous letter proved that he numbered among his acquaintances a person capable of villainy, but he could see no more reason why that villainy should be hidden in the unfathomed depths of the character of the man with a warm heart rather than of the unfeeling man, the artist rather than the bourgeois, the great lord rather than the valet. What criterion should one adopt to judge one's fellows? In truth, there was not a single person among those he knew who might not be capable of infamy. Must he then stop seeing them all? His mind clouded over; he drew his hands two or three times across his brow, wiped the lenses of his pince-nez with his handkerchief, and reflecting that, after all, men as good as himself associated with Monsieur de Charlus, the Prince des Laumes, and the rest, he persuaded himself that this meant, if not that they were incapable of infamy, at least that it was a necessity of life, to which everyone must submit, to associate with people who were perhaps not incapable of it. And he continued to shake hands with all the friends he had suspected, with the purely formal reservation that each one of them had possibly sought to drive him to despair. As for the actual content of the letter, he did not worry about it, because not one of the charges levelled against Odette had the faintest plausibility. Like many people, Swann had a lazy mind and lacked imagination. He knew very well as a general truth that people's lives are full of contrasts, but for each particular individual he imagined the part of his or her life of which he knew nothing as being identical to the part he knew. He imagined what he was not told on the basis of what he was told. During the times when Odette was with him, if their conversation turned to some dishonest act committed or some unworthy sentiment expressed by a third party, she would condemn them by virtue of the same principles that Swann had heard professed by his parents and to which he had always remained faithful; and then she would arrange her flowers, drink a cup of tea, or enquire after Swann's work. So Swann extended these habits to the rest of Odette's life, and saw her going through these motions whenever he wanted to picture to himself the times when she was away from him. If anyone had portrayed her to him as she was, or rather as she had been with him for so long, but with another man, he would have been distressed, because that picture of her would have seemed quite plausible. But the idea that she went to procuresses, took part in orgies with other women, and led the dissolute life of the most abject creatures—what an insane aberration, for the realization of which, thank God, the imagined chrysanthemums, the endless partaking of tea, the virtuous indignation left no room! However, from time to time he would give Odette to understand that, for some malicious reason, someone had been reporting to him about everything she did; and by making use of an insignificant but true detail which he had learned by chance, he would imply that he had accidentally divulged a tiny fragment, among a great many others, of a complete reconstruction of Odette's life which he held in his mind, thus making her suppose that he was well informed about things that in reality he did not know or even suspect, for if quite often he adjured Odette never to tamper with the truth, it was only, whether he realized it or not, so that she would tell him everything she did. No doubt, as he said to Odette, he loved sincerity, but he loved it as a procuress who could keep him informed about his mistress's life. And so his love of sincerity, not being disinterested, had not made him a better person. The truth he cherished was the truth Odette could tell him; but, to obtain that truth, he was not afraid to resort to falsehood, the very falsehood which he never stopped portraying to Odette as leading every human being to degradation. In short, he lied as much as Odette because, while unhappier than she, he was no less selfish. And she, hearing Swann tell her the things she had done, would stare at him with a look of mistrust, and put a touch of annoyance into her expression just in case, so as not to appear to be humiliated and to be blushing for her actions.

One day, during the longest period of calm he had yet been able to go through without suffering fresh attacks of jealousy, he had agreed to go to the theatre that evening with the Princesse des Laumes. Having opened his newspaper to find out what was being played, the sight of the title, *Les Filles de Marbre** by Théodore Barrière, struck him such a painful blow that he recoiled and turned his head away. Illuminated as though by footlights, in the new spot where it now appeared, the word 'marble', which he had lost the ability to distinguish, so accustomed was he to seeing it before his eyes, had suddenly become visible again, and had immediately reminded him of the story Odette had told him long ago of a visit she had paid to the Salon at the Palais de l'Industrie with Madame Verdurin, who had said to her: 'Be careful, now! I know how to melt you. You're not made of marble, you know.' Odette had sworn it was only a joke, and he had attached no importance to it at the time. But he had had more confidence in her then than he had now. And the anonymous letter had indeed alluded to affairs of that kind. Not daring to lift his eyes to the newspaper again, he unfolded it, turned a page in order not to see the words '*Les Filles de Marbre*', and mechanically began to read the news from the provinces. There had been a storm in the Channel, damage was reported in Dieppe, Cabourg, and Beuzeval.* Immediately he recoiled again in horror.

The name Beuzeval had reminded him of another place in the same area, Beuzeville, whose name is linked by a hyphen to another, Bréauté, which he had often seen on maps, but without ever noticing that it was the same as that of his friend Monsieur de Bréauté, whom the anonymous letter mentioned as having been Odette's lover. After all, in the case of Monsieur de Bréauté, there was nothing implausible about the charge; but as far as Madame Verdurin was concerned, it was a sheer impossibility. The fact that Odette sometimes lied did not mean one could assume she never told the truth, and in the remarks she had exchanged with Madame Verdurin and which she herself had described to Swann, he had recognized one of those pointless and dangerous little pleasantries which, from inexperience of life and ignorance of vice, are made by women whose very innocence they reveal and who—like Odette for instance—are least likely to feel passionate love for another woman. Whereas on the contrary the indignation with which she had denied the suspicions she had unintentionally aroused in him for a moment with her account accorded with everything he knew about his mistress's tastes and temperament. But at this moment, through one of those inspirations typical of jealous men, analogous to the inspiration which reveals to a poet or a scientist who thus far has nothing but a single rhyme or observation, the idea or law that will give them all the power they need, Swann recalled for the first time a remark Odette had made to him at least two years before: 'All Madame Verdurin thinks about these days is me! I'm her little pet. She kisses me, she wants me to go shopping with her, and to call her *tu*.' Far from seeing, at the time, any connection between this comment and the silly remark reported to him by Odette and meant to suggest some sort of depravity, he had welcomed it as proof of a warm friendship. But now the memory of Madame Verdurin's expressions of affection had suddenly blended with the memory of her unseemly conversation. He could no longer separate them in his mind, and saw them mingled in reality too, the affection lending a certain seriousness and importance to the pleasantry which, in turn, made the affection seem somewhat less innocent. He went to see Odette at her house. He sat down at a distance from her. He did not dare kiss her, not knowing whether it would be affection or anger that a kiss would provoke, either in her or in himself. He sat there, saying nothing, watching their love die. Suddenly he made up his mind.

'Odette, my dear,' he said, 'I know I'm being awful, but there are a few things I must ask you. Do you remember the idea I got into my head about you and Madame Verdurin? Tell me, was it true, with her or with anyone else?'

She shook her head, pursing her lips, a sign people often use to indicate that they will not go, because it bores them, if someone asks: 'Are you coming to watch the procession go past? Will you be at the review?' But a shake of the head usually applied to an event in the future, by that very fact, imparts a degree of uncertainty to the denial of an event in the past. Furthermore, it suggests only reasons of personal expediency rather than disapproval or moral impossibility. When he saw Odette thus signal to him that it was untrue, Swann realized it might well be true.

'I've told you. You know very well,' she added, looking irritated and unhappy.

'Yes, I know, but are you sure? Don't say, "You know very well"; say, "I have never done anything of that sort with any woman." '

She repeated his words, as though it were a school lesson, ironically, and as if she wanted to get rid of him: 'I have never done anything of that sort with any woman.'

'Can you swear it on your medal of Our Lady of Laghet?'

Swann knew Odette would never swear a false oath on that medal.

'Oh, stop being so horrible to me!' she exclaimed, swiftly sidestepping his question. 'How long is this going to go on? What's the matter with you today? You seem determined to make me hate you, make me absolutely loathe you. I wanted to have a nice time with you again, the way we used to, and this is how you thank me!'

But Swann, not letting go, like a surgeon waiting for a spasm to subside that has interrupted his operation but will not make him abandon it, continued:

'You'd be quite wrong if you thought I'd hold it in any way against you, Odette,' he said to her with a persuasive and deceptive gentleness. 'I only talk to you about things I know, and I always know much more than I say. But only you can mitigate by your confession what will go on making me hate you as long as I only have other people's word for it. Any anger I might feel has nothing to do with your actions, I forgive you everything because I love you; it's because of your duplicity, the ridiculous duplicity that makes you persist in denying things I know to be true. How can you expect me to go on loving you when I see you insisting on, swearing to, something I know is untrue? Odette, don't prolong this moment which is agony for both of us. If you want to, you can end it in a second, you'll be free of it for ever. Tell me on your medal, yes or no, if you have ever done these things.'

'But I have no idea!' she exclaimed angrily. 'Perhaps a very long time ago, without knowing what I was doing. Perhaps two or three times.'

Swann had considered in advance every possibility. Reality must therefore be something that bears no relation to possibilities, any more than the thrust of a knife into one's body bears any relation to the gradual movement of the clouds overhead, for the words 'two or three times' carved a kind of cross in the tissues of his heart. How strange that the words 'two or three times', mere words, words spoken into the air, at a distance, could so lacerate the heart, as if they had actually touched it, could make a man ill, as if he had swallowed poison. Instinctively Swann thought of the remark he had heard at Madame de Saint-Euverte's: 'I've never seen anything like it since the table-turning.' The pain he now felt was unlike anything he had thought possible. Not only because, even in his moments of deepest distrust, he had rarely imagined such an extremity of evil, but because, even when he did imagine it, it remained vague, ambiguous, not clothed in the particular horror that had arisen from the words 'perhaps two or three times', not armed with that specific cruelty, as different from anything he had ever known as a disease with which one is stricken for the first time. And yet Odette, the source of all his pain, was no less dear to him, was on the contrary more precious, as if, as his suffering increased, so did the value of the sedative, of the antidote which this woman alone possessed. He wanted to devote more care to her, as to a disease one suddenly discovers is more serious. He wanted the terrible thing she had told him she had done 'two or three times' not to happen again. To ensure this, he had to watch over Odette. People often say that when we tell a friend about the misdeeds of his mistress, we succeed only in making him more attached to her, because he does not believe what he is told; but how much more so if he does! But, Swann wondered, how could he manage to protect her? He could perhaps keep her safe from a particular woman, but there were hundreds of others, and he realized what madness had come over him when, on the evening when he had not found Odette at the Verdurins', he had begun to want something that was always impossible—to possess another person. Happily for Swann, underneath the new sufferings that had entered his soul like an invading horde, there lay a natural foundation, older, gentler, and quietly industrious, like the cells of a damaged organ that at once prepare to mend the affected tissues, or like the muscles of a paralysed limb that strive to recover their normal movements. For a time, these older, more autochthonous inhabitants of his soul employed all Swann's strength in the mysterious labour of reparation that gives one an illusion of relief during convalescence, or after an operation. This time it was not so much, as it usually was, in Swann's mind that this respite, through exhaustion, took effect, it was rather in his heart. But all the things that have ever existed in life tend to recur, and like a dying animal seized anew by the force of a convulsion that had seemed over, on Swann's heart, spared for a moment, the same agony returned of its own accord to retrace the same cross. He remembered those moonlit evenings when, leaning back in the victoria that was taking him to the Rue La Pérouse, he would voluptuously savour the emotions of a man in love, unaware of the poisoned fruit they would inevitably bear. But all these thoughts lasted no more than a second, the time it took him to raise his hand to his heart, catch his breath, and manage a smile to hide his torment. Already he was beginning to ask further questions. For his jealousy, which had taken more pains than an enemy would have done to strike this blow, to make him feel the most intense suffering he had yet known, was not satisfied that he had suffered enough, and sought to expose him to a wound that was deeper still. Thus, like a malevolent deity, Swann's jealousy inspired him, driving him on towards his ruin. It was not his fault, but Odette's alone, if at first his torment did not grow worse.

'My darling,' he said, 'it's all in the past now. Was it with anyone I know?'

'No, no, I swear it wasn't. Anyway, I think I exaggerated, I don't think I went that far.'

He smiled and went on: 'As you like. It doesn't really matter, but it's a shame you can't tell me the name. If I could picture the person it would keep me from ever thinking about it again. I say this for your sake, because then I wouldn't bother you about it any more. It's such a relief to be able to picture something in your mind! The things that are really horrible are those you can't imagine. But you've already been so nice about it, I don't want to keep on at you. I'm so very grateful to you for being so good to me. I've quite finished now. Just one more thing, though: how long ago was it?'

'Oh, Charles, can't you see you're killing me? It was all so long ago. I never gave it another thought. And now it's as if you're determined to put those ideas in my head again.' And with unconscious stupidity but deliberate spite, she added: 'A lot of good it'll do you!'

'Oh, I only wanted to know if it had happened since I've known you! It would be natural enough. Did it happen here? Can't you tell me which particular evening, so I can picture what I was doing at the time? You must realize it isn't possible that you don't remember who it was with, Odette, my love.'

'But I don't, really I don't; I think it was in the Bois one evening when you came to meet us on the island. You'd had dinner with the Princesse des Laumes,' she added, happy to give him a specific detail that would attest to her truthfulness. 'There was a woman at the next table I hadn't seen for ages. She said: "Come round behind that little rock and see how the moonlight looks on the water." At first I just yawned, and said: "No, I'm tired, I'm quite happy where I am." She insisted there had never been moonlight quite like it. "Oh, come off it!" I said. I knew very well what she was after.'

Odette was almost laughing as she related this, either because it seemed to her quite natural, or because she thought she would thereby make it seem less important, or so as not to appear humiliated. But, at the sight of Swann's face, she changed her tone:

'You're a beast, you enjoy torturing me, making me tell you lies, so you'll leave me in peace.'

This second blow was even more terrible for Swann than the first. Never had he supposed it to have been so recent, hidden from his eyes that had failed to discover it, not in a past he had not known, but in the course of evenings he could recall so clearly, evenings he had spent with Odette, which he had believed he knew all about but now seemed, in retrospect, horrible and full of deceit; among them, suddenly, there opened up a great chasm, that moment on the island in the Bois. Odette, without being intelligent, had the charm of naturalness. She had described, she had mimed the scene with such simplicity that Swann, breathless, saw everything: Odette's yawn, the little rock. He heard her answer—gaily, alas!—: 'Oh, come off it!' He felt she would tell him nothing more that evening, that no further revelation could be expected for the moment; so he said: 'My poor darling, please forgive me, I can see I've hurt you; but it's all over now, and I won't think about it any more.'

But she saw that his eyes remained fixed on the things he did not know and on that past time of their love, monotonous and sweet in his memory because it was vague, which was now being torn open like a wound by that moment on the island in the Bois, in the moonlight, after his dinner with the Princesse des Laumes. But he was so accustomed to finding life interesting—to admiring the strange discoveries one can make—that even while suffering to the point of thinking he could not endure such pain for long, he said to himself: 'Life is really astonishing; it is full of great surprises; immorality is actually more common than one would think. Here's a woman I trusted, who seems so simple, so honest in any case, even though her morals were a little loose, who seemed quite normal and healthy in her tastes; after an implausible denunciation, I question her, and the little she admits reveals far more than I would ever have suspected.' But he could not confine himself to these detached observations. He tried to form a precise estimate of the significance of what she had told him, in order to know if he ought to conclude that she had done these things often and was likely to do them again. He repeated her words to himself: 'I knew very well what she was after', 'two or three times', 'Oh, come off it!', but they did not reappear in his memory unarmed, each of them held a knife and with it struck him another blow. For a long time, just as a sick man cannot stop himself from trying repeatedly to make the motion that causes him pain, he kept saying these words to himself: 'I'm quite happy where I am', 'Oh, come off it!', but the pain was so intense that he had to stop. He was amazed that acts he had always dismissed light-heartedly as being quite trivial had now become as serious as a mortal illness. He knew many women he could have asked to keep an eye on Odette. But how could he expect them to adopt the point of view he now had and not hold on to the point of view he had had for so long, that had always guided him in love affairs, and not say to him, with a laugh: 'You awful jealous man, trying to rob other people of their pleasure'? Through what trap-door, suddenly opened, had he (who in the past had derived only refined pleasures from his love for Odette) been plunged into this new circle of hell from which he could not see how he would ever escape? Poor Odette! He did not hold it against her. She was only half to blame. Didn't people say it was her own mother who had handed her over to a rich Englishman in Nice when she was still little more than a child? But what painful truth was now contained for him in those lines from Alfred de Vigny's *Journal d'un poète* which in the past had left him quite unmoved: 'When you feel you are falling in love with a woman, you should say to yourself: Who are her friends? What kind of life has she led? All one's future happiness depends upon the answers.'* Swann was surprised that simple statements spelled out by his mind, like 'Oh, come off it!', or 'I could see very well what she was after', could hurt him so much. But he realized that what he believed to be simple statements were merely parts of the framework that still contained, and could still bring back to him, the pain he had felt when Odette was telling her story. For it was indeed the same pain that he was now feeling again. Even though he now knew—and even if, with the passage of time, he had forgotten a little, and forgiven—the moment he repeated these words to himself all his old suffering turned him once again into the person he had been before Odette had spoken: ignorant, trustful; his cruel jealousy placed him once again, so that he might be hurt all the more by Odette's confession, in the position of a man who does not yet know, and after several months this old story still bowled him over like a revelation. He marvelled at the terrible re-creative power of his memory. It was only by the weakening of that generative force, whose fecundity diminishes with age, that he could hope for an easing of his torment. But as soon as the power of any one of Odette's remarks to make him suffer seemed nearly exhausted, one of those on which Swann's mind had dwelt less until then, a remark that was almost new, would come to relieve the others and strike at him with undiminished vigour. The memory of the evening when he had dined with the Princesse des Laumes was painful to him, but it was only the core of his sickness, which spread out confusedly all around into the days before and after it. And whatever point in it he tried to touch in his memories, it was the whole of that season, during which the Verdurins had dined so often on the island in the Bois, that hurt him. So badly, that the curiosity which his jealousy kept provoking in him was gradually neutralized by his fear of the new torments he would inflict on himself by satisfying it. He realized that the entire period of Odette's life that had elapsed before she met him, a period he had never tried to picture, was not the abstract expanse he could vaguely see, but had consisted of specific years, each one filled with concrete incidents. But if he were to learn more of them, he was afraid that that past of hers, colourless, fluid, and tolerable, might assume a hideous, tangible form, a face that was individual and diabolical. And he continued to refrain from trying to imagine it, no longer from laziness of mind, but from fear of suffering. He hoped that, one day, he might at last be able to hear mention of the island in the Bois or the Princesse des Laumes without feeling the old rending of his heart, and thought it would be imprudent to provoke Odette into supplying him with more words spoken, names of places, and different circumstances which, when his suffering had barely abated, would rouse it again in another form.

But often the things he did not know, that he dreaded now to learn, were revealed spontaneously by Odette herself, and without her realizing it; in fact the gap that depravity put between Odette's real life and the comparatively innocent life which Swann had believed, and often still believed, his mistress to lead, was far wider than she realized: a depraved person, always affecting the same virtue in the eyes of the people by whom he does not want his vices to be suspected, has no gauge by which to recognize how far those vices, whose continuous growth is imperceptible to himself, are gradually drawing him away from normal ways of living. In the course of their cohabitation, in Odette's mind, along with the memory of the acts she was hiding from Swann, other actions were gradually coloured by them, infected by them, without her being able to see anything strange about them, without their seeming out of place in the particular surroundings where she kept them inside her; but if she described them to Swann, he would be horrified by the revelation of the environment they betrayed. One day he was trying, without hurting Odette, to ask her if she had ever had any dealings with a procuress. He was convinced, in fact, that she had not; the anonymous letter had lodged the idea in his mind, but in a mechanical way; it had met with no credence there, but had in fact remained there, and Swann, in order to be rid of the purely material but nonetheless awkward presence of the suspicion, wanted Odette to remove it. 'Oh, no! Not that they don't pester me,' she added with a smile of satisfied vanity, no longer able to realize it could not seem acceptable to Swann. 'There was one here yesterday who stayed more than two hours waiting for me, offered me any amount I wanted. Apparently some ambassador had said to her: "I'll kill myself if you don't bring her to me." They told her I'd gone out. In the end I went and spoke to her myself so she would go away. I wish you could have seen the way I treated her; my maid could hear me from the next room and said I was shouting at the top of my voice: "Haven't I told you?" I said. "I don't want to! That's how it is, I just don't feel like it! Really, I should hope I'm still free to do as I please! If I needed the money, I could understand . . ." The concierge has orders not to let her in again. He's to say I've gone to the country. Oh, I wish you'd been hiding somewhere. I think you'd have been pleased, my dear. Your little

Odette has some good in her, you see, even though some people don't appreciate her at all.'

Moreover, her very admissions, when she made any, of faults that she supposed he had discovered, served Swann as starting-points for new doubts rather than putting an end to the old. For they never exactly matched his suspicions. Though Odette might remove from her confession all the essentials, there remained in the accessory part something Swann had never imagined, that crushed him with its newness, and would enable him to alter the terms of the problem of his jealousy. And these admissions he could never forget. His soul bore them along, cast them aside, cradled them like dead bodies, and was poisoned by them.

On one occasion she mentioned a visit Forcheville had paid her on the day of the Paris-Murcia Fête. 'What? You already knew him then? Oh, yes, of course you did,' he said, correcting himself so as not to show that he had not known. And suddenly he began to tremble at the thought that, on the day of the Paris-Murcia Fête, when he had received from her the letter he had kept so carefully, she had perhaps been having lunch with Forcheville at the Maison d'Or. She swore she had not. 'But the Maison d'Or does remind me of something or other which I found out later wasn't true,' he said in order to frighten her. 'Yes, that I hadn't been there at all that evening when I told you I had just come from there, and you had been looking for me at Prévost's,' she replied (thinking from his manner that he knew this) with a decisiveness in which there was, not cynicism, but rather timidity, a fear of upsetting Swann, which out of self-respect she wanted to hide, as well as a desire to show him that she was capable of being frank. And so she struck with the precision and force of an executioner, though quite without cruelty, for she was not conscious of the hurt she was causing Swann; and she even began to laugh, but perhaps, it is true, chiefly so as not to appear apologetic or embarrassed. 'It's quite true, I hadn't been to the Maison Dorée; I was coming away from Forcheville's house. I actually had been to Prévost's, I didn't make that up, and he met me there and asked me to come in and look at his engravings. But someone else came to see him. I told you I was coming from the Maison d'Or because I was afraid you would be annoyed. You see? That was rather kind of me, wasn't it? Even if it was wrong of me, at least I'm telling you all about it now. What would I have to gain by not telling you I had lunch with him the day of the Paris-Murcia Fête, if it was true? Especially since, at the time, we didn't know each other very well, did we, darling?' He smiled at her with the sudden, craven weakness of the broken creature these crushing words had made of him. So, even during the months he had never dared to think about again because they had been too happy, during those months when she had loved him, she was already lying to him! Besides the time (the first evening they had 'done a cattleya') when she had told him she had just come from the Maison Dorée, how many others there must have been, each of them also concealing a lie which Swann had not suspected. He remembered that one day she had said to him: 'I would just tell Madame Verdurin my dress wasn't ready, or my cab came late. One can always think of some excuse.' From him too, probably, when she had murmured the little phrases that explain a delay or justify changing the time of a meeting, they must often have concealed, without his suspecting it then, something she was going to do with another man, a man to whom she had said: 'I'll just tell Swann my dress wasn't ready, or my cab came late. One can always think of some excuse.' And beneath all Swann's most tender memories, beneath the simplest words Odette had said to him in those early days, which he had believed like the words of the gospel, beneath the daily actions she had recounted to him, beneath the most ordinary places, her dressmaker's apartment, the Avenue du Bois, the Hippodrome, he could sense, concealed within the superfluity of time which even in the busiest days still leaves some play, some room, and can serve as hiding places for certain actions, he could sense the intrusion of a possible undercurrent of lies that debased all that had remained most dear to him (his best evenings, the Rue La Pérouse itself, which Odette must always have left at other hours than those she had reported to him), spreading everywhere a little of the murky horror he had felt on hearing her admission about the Maison Dorée, and, like the loathsome creatures in the Desolation of Nineveh,* dismantling stone by stone his entire past. And now, if he turned away each time his memory spoke the cruel name of the Maison Dorée, it was because what it now recalled was no longer, as but recently at Madame de Saint-Euverte's party, a happiness he had long since lost, but an unhappiness of which he had only just become aware. Then the same thing happened with the name of the Maison Dorée as with that of the island in the Bois, it gradually lost its power to inflict pain on Swann. For what we believe to be our love, or our jealousy, is not a single passion, continuous and indivisible. It is composed of an infinity of successive loves, of different jealousies, which are ephemeral but by their uninterrupted multiplicity give the impression of continuity, the illusion of unity. The life of Swann's love, the fidelity of his jealousy, were formed of the death, the infidelity, of innumerable desires, innumerable doubts, all of which had Odette as their object. If he had not seen her for a long time, those that died would not have been replaced by others. But the presence of Odette continued to sow in Swann's heart alternate seeds of affection and suspicion.

On certain evenings she would suddenly be full of affection towards him again, and would warn him severely that he ought to take advantage of it right away, under penalty of not seeing it repeated for years to come; they had to go back to her house immediately to 'do a cattleya', and this desire which she claimed to feel for him was so sudden, so inexplicable, so imperious, the caresses she lavished on him so demonstrative and so unwonted that this brutal and improbable fondness made Swann as unhappy as a lie or an unkindness. One evening when he had once again, in obedience to her command, gone home with her and she was kissing him and whispering to him with a passion quite unlike her usual coldness, he suddenly thought he heard a noise; he got up, looked everywhere, found no one, but could not bring himself to lie down again next to her, whereupon she flew into a rage, broke a vase, and said to Swann: 'It's impossible to do anything right with you!' And he was left wondering whether she had not hidden some man in the room with the aim of provoking his jealousy or inflaming his senses.

Sometimes he visited brothels in the hope of learning something about her, though without daring to say her name. 'I've got a nice little one I know you'll like,' the Madam would say. And he would stay there for an hour chatting gloomily to some poor girl who was surprised that he went no further. One who was very young and beautiful said to him one day: 'What I'd like would be to find a man who'd be a real friend to me; then he could be sure I'd never go with another man again.'

'Really? Do you think it's possible for a woman to be touched that a man loves her, and never be unfaithful to him?' Swann asked anxiously.

'Oh yes! It would all depend, though, on what she's like!'

Swann could not help saying to these girls the sorts of things the Princesse des Laumes would have enjoyed. To the one who was looking for a friend, he said with a smile: 'How nice, you've put on blue eyes to go with your sash.'

'And you too, you're wearing blue cuffs.'

'What a nice conversation we're having, in a place like this! I'm not boring you, am I? Or stopping you from doing something else?'

'No, I've got plenty of time. If you'd been boring me, I'd have said so. I like listening to you.'

'I'm very flattered . . . Aren't we having a nice little chat?' he said to the Madam, who had just come in.

'Yes, that's just what I was thinking to myself. How good they're being, I thought! People are coming here now just to talk. The Prince was telling me just the other day that it's much nicer here than at his wife's house. It seems that nowadays all the society women put on such airs. It shouldn't be allowed! But I'll leave you in peace, I know when I'm not wanted.' And she left Swann alone with the girl with blue eyes. But soon he stood up and took his leave. She no longer interested him, she did not know Odette.

The painter had been unwell, and Dr Cottard recommended that he go on a sea-voyage; several of the faithful said they would go with him; the Verdurins could not face the prospect of being left alone, they rented a yacht, then purchased it; thus Odette went on frequent cruises. Each time she had been gone for a little while, Swann felt he was beginning to detach himself from her, but as if this mental distance were proportional to the physical distance, as soon as he heard that Odette was back, he could not rest without seeing her. Once, having gone off for only a month, so they thought, either because they were tempted in the course of the journey, or because Monsieur Verdurin had cunningly arranged things beforehand to please his wife and had informed the faithful only bit by bit as they went along, from Algiers they went to Tunis, then to Italy, then to Greece, to Constantinople, to Asia Minor. The trip had lasted for nearly a year. Swann felt perfectly relaxed, almost happy. Even though Madame Verdurin had tried to persuade the pianist and Dr Cottard that the aunt of the one and the patients of the other had no need of them, and that in any case it was unwise to let Madame Cottard return to Paris which, Monsieur Verdurin assured them, was in the throes of a revolution, she was obliged to grant them their freedom at Constantinople.

And the painter left with them. One day, shortly after the return of the three travellers,* Swann, seeing an omnibus go by heading for the Luxembourg, where he had some business, had jumped on and found himself sitting opposite Madame Cottard, who was doing the rounds of the ladies whose 'day' it was; she was in full dress uniform, an ostrich feather in her hat, a silk dress, a muff, a parasol, a calling-card case, and freshly laundered white gloves. Arrayed with these insignia, in fine weather she would go on foot from one house to the next in the same neighbourhood, but when she had to proceed to a different neighbourhood would use the omnibus system, changing as necessary. For a few minutes, before the woman's native amiability broke through the starched surface of the petty bourgeoisie, and not being sure whether she ought to talk about the Verdurins to Swann, she produced quite naturally, in her awkward, slow, soft voice, which from time to time was drowned out completely by the rattling of the omnibus, remarks selected from those she had heard and repeated in the twenty-five houses whose stairs she climbed in the course of a day.

'I don't need to ask you, Monsieur, if a man so in the swim as yourself has been to the Mirlitons to see the portrait by Machard* which the whole of Paris is rushing to see? Do tell me what you think of it. Whose camp are you in, those who approve or those who don't? It's the same in every house now, the only thing they talk about is Machard's portrait; you aren't fashionable, you aren't really cultured, you aren't up-to-date unless you can give your opinion of Machard's portrait.'

Swann replied that he had not seen the portrait, and Madame Cottard was afraid she had offended him by obliging him to confess it.

'Well, that's all right! At least you admit it straightaway, you don't think you're in disgrace because you haven't seen Machard's portrait. I think that's admirable of you. Well, I have seen it. Opinion is divided, you know, some people think it's too polished, rather like whipped cream, but I think it's just perfect. Of course, she's not like the blue-and-yellow women of our friend Biche. But I must tell you frankly (you'll think I'm terribly old-fashioned, but I always say what I think): I don't understand his work. Of course, I can see the good points in his portrait of my husband, it's not as strange as what he usually does, but even so he had to go and give him a blue moustache. Whereas Machard! Just imagine, the husband of the friend I'm just on my way to see now (which has given me the great pleasure of your company) has promised her that, if he's elected to the Academy (he's one of the Doctor's colleagues) he'll get Machard to paint her portrait. Now that's a really lovely idea! I've got another friend who says she really prefers Leloir.* I'm just an ignoramus, and for all I know Leloir may be better technically. But I think the most important thing in a portrait, especially when it's going to cost 10,000 francs, is that it should be a good likeness, and nice to look at.'

Having made these pronouncements, to which she had been inspired by the loftiness of her plume, the monogram on her card-case, the little number inked inside her gloves by the cleaner, and the embarrassment of speaking to Swann about the Verdurins, Madame Cottard, seeing that the omnibus was still a fair distance away from the corner of the Rue Bonaparte, where the driver was to let her off, listened to her heart, which counselled other words.

'Your ears must have been burning, Monsieur,' she said, 'while we were on our voyage with Madame Verdurin. We talked about you all the time.'

This came as a great surprise to Swann, for he assumed his name was never uttered in the presence of the Verdurins.

'Of course,' Madame Cottard went on, 'Madame de Crécy was there, and that says it all. Wherever Odette is, she can never go for long without talking about you. And you can well imagine it's never unfavourably. What! You don't believe me?' she said, seeing that Swann looked sceptical.

And, carried away by the sincerity of her conviction, and giving no negative dimension to the word, which she used purely in the sense in which one employs it to speak of the affection between friends, she continued: 'She *adores* you! Oh, I'm quite sure one could never say a bad word about you in front of her! That would spell trouble! Apropos of anything at all, if we were looking at a painting, for instance, she would say: "Now, if he was here, he'd be able to tell us whether it's genuine or not. There's nobody like him for that." And she'd be constantly saying: "I wonder what he's doing at this moment? If only he would do a little work! It's dreadful that a man with such gifts should be so lazy." (You'll forgive me, won't you?) "I can see him now, he's thinking about us, he's wondering where we are." And one thing she said I found quite charming: Monsieur Verdurin said to her: "How on earth can you see what he's doing at this moment, when he's a thousand miles away?" And Odette replied: "To the eye of a friend, nothing is impossible." No, I swear, I'm not saying this just to flatter you; you have a true friend in her, such as you don't often find. I can tell you, too, that if you don't know it, you're the only one who doesn't. Madame Verdurin told me as much herself on our last day with them (you know how it is, one always talks more freely just before saying goodbye): "I'm not saying Odette isn't fond of us, but anything we might say to her doesn't count for much compared to what Monsieur Swann might say." Oh, my goodness! The driver's stopping for me! I've been chatting away so much, I nearly missed the Rue Bonaparte . . . Would you be so kind as to tell me if my feather's straight?'

And Madame Cottard withdrew from her muff, and proffered to Swann a white-gloved hand from which there escaped, along with a transfer ticket, a vision of upper-class life that filled the omnibus, mingled with the smell of newly cleaned kid. And Swann felt himself overflowing with affection for her, as much as for Madame Verdurin (and almost as much as for Odette, for the feeling he now had for her, being no longer mingled with pain, was hardly love any more), while from the platform of the omnibus he followed her with fond eyes as she boldly made her way up the Rue Bonaparte, her plume erect, her skirt lifted in one hand, while in the other she held her parasol and her card-case with its monogram fully displayed, her muff dancing in front of her as she went.

To counteract the morbid feelings Swann had for Odette, Madame Cottard, in this respect a better physician than her husband would have been, had grafted onto them other feelings, normal ones, of gratitude and friendship, feelings which in Swann's mind would make Odette appear more human (more like other women, because other women too could inspire these feelings in him), and would hasten her final transformation into the Odette he had loved with untroubled affection, who had brought him back one evening after a party at the painter's home to drink a glass of orangeade with Forcheville, the Odette with whom Swann had glimpsed the possibility of living in happiness.

In the past, having often thought with terror that one day he would cease to be in love with Odette, he had resolved to be vigilant and, as soon as he felt his love was beginning to leave him, to cling to it and hold it back. But now, to the weakening of his love there corresponded a simultaneous weakening of his desire to remain in love. For a person cannot change, that is to say become someone else, while continuing to be governed by the feelings of the person they no longer are. Occasionally a name glimpsed in a newspaper, that of one of the men he thought might have been Odette's lovers, revived his jealousy. But it was very mild, and as it proved to him that he had not yet completely emerged from the time when he had suffered so much—but when he had also known so voluptuous a way of feeling—and that the hazards of the road ahead might still enable him to catch a furtive, distant glimpse of its beauties, this jealousy actually gave him a pleasant thrill, just as to the sad Parisian leaving Venice to return to France a last mosquito proves that Italy and the summer are still not too remote. But more often than not, when he made the effort, if not to remain in that particularly distinctive period of his life from which he was emerging, at least to retain a clear view of it while he still could, he discovered that already it was not possible; he would have liked to observe, as if it were a landscape about to disappear, that love which he had just left behind; but it is so difficult to assume a kind of double vision and create for oneself an accurate representation of a feeling one no longer has that soon, darkness gathering in his brain, he could see nothing at all, gave up looking, took off his pince-nez, wiped its lenses; he told himself that it would be better to rest a little, that there would be time enough later on, and settled back with the incuriosity, the torpor of the drowsy traveller who pulls his hat down over his eyes in order to sleep in the railway carriage as he feels it carrying him faster and faster away from the country where he has lived for so long and which he had vowed not to let slip past without giving it a last farewell. Indeed, like the same traveller if he does not wake until he is back in France, when Swann chanced upon proof close at hand that Forcheville had been Odette's lover, he realized that it caused him no pain, that his love was now far away, and he was sorry that he had had no warning of the moment when he was about to leave it behind for ever. And just as, before kissing Odette for the first time, he had tried to imprint on his memory the face which had been familiar to him for so long and was about to be transformed by the memory of that kiss, so he would have wanted, in his thoughts at least, to have been able to make his farewells, while she still existed, to the Odette who had inspired him with love and jealousy, to the Odette who had made him suffer and whom he would now never see again. He was mistaken. He did see her again, one more time, a few weeks later. It was while he was asleep, in the twilight of a dream. He was walking with Madame

Verdurin, Dr Cottard, a young man in a fez whom he could not identify, the painter, Odette, Napoleon III, and my grandfather, along
a path that followed the line of the coast and overhung the sea, at
times by a great height, at others by just a few metres, so that they
were constantly climbing and descending; those who were descending were already no longer visible to those who were still climbing;
what little daylight remained was failing, and it seemed as though
they were about to be shrouded in darkest night. At times the waves
leapt right up to the edge, and Swann could feel the spray of icy water
on his cheek. Odette told him to wipe it off, but he could not, and was
embarrassed by this in front of her, as he was embarrassed to be in his
nightshirt. He hoped that, in the darkness, no one would notice, but
Madame Verdurin gave him a long stare of surprise during which he
saw her face change shape, her nose grow longer, and she sprouted
a large moustache. He turned away to look at Odette, her cheeks were
pale, with little red spots, her features drawn, ringed with shadows,
but she was looking at him with eyes full of tenderness that were
about to fall upon him like teardrops, and he felt he loved her so much
that he would have liked to take her away with him at once. Suddenly
Odette turned her wrist, glanced at a tiny watch, and said: 'I must go.'
She took leave of everyone, in the same manner, but without taking
Swann aside, without telling him where they were to meet that evening, or another day. He did not dare to ask her; he would have liked
to follow her but was obliged, without turning back towards her, to
answer with a smile a question from Madame Verdurin, but his heart
was pounding horribly, he felt he hated Odette, he would gladly have
gouged out those eyes that he had loved so much just a moment ago,
and crushed those pale cheeks. He walked on up the slope with
Madame Verdurin, which meant that with each step he moved further
away from Odette, who was going back down the way they had come.
One second later she had been gone for hours. The painter remarked
to Swann that Napoleon III had disappeared a moment after she had.
'They obviously arranged it in advance,' he added. 'They must have
met at the foot of the cliff, but they didn't want to say goodbye at the
same time for the sake of appearances. She's his mistress.' The young
stranger began to cry. Swann tried to comfort him. 'You know, what
she's doing is for the best,' he said, drying his eyes and taking off his
fez to make him feel more at ease. 'I told her dozens of times she
should do it. So why be upset about it? He's the one who can really

understand her.' Thus did Swann reason with himself, for the young man he had failed to identify at first was also himself; like certain novelists, he had divided his personality between two characters, the one having the dream, and the other he saw before him wearing a fez.

As for Napoleon III, it was to Forcheville that a vague association of ideas, then a certain change in the Baron's usual features, and lastly the broad ribbon of the Legion of Honour on his chest, had made him give that name; but in reality, and in everything that the character in the dream represented and reminded him of, it was indeed Forcheville. For, from incomplete and changing images, Swann in his sleep drew false deductions, having for a moment such creative power that he reproduced himself by simple division, like certain lower organisms; with the warmth he felt in his own palm he modelled the hollow of an imaginary hand which he thought he was holding, and from feelings and impressions of which he was not yet conscious he produced peripeteias of a sort which, through their sequential logic, would engender at just the right moment in his sleep the person required to receive his love or make him wake up. In an instant utter darkness descended upon him, an alarm sounded, people ran past him, escaping from their blazing houses; Swann heard the sound of the surging waves, and of his own heart, which with equal violence was pounding anxiously in his breast. Suddenly these palpitations quickened, he felt an inexplicable pain and nausea; a peasant, covered in burns, called out as he ran: 'Come and ask Charlus where Odette ended up this evening with her friend. He used to go about with her at one time, and she tells him everything. It's them that started the fire.' It was his valet, who had come to wake him and was saying:

'Monsieur, it's eight o'clock and the hairdresser is here. I've told him to come back in an hour.'

But these words, reaching Swann through the waves of sleep in which he was submerged, had reached his consciousness only by undergoing that refraction that causes a ray of light in the depths of water to appear to be a sun, just as, a moment earlier, the sound of the doorbell, resounding in the depths with the sonority of an alarm, had given birth to the episode of the fire. Meanwhile, the scene before his eyes turned to dust, he opened his eyes, heard one last time the sound of a wave in the sea as it receded. He touched his cheek. It was dry. And yet he could remember the sensation of the cold spray and the taste of the salt. He got out of bed and dressed. He had asked

the hairdresser to come early because he had written to my grandfather
the day before to say he would be going to Combray in the afternoon, having learned that Madame de Cambremer—Mademoiselle
Legrandin—was spending a few days there. The association in his
memory of the charm of that young face with the charm of a countryside he had not visited for so long offered him a combined attraction
that had made him decide to leave Paris for a few days at least. As the
different chance events that bring us into contact with certain people
do not coincide with the time during which we are in love with them,
but, overlapping it, may occur before love has begun and may be
repeated after it has ended, the earliest appearances in our lives of
a person destined to attract us later on assume retrospectively in our
eyes the significance of an omen, a portent. This was how Swann had
often looked back at the image of Odette when he met her at the theatre,
on that first evening when he had not dreamed he would ever see her
again—and how he now recalled the party at Madame de Saint-
Euverte's at which he had introduced General de Froberville to
Madame de Cambremer. So many are our interests in life that it is not
uncommon, on the self-same occasion, for the foundations of a happiness that does not yet exist to be laid down alongside the aggrava-
tion of a sorrow from which we are still suffering. And undoubtedly
this could have happened to Swann elsewhere than at Madame de
Saint-Euverte's. Who indeed can say whether, had he found himself
elsewhere that evening, if other happinesses, other sorrows might not
have come to him, which later would have appeared to him to have
been inevitable? But what did seem to him to have been inevitable was
what had taken place, and he was not far short of seeing something
providential in the fact that he had decided to go to Madame de Saint-
Euverte's party, because his mind, anxious to admire life's rich possibilities, and incapable of engaging for long with a difficult question,
such as the question of what was most to be wished for, felt that in
the sufferings he had experienced that evening and in the pleasures,
as yet unsuspected, that were already germinating—between which
the balance was too difficult to establish—there was a sort of necessary
connection.

But while, an hour after he had woken, he was giving instructions
to the hairdresser to see that his newly cut hair should not become
disarranged on the train, he thought about his dream again, and
saw once again, as he had felt them close behind him, Odette's pale

complexion, her too thin cheeks, her drawn features, her tired eyes, everything that—in the course of the successive expressions of affection which had made of his abiding love for Odette a long oblivion of the first image he had formed of her—he had ceased to notice since the earliest days of their affair, days to which, no doubt, while he slept, his memory had returned to seek their exact sensation. And with the intermittent boorishness that reappeared in him as soon as he was no longer unhappy and his moral standards dropped accordingly, he exclaimed to himself: 'To think I've wasted years of my life, that I wanted to die, that I felt my deepest love, for a woman who didn't really appeal to me, who wasn't my type!'

EXPLANATORY NOTES

3 *play Wagner as well as that . . . Potain*: the music of the German composer
Richard Wagner (1813–83) became particularly popular in France in the
late 1870s. Francis Planté (1839–1934) was a French pianist and composer
whose concerts drew significant audiences in the 1870s; Anton
Grigorievitch Rubinstein (1825–94) was one of the finest pianists of the
nineteenth century and founded the conservatories of St Petersburg and
Moscow. Pierre-Charles-Edouard Potain (1825–1901) was a celebrated
cardiologist elected to the French Academy of Medicine in 1882 and to the
Institut de France in 1893. That Madame Verdurin should hold that her
'young pianist' and Dr Cottard are 'streets ahead' of these luminary figures in their respective fields is an early indication of the somewhat blin-
kered over-confidence of the hostess in her coterie.

Madame de Crécy: Odette, as the narrator learns much later, in *The Captive*,
goes at this time by the name of Madame de Crécy as the result of an earlier marriage to Pierre de Verjus, Comte de Crécy, a man whose wealth,
according to the narrator's source, Odette drained to the last centime
before separating from him.

4 *ride of the Valkyrie . . . prelude to Tristan*: the Ride of the Valkyries (the plural is
now generally used) is one of Wagner's best-known compositions: it features at the opening of the third act of *Die Walküre*, the second opera in
Wagner's four-part epic cycle *Der Ring des Nibelungen* (*The Ring of the
Nibelung*, first performed as a cycle in 1876). 'Tristan' refers to Wagner's
earlier, hugely influential opera, *Tristan and Isolde*, first performed in
1865.

5 *fishing for compliments*: Odette is in the habit of dropping English words
and phrases into conversation, an affectation which she believes brings
an allure of culture and mystique. We have italicized these where they
appear in the text.

6 *naturalization papers*: the mention here of official documents confirming
Swann's status as a naturalized French citizen is a reminder of his complex identity as Jewish, French, and as an unusual individual who moves
back and forth between quite distinct social milieux.

8 *when I began to take an interest*: this is the first of a small number of intru-
sions of the first-person pronoun into the narration of *Swann in Love*,
which is otherwise focalized exclusively on Charles Swann. The 'I' in
question (as outlined in the Introduction) is the narrator-hero of *In Search of
Lost Time*, the much longer novel of which *Swann in Love* is part. Since its
events pre-date the birth of the narrator of Proust's longer novel, *Swann
in Love* is effectively a lengthy flashback, which fills in the backstory to the
life of Charles Swann, who is an influential figure for Proust's narrator.

9 *Quel est donc ce mystère?* | *Je n'y puis rien comprendre*: 'What then is this mystery? | I can't make head nor tail of it.' The grandfather here is quoting lines from the end of the first act of *La Dame Blanche* (1825), a comic opera by François-Adrien Boieldieu, with a libretto by Eugène Scribe based on scenes from a variety of works by Sir Walter Scott.

Vision fugitive: 'fugitive vision'. Allusion to an aria sung by Herod in Jules Massenet's opera *Hérodiade* (1881).

Dans ces affaires | *Le mieux est de ne rien voir*: 'in these matters | it is best not to see anything'. A quotation from the closing lines of André Grétry's comic opera *Amphitryon* (1786), which itself echoes Molière's comedy of the same title. By humming snatches of music from works that deal with complex amorous affairs involving mystery, betrayal, and deception, the narrator's grandfather is gently mocking Swann's way of conducting his own affairs.

12 *Vermeer of Delft*: Johannes (or Jan) Vermeer (1632–75) is recognized as one of the finest painters of the Dutch Golden Age. Little known in his life-time and with only thirty-four works attributed to his name, Vermeer was rediscovered by scholars in the nineteenth century. Proust saw the *View of Delft* (1660–1) during a trip to Holland in 1902 and again towards the end of his life at an exhibition in Paris in 1921. In *The Captive*, the fifth volume of *In Search of Lost Time*, in a characteristic moment of one art-form illuminating another, the fictional writer Bergotte experiences a blissful aesthetic revelation of how he should have written his novels whilst contemplating the *View of Delft*, shortly before expiring in front of the bewitching canvas.

Areopagus: a large outcrop of rock north-west of the Acropolis in Athens, Greece, which, prior to the fifth century BC, served as the site of the council of elders of the city. It later became the site of criminal trials. Odette's reference to a frog here is unclear: a number of Jean de la Fontaine's *Fables* (1668–94) include frogs, such as 'Les grenouilles qui demandent un roi' ('The frogs who desired a king'), which is a rewriting of one of Aesop's fables, but none features the Areopagus.

15 *Sarah Bernhardt*: 'La divine Sarah', as she came to be known, was the foremost theatrical actress of her era (1844–1923) and a cultural icon not only in France but across the globe, as a result of her touring widely. Bernhardt is referred to on a number of occasions in *In Search of Lost Time*; she coexists with the actress 'La Berma', a fictional creation whose life displays many parallels with that of Bernhardt. 'Golden voice' ('la voix d'or') is the name reportedly given to the actress by Victor Hugo after her rousing performance in the role of the queen in his play *Ruy Blas* in 1872.

20 *the Ninth . . . the Meistersingers*: just as she holds her pianist to be better than the most lauded practitioners of the time, as we learn on the opening page of *Swann in Love*, here, by mentioning the finale of Beethoven's *Ninth Symphony* (1824, the last he completed in his lifetime) and the overture to Wagner's *Die Meistersinger von Nürnburg* (*The Mastersingers of Nuremburg*,

first performed 1868), Madame Verdurin is placing the sonata she has 'discovered' in the company of the very best-known parts of some of the most influential and celebrated musical compositions of her century.

neurasthenic symptoms: neurasthenia was a category used in the late nineteenth and early twentieth centuries to describe a range of ailments and complaints believed to be related to nervousness and often suffered in combination. Neurasthenia was the subject of a medical self-help book published by Proust's father in collaboration with Gilbert Ballet in 1897: *L'Hygiène du neurasthénique* (*How to Live with Neurasthenia*). Proust himself displayed many symptoms that contemporary medicine diagnosed as neurasthenic, and the condition was often associated with hypersensitivity of the sort repeatedly displayed by the protagonist of *In Search of Lost Time*.

21 *Beauvais*: the name of the town in Picardy, in Northern France, is used attributively to describe tapestries, and furniture (often upholstered with tapestry), manufactured there since the seventeenth century. The Director of the Beauvais tapestry works produced a series of designs drawing on La Fontaine's *Fables* in the 1730s, though none of these includes Madame Verdurin's 'Bear and the Grapes'. She (or Proust) may be misremembering La Fontaine's 'L'ours et l'amateur des jardins' ('The Bear and the Gardener') or 'Le renard et les raisins' ('The Fox and the Grapes').

22 *sine materia*: without substance (Latin). The phrase encapsulates the immaterial, evanescent nature of the pleasure imparted by the experience of listening to a piece of music.

25 *Vinteuil*: first encountered in 'Combray' as the old piano teacher who lives at Montjouvain, Vinteuil is a fictional figure (like the painter, Elstir, and the novelist, Bergotte).

26 *di primo cartello*: Italian term relating to performers of the very highest quality, who take 'top billing'.

28 *Gambetta's funeral*: Léon Gambetta (1838–82), lawyer and political leader, Prime Minister of France 1881–2; his state funeral took place on 6 January 1883.

Les Danicheff: a play first performed in 1876, *Les Danicheff* was a collaboration between Pierre de Corvin-Koukowsky and Alexandre Dumas *fils*.

where Monsieur Grévy lives: Jules Grévy (1807–91), President of France 1879–87.

31 *Peter De Hooch*: (1629–84), a contemporary of Vermeer and a major figure in seventeenth-century Dutch painting.

34 *Notre-Dame de Laghet*: Laghet is a place of Christian pilgrimage in the Alpes-Maritimes, near Nice where Odette used to live; the church and monastery were founded in the seventeenth century.

35 *Sistine Chapel*: Zipporah, daughter of Jethro and wife of Moses, appears in a fresco by Botticelli (?1455–1510) on the ceiling of the Sistine Chapel, depicting the 'Life of Moses'.

35 *Antonio Rizzo*: the Correr Museum in Venice holds a bronze bust of Andrea Loredan (who was not in fact a *doge*) by the Paduan sculptor Andrea Briosse (1471–1532), who was known as 'il Riccio' or 'il Rizzo'.

Ghirlandaio: (1449–94), a Florentine Renaissance painter of the same generation as Botticelli. Michelangelo (1475–1564) was for a time an apprentice in Ghirlandaio's workshop.

Tintoretto: (1518–94), a Venetian Renaissance painter whose self-portrait, with prominent nose, heavily bearded face, and 'piercing gaze', hung in the Louvre in Proust's time.

37 *La Maison Dorée*: an elegant restaurant established in 1840 (which Proust sometimes renders La Maison d'Or). This and the other establishments mentioned subsequently (Prévost's, Tortoni's, and the Café Anglais) were all popular, respectable Parisian establishments.

the Paris-Murcia Fête: a fund-raising 'fête' held in Paris on 18 December 1879 following serious flooding in the province of Murcia in south-east Spain in October that year.

42 *Eurydice*: in Greek mythology, Eurydice, wife of Orpheus, was killed by a snake-bite on her wedding day. Orpheus, through the power of his singing, persuaded the Gods to allow him to bring Eurydice back from Hades, but they imposed the condition that he should not take a backward glance towards her as they climbed up from the underworld. Unable to resist the compulsion to turn back towards his beloved, Orpheus lost Eurydice a second time, for ever.

46 *victoria*: a four-wheeled, horse-drawn open carriage.

47 *Tagliafico*: the *Valse des Roses* (*Waltz of the Roses*) is the best-known composition of Olivier Métra (1830–89), who was notably the conductor at the Folies-Bergères in the 1870s. The *Pauvre fou* (actually titled *Pauvres fous*, 'The Poor Lunatics'), is a song written by the French-Italian opera singer Joseph Dieudonné Tagliafico (1821–1900), who performed at the Théâtre des Italiens in Paris from the 1840s. That these pieces of music should be Odette's 'favourites' gives a snapshot of what, to Swann and the elevated circles in which he habitually moves, are her undiscerning aesthetic tastes.

51 *Watteau*: Antoine Watteau (1684–1721), a major French painter of the eighteenth century, credited in particular with developing the genre known as 'fêtes galantes', outdoor scenes of playful, amorous adventures. In an essay on the painter Proust described his work as 'the apotheosis of love and pleasure'.

in the style of the Vicomte de Borelli: Vicomte Raymond de Borrelli (1827–1906)—Proust misspells his name—was a society poet and, like the *Valse des Roses*, is here representative of Odette's unrefined taste.

53 *Hippodrome*: a horse-racing arena in the Bois de Vincennes in Paris, established in 1863 and rebuilt in 1879 after significant damage during the Franco-Prussian war.

56 *La Reine Topaze*: comic opera by Victor Massé (1822–84), first performed in 1856.

57 *Serge Panine*: novel published in 1881 by George Ohnet (1848–1918), which was adapted for the stage the following year: it was enjoyed by the public but not by the critics.

Olivier Métra: conductor, composer of the *Valse des Roses* mentioned previously.

59 *École du Louvre*: establishment founded in 1881 for the training of museum conservators.

61 *Blanche de Castille*: (1188–1252), daughter of Alphonso VIII of Castille and Eleanor of England. She was Queen of France as wife of Louis VIII and regent during the reign of her son, Louis IX (1214–70), who was canonized Saint Louis in 1297.

62 *Suger and other Saint Bernards*: the *Chronicle of Saint-Denis* (the popular title for the *Grandes chroniques de France*), a history of the kings of France, was begun by the Abbé Suger (1081–1151) in the twelfth century. Brichot is somewhat confused with his 'impeccably reliable source' here, since both Suger and Bernard de Clairvaux (1091–1153, canonized in 1174) died more than thirty years before Blanche de Castille was born.

64 *even better than Rembrandt or Hals*: the painter here compares the contemporary canvases he has seen at the exhibition with long-established masterpieces whose accomplishment resists analysis: *The Night Watch* (1642) by Rembrandt (1606–69) and *The Regentesses of the Old Men's Almshouse, Haarlem* (?1664) by Franz Hals (1580–1666).

the 'Ninth' and the Winged Victory: to Beethoven's *Ninth Symphony*, previously mentioned as the archetypal masterpiece, is added *The Winged Victory of Samothrace*, a sculpture of the Greek goddess Nike, discovered in 1863 on the island of Samothrace and exhibited in the Louvre since 1884.

66 *Francillon*: a recurring topic of conversation in the Verdurin circle is contemporary art, though, as is quite clear, the guests' engagement is frequently superficial. Madame Cottard is keen to show that she is up-to-date here, by mentioning *Francillon* (first performed in 1887) by Alexandre Dumas *fils*, a play she has not yet seen. The play contains a scene where a 'Japanese salad' is prepared: it is a salad of cooked potatoes and mussels, dressed with olive oil, vinegar, a glass of Château d'Yquem, and finely sliced truffles. The name simply reflects the prevailing 'japonisme' of the period, the fascination with all things Japanese.

Le Maître de Forges: (*The Owner of the Iron Works*), a sentimental novel of 1882 by Georges Ohnet, whose *Serge Panine* is mentioned here and a little earlier in the text.

68 *Palais de l'Industrie*: (Palace of Industry), built for the World's Fair in Paris in 1855. It was where the annual 'Salons' (exhibitions) of painting and

sculpture were held until it was demolished in 1897 to make way for the Grand Palais and the Petit Palais, built for the World's Fair of 1900 and still standing today.

68 *the La Trémoïlles and the Laumes*: two families are mentioned here: one real and one fictional. The La Trémoïlles were one of France's oldest aristocratic families, with a history dating back to the eleventh century. The Laumes are Proust's invention and similarly formidable in their history: they are a branch of the Guermantes family that lends its name to the third volume of Proust's novel, *Le Côté de Guermantes* (*The Guermantes Way*). Since *Swann in Love* narrates a time prior to Proust's narrator's childhood, readers of 'Combray', the preceding section of the novel, there encounter the Prince and Princesse des Laumes as the Duc and Duchesse de Guermantes (titles inherited upon the death of the Prince's father); their ancestral home lies adjacent to Combray, the village where the narrator's family spend their summers during his childhood.

69 *'That gentle anarchist Fénelon'*: François de Salignac de la Mothe-Fénelon (1651–1715), theologian and tutor to Louis XIV's grandson, the Duc de Bourgogne (1682–1712). Fénelon is described here playfully as a 'gentle anarchist' since some of his writings, including his book *Les Aventures de Télémaque* (*The Adventures of Telemachus*, 1699), intended for the instruction and education of the young Duc, contained criticisms of the reign of Louis XIV.

70 *Those de la Trémouilles*: Brichot inadvertently shows his ignorance here by mispronouncing Trémouïlles, without the diaeresis.

George Sand: nom de plume of the celebrated female novelist Amantine-Lucile-Aurore Dupin (1804–76). Sand's novel *François le Champi* (1847) plays a pivotal role in the narrator's childhood development in 'Combray'.

71 *Se non è vero*: truncated version of the Italian 'se non è vero è ben trovato'—even if it's not true, it's a good story.

72 *it's not serpent à sonates*: there is a play on words in the French here that alludes to an acquaintance of Proust's. Marquise Diane de Saint-Paul was a gifted pianist with a reputation as an uncompromising gossip, known therefore as the 'serpent à sonates' or 'sonata snake', playing on the term for rattlesnake, 'serpent à sonnettes'.

76 *Gustave Moreau*: 1826–98, best known as a Symbolist painter whose canvases lavishly depict mythological and biblical themes and motifs such as *Oedipus and the Sphinx* (1864) or *Salomé* (1876).

78 *Île des Cygnes*: 'Island of the Swans', an island in the larger of the two lakes in the Bois de Boulogne.

80 *brougham*: a four-wheeled, horse-drawn closed carriage, typically with two seats.

87 *the painter of the 'Primavera'*: the reference is once again to Botticelli. The 'Primavera' (?1482) is one of his most celebrated works; also known in

English as the 'Allegory of Spring', it can be seen in the Uffizi Gallery in Florence.

88 *watch Moses pour water into a trough*: another allusion to Botticelli, this time to his *Madonna of the Pomegranate* (?1487), also in the Uffizi, and to the *Life of Moses* frescoes in the Sistine Chapel.

91 *Moonlight Sonata*: Beethoven's Opus 27, no. 2, the Piano Sonata no. 14 in C sharp minor (composed in 1801), has, since the mid-nineteenth century, been popularly referred to as 'the Moonlight Sonata', after a critic likened the effect of the sonata's first movement to moonlight on Lake Lucerne.

92 *the peasant who is engaged in slaughtering it*: the narrator here refers to an incident in 'Combray', the first part of *Swann's Way*, in which the child protagonist witnesses the family servant Françoise killing a chicken for the family table. Unexpectedly the child is suddenly plunged into the adult world of ethics: the woman he had hitherto considered to be saintly is seen to be capable of a violent act of slaughter, yet the young protagonist cannot condemn her actions outright since he realizes that he has long been a beneficiary of them, enjoying as he does the succulent roast chickens that Françoise prepares.

93 *a play by Labiche*: Eugène Labiche (1815–88), dramatic author of vaudeville and farce, whose plays poked fun at the bourgeoisie.

94 *Plato and Bossuet, and the old system of education in France*: Plato famously condemns artists on moral grounds in book ten of *Republic*, which Bossuet (1627–1704), a theologian, moralist, and orator, cites in his *Maximes et réflexions sur la comédie* (1694). French school education underwent major changes in the 1880s as a result of reforms and innovations implemented by Jules Ferry (1832–93), then Minister of Education.

the last circle of Dante: in Dante's *Divine Comedy* (1320), the last (ninth) circle of Hell is reserved for those sinners guilty of treachery, the misdeed Swann is railing at here.

Noli me tangere: 'Don't touch me' (Latin). Reported in John 20:17 as the words of Christ, spoken to Mary Magdalen after the resurrection.

96 *Une nuit de Cléopâtre*: opera (first performed in 1885) by Victor Massé, whose other works include *La Reine Topaze*, previously mentioned.

101 *Carte du Tendre*: ('the Map of Love') in *Clélie* (written between 1654 and 1660), Madame de Scudéry (1607–1701) incorporated an allegorical map of the different paths that can be taken to arrive at true love.

102 *the reality of the external world or the immortality of the soul*: Swann's state here is likened to that of people who have 'worn themselves out' with philosophical reflection. Precisely such reflections fill the pages of Descartes (1596–1650), Pascal (1623–62), and Kant (1724–1804), thinkers with whose work Proust was familiar; these preoccupations are also those we encounter as we are plunged into the thoughts of Proust's restless narrator on the very first page of *Swann's Way*.

102 *Philippe le Beau . . . Margaret of Austria*: the church at Brou, in Bourg-en-Bresse, was built on the order of Marguerite of Austria (1480–1530) to commemorate her husband, Philibert le Beau (1480–1504), Duc de Savoie, who was killed in a hunting accident.

103 *'Bal des Incohérents'*: the 'Ball of the Incoherents', a public event first held in Paris in 1885. The 'Incoherents' were artists who mocked the official 'Salon' exhibitions and staged very successful exhibitions of their own, the opening of which was marked by a costumed ball.

106 *landau*: a four-wheeled, horse-drawn, convertible carriage.

Bayreuth: by the 1880s the annual *Bayreuther Festspiele* (Bayreuth Festival), dedicated to performances of Wagner's works in a specially designed concert-house inaugurated in 1876, was a fashionable destination for cultural tourists from Europe and further afield.

107 *the difference between Bach and Clapisson*: Johann Sebastian Bach (1685–1750), immensely influential German Baroque composer; Antonin-Louis Clapisson (1808–66) was a minor French composer of comic operas.

114 *Saint-Simon . . . Madame de Maintenon . . . Lulli*: the Duc de Saint-Simon (1675–1755) wrote at great length and in remarkable detail about life in Louis XIV's court at Versailles. One section of his *Mémoires* (which span the period 1691–1723) is dedicated to the dinners held by Madame de Maintenon (1635–1719). Jean-Baptiste Lulli (1632–87) was an important composer of the period.

115 *the art of placing an order*: Crapotte (Proust misspells this) and Jauret were Parisian fruiterers popular with the elegant hostesses of the period; Chevet was a 'traiteur' or upmarket grocer/caterer.

118 *the Septennate*: the French Presidential term was historically seven years. The 'septennate' referred to here is most likely that of Edmé Patrice, Comte de Mac-Mahon, which began in 1873, though did not run its full course: Mac-Mahon resigned from office in 1879.

Botticelli's Primavera, his fair Vanna, or his Venus: Primavera, the goddess of spring, appears in the painting of that name previously mentioned; the 'fair Vanna' refers to *Giovanna Tornabuoni and the Three Graces* (?1480), which Proust could have seen in the Louvre; and 'his Venus' is a reference to the famous *Birth of Venus* (1484–6).

119 *second part of this story*: a projection forward to the latter part of *Swann's Way*, 'Place-names: the Name', in which Swann and Odette are married.

120 *Mémé old chap*: a familiar, diminutive form of 'Palamède', the Baron de Charlus's given name, used only by those who are close to him.

127 *Balzac's 'tigers'*: in the early to middle years of the nineteenth century, explored in the fictions of Honoré de Balzac (1799–1850), a 'tigre' (or 'tiger': the term was used in English) was an elegant gentleman's groom (a young male servant or attendant).

128 *Mantegna*: Andrea Mantegna (?1430–1506), Italian painter and engraver who was part of the team of artists who decorated the Church of the

Eremitani at Padua between 1449 and 1456: here, in the Ovetari Chapel, one can see 'Scenes from the life of Saint John and Saint Christopher'. In the 'Martyrdom of Saint John', a warrior is depicted deep in thought, leaning on his shield as Proust describes here. Mantegna also painted the altarpiece of San Zeno in Verona, between 1456 and 1459.

one of Albrecht Dürer's Saxons: Albrecht Dürer (1471–1528), German painter and artist, a key figure in the Northern Renaissance, who was influenced by Mantegna and made copies of his engravings.

the Doges' Palace—'The Giants' Staircase': the staircase in the central courtyard of the Ducal Palace in Venice takes its name from the huge statues of Mars and Neptune that flank it. The English art historian John Ruskin (1819–1900), whose works Proust read with great care, dedicates a significant section of his study of Venetian architecture, *The Stones of Venice* (1851–3), to the Doges' Palace. Proust, with the assistance of his mother and an English-speaking cousin of his friend Reynaldo Hahn, published translations of Ruskin's *The Bible of Amiens* (1885) and *Sesame and Lilies* (1865) in 1904 and 1906 respectively.

129 *like one of Goya's sextons*: Proust was familiar with the work of the Spanish painter Francisco de Goya (1746–1828), though it is not clear which work he has in mind when evoking a representation of sextons.

like some priceless effigy by Benvenuto Cellini: Cellini (1500–71), sculptor and goldsmith from Florence. As with the preceding reference to Goya, it is not certain to which work Proust is alluding here.

Aubusson tapestries: tapestries and carpets have been manufactured at Aubusson in the Creuse department since the fourteenth century.

130 *Jockey Club*: one of the most exclusive private clubs in Paris. Established in 1833, for Proust it represented the epitome of the elite, closed group, with its own rules and codes of conduct. That Swann, Jewish and neither an aristocrat nor a leader of industry, should have attained election indicates how well connected he is in the highest circles of society.

131 *Giotto's Vices and Virtues at Padua*: the Scrovegni Chapel, also known as the Arena Chapel, in Padua, contains a fresco series by Giotto di Bondone (?1266–1337), which includes allegorical depictions of the seven vices and virtues. Swann gives the young protagonist reproductions of these images in *Swann's Way* and we learn that, just as he had earlier associated Odette with Botticelli's Zipporah, he then sees in the protagonist's family's kitchen maid an embodiment of Giotto's figure of Charity.

an aria from Orfeo: the reference here is to the opera *Orpheus and Eurydice* (1762) by Gluck (1714–87).

Liszt's 'Saint Francis Preaching to the Birds': Franz Liszt (1811–86) composed two pieces of music for solo piano in 1863 inspired by 'legends': 'Saint Francis of Assisi preaching to the birds' and 'Saint Francis of Paola walking on the waves'.

132 *her ultra-Legitimist family would never have forgiven her*: Madame de Gallardon here worries that meeting Princess Mathilde (1820–1904), the niece of Emperor Napoleon I, would horrify her family who, as 'ultra-Legitimists', would want nothing to do with those associated with the usurping of the power of the old regime aristocracy.

137 *Mérimée . . . the plays of Meilhac and Halévy*: the Guermantes' wit is a recurring theme in Proust's novel as a whole and here we are provided with a literary frame of reference for it. Prosper Mérimée (1803–70) was a dramatist and writer of short fiction, notably the novella *Carmen* (1845) which was the basis for Bizet's opera (1875). The libretto for this latter was written by Henri Meilhac (1831–97) and Ludovic Halévy (1834–1908), father of Proust's schoolfriend Daniel Halévy (1872–1962). Meilhac and Halévy's collaborations are characterized by their lively and often satirical nature.

140 *the Belloir agency*: Belloir was a company that rented chairs and sundries for receptions and parties.

     the name of a victory before it was a bridge: Napoleon I's forces defeated the Prussian army in the Battle of Jena in October 1806. To commemorate the victory, Napoleon ordered the construction of the bridge, which was formally opened in 1814.

141 *famous mosaic table . . . Treaty of*: Proust is most likely referring here to the table variously referred to as the 'Breteuil Table', the 'Teschen Table', and the 'Table of Peace', presented to the Baron de Breteuil (1730–1807) to mark the role he played in negotiating the Teschen Treaty of 1779, which established principles of collective security in Europe that ultimately formed the basis of the Covenant of the League of Nations and the Charter of the United Nations. The table can be seen in the Louvre Museum in Paris, which acquired the table via a crowd-funding initiative in January 2015.

142 *Vercingetorix*: (?82–46 BC) fearsome warrior king who commanded the combined Gallic tribes against Julius Caesar.

144 *The double abbreviation . . .* : Swann and the Princesse des Laumes are having fun with the sound of the name 'Cambremer', which 'ends just in time' in that it doesn't quite spell 'merde' (shit). 'It doesn't begin any better', notes Swann, since the first part of the name is shared with that of a General in Napoleon's army, Pierre Cambronne, who, it is said, cried 'Merde!' when demanded to surrender at Waterloo. To speak of 'le mot de Cambronne' (Cambronne's word) was a genteel, euphemistic way of saying 'shit'.

145 *that old Bérénice*: 'That awful Rampillon woman' has been 'dropped by her prince', which leads the Princesse des Laumes to make an allusion to Racine's play *Bérénice* (1670), whose title character is to be married to the Emperor Titus, but is jilted because the Roman public cannot tolerate a foreign queen.

146 *La Pérouse*: Jean-François de Galaup, Comte de la Pérouse (1741–?1788), was a naval officer appointed by Louis XVI to lead a round-the-world expedition. He set off in August 1785, reaching Chile, Hawaii, Alaska,

California, Macau, Korea, Japan, Russia, and Australia before he and his crew disappeared without trace; their last correspondence dates from February 1788.

151 *as he would that of La Princesse de Clèves or of René*: Swann's points of reference speak volumes about his tortured state of mind. He associates the sonata with 'a conception of love and happiness' as distinctive as that found in two literary classics: *La Princesse de Clèves* (1678), a novel by Madame de La Fayette (1634–93), which tells of the frustrated love of a married woman for another man, and the short novel *René* (1805), by Chateaubriand (1768–1848), whose plot concerns the romantic hero René and his sister Amélie's incestuous love for him.

152 *like some theme in Tristan*: Wagner's *Tristan and Isolde* (first performed in 1865), in a similar vein to the literary allusions indicated in the previous note, tells the story of a forbidden love affair that ends in tragedy.

153 *as inspired, perhaps, as Lavoisier or Ampère*: Proust's comparisons often straddle disciplinary boundaries and bring together that which might conventionally be thought of as quite distinct. Here the creative powers of the artist are compared to two of the eighteenth and nineteenth centuries' greatest scientists: Antoine-Laurent de Lavoisier (1743–94) is considered to be the founder of modern chemistry, whilst André Marie Ampère (1775–1836) was a mathematician and physicist who formulated the theory of electromagnetism.

155 *convinced that . . . was in fact a Vermeer*: at the sale Proust mentions (which took place in 1876), the painting in question was indeed sold to the Mauritshuis Museum in the Hague and was believed at the time to be the work of Nicolas Maes (?1634–93); an 1891 catalogue for the Mauritshuis indicates that the painting by that time had been re-attributed to Vermeer.

156 *You're never as unhappy as you think*: likely allusion to La Rochefoucauld's maxim 'On n'est jamais si heureux ni si malheureux qu'on s'imagine' (You are never as happy nor as unhappy as you imagine). The Duc de La Rochefoucauld (1613–80) was a moralist and author of the widely-read *Maximes* (1665).

Mohammed II, whose portrait by Bellini he liked so much: earlier, in the 'Combray' part of *Swann's Way*, Swann likens the narrator's friend Bloch to this portrait, painted in 1479 by the Venetian artist Gentile Bellini (?1429–1507).

157 *Whitsun*: Whitsun, or Pentecost, is celebrated on the seventh Sunday after Easter in the Christian calendar.

161 *Les Filles de Marbre*: first performed in 1853, this successful play (*Girls of Marble*), by Théodore Barrière, treats the life of courtesans, who are characterized as heartless and cold.

Dieppe, Cabourg, and Beuzeval: towns on the north coast of France. Between 1907 and 1914, Proust holidayed every year at Cabourg, which lends many traits to the fictional resort town of Balbec in his novel.

167 *Alfred de Vigny's Journal d'un poète . . . happiness depends upon the answers*: the lines mentioned here are an accurate quotation from the posthumously published notes of the French Romantic poet, novelist, and dramatist Alfred de Vigny (1797–1863), titled *Journal d'un poète* (*A Poet's Diary*, 1867).

171 *like the loathsome creatures in the Desolation of Nineveh*: Proust alludes here (somewhat obliquely) to a biblical story via John Ruskin's *The Bible of Amiens* (1884), which he had translated in 1904. In his description of the façade of the cathedral Ruskin points out statues of minor prophets standing above carved allusions to their respective prophecies: the animals left inhabiting the desolated, God-forsaken city of Nineveh figure among the prophecies of Zephaniah. The motif of desolation serves to communicate Swann's frame of mind.

174 *the three travellers*: there are in fact four: Monsieur and Madame Verdurin, Madame Cottard, and Odette.

the Mirlitons . . . Machard: the Mirlitons was an annual art exhibition organized by the 'Cercle de l'Union Artistique' (The Circle of the Artistic Union). Jules-Louis Machard (1839–1900) was a portrait painter of great renown who first exhibited at the Mirlitons in 1863.

175 *Leloir*: Jean-Baptiste-Auguste Leloir (1809–92), primarily a painter of historical and religious subjects, though he did produce a number of portraits.

The Oxford World's Classics Website

www.worldsclassics.co.uk

- Browse the full range of Oxford World's Classics online

- Sign up for our monthly e-alert to receive information on new titles

- Read extracts from the Introductions

- Listen to our editors and translators talk about the world's greatest literature with our Oxford World's Classics audio guides

- Join the conversation, follow us on Twitter at OWC_Oxford

- Teachers and lecturers can order inspection copies quickly and simply via our website

www.worldsclassics.co.uk

American Literature

British and Irish Literature

Children's Literature

Classics and Ancient Literature

Colonial Literature

Eastern Literature

European Literature

Gothic Literature

History

Medieval Literature

Oxford English Drama

Philosophy

Poetry

Politics

Religion

The Oxford Shakespeare

A complete list of Oxford World's Classics, including Authors in Context, Oxford English Drama, and the Oxford Shakespeare, is available in the UK from the Marketing Services Department, Oxford University Press, Great Clarendon Street, Oxford OX2 6DP, or visit the website at www.oup.com/uk/worldsclassics.

In the USA, visit www.oup.com/us/owc for a complete title list.

Oxford World's Classics are available from all good bookshops. In case of difficulty, customers in the UK should contact Oxford University Press Bookshop, 116 High Street, Oxford OX1 4BR.

ÉMILE ZOLA

L'Assommoir
The Belly of Paris
La Bête humaine
The Conquest of Plassans
The Fortune of the Rougons
Germinal
The Kill
The Ladies' Paradise
The Masterpiece
Money
Nana
Pot Luck
Thérèse Raquin